WAGE DETERMINATION AND DISTRIBUTION IN JAPAN

Wage Determination and Distribution in Japan

TOSHIAKI TACHIBANAKI

This publication was supported by a generous donation from The Daido Life Foundation

CLARENDON PRESS · OXFORD
1996

Oxford University Press, Walton Street, Oxford OX2 6DP
Oxford New York
Athens Auckland Bangkok Bombay
Calcutta Cape Town Dar es Salaam Delhi
Florence Hong Kong Istanbul Karachi
Kuala Lumpur Madras Madrid Melbourne
Mexico City Nairobi Paris Singapore
Taipei Tokyo Toronto
and associated companies in
Berlin Ibadan

Oxford is a trade mark of Oxford University Press

Published in the United States
by Oxford University Press Inc., New York

© Toshiaki Tachibanaki, 1996

All rights reserved. No part of this publication may be reproduced,
stored in a retrieval system, or transmitted, in any form or by any means,
without the prior permission in writing of Oxford University Press.
Within the UK, exceptions are allowed in respect of any fair dealing for the
purpose of research or private study, or criticism or review, as permitted
under the Copyright, Designs and Patents Act, 1988, or in the case of
reprographic reproduction in accordance with the terms of the licences
issued by the Copyright Licensing Agency. Enquiries concerning
reproduction outside these terms and in other countries should be
sent to the Rights Department, Oxford University Press,
at the address above

British Library Cataloguing in Publication Data
Data available

Library of Congress Cataloging in Publication Data
Tachibanaki, Toshiaki, 1943–
Wage determination and distribution in Japan / Toshiaki Tachibanaki.
Includes bibliographical references and index.
1. Wages—Japan. 2. Compensation management—Japan. I. Title.
HD5077.T234 1996   95-38882
331.2'952—dc20
ISBN 0-19-828865-4

1 3 5 7 9 10 8 6 4 2

Typeset by Best-set Typesetter Ltd., Hong Kong
Printed in Great Britain
on acid-free paper by
Biddles Ltd., Guildford & King's Lynn

PREFACE

Wages are very important determinants of the level of employment and unemployment, incentives, and earnings distribution. As they form the principal source of income for nearly all employees, wages are the most crucial variables which determine not only the working of the labour market in general but also the living standards of many people. The principal purpose of this book is to investigate various aspects of wages in Japan in order to shed light on the issue. Emphasis is placed upon investigating the way in which wages are determined, and how they are distributed among workers. At the same time, the causes and socioeconomic implications of wage determination and wage differentials are examined and discussed.

Japan differs from the Euro-American countries in various aspects of the labour market and industrial relations. These features provide Japan with unique characteristics, which are examined carefully in order to evaluate whether or not economic rationality is the principal motive for them. The method of investigating the various issues is both theoretical and empirical.

I have been working on these issues for a number of years, and have published several articles in academic journals. A substantial part of this material has been used in the writing of this book, although I have done substantial rewriting to create a monograph which can be read from beginning to end as a continuous story and stream. Some of the articles were co-authored, and I am very grateful to the co-authors for kindly permitting me to use these materials: Naosumi Atoda, Y. Kawashima Horn, Souichi Ohta, and Atsuhiro Taki. The book also includes new material which has not been published elsewhere.

This book is the first book I have written in English. So I would like to thank my teachers in various places and at various times in Japan and the USA, including Kinya Nishikawa, Hisao Kumagai, Michio Hatanaka, Shinichi Ichimura, Carl F. Christ, Charles R. Hulten, and Dale W. Jorgenson. These professors taught me economics and econometrics during my study for the BA, MA, and Ph.D. degrees, and were very influential in increasing my human capital.

After completing my degree, I received help and useful comments on my articles from a large number of colleagues, friends, co-researchers, and students, who are too numerous to mention. It is necessary, however, for me to thank the following for professional and personal advice at various stages of my career: Takeshi Amemiya, Masahiko Aoki, Charles Brown, Richard B. Freeman, Zvi Griliches, Robert J. Gordon, Tatsuo Hatta, Bertil Holmlund, Tsuneo Ishikawa, Takenori Inoki, Kazuo Koike, Ryutaro Komiya, Richard Layard, Pascal Mazodier, Jacques Mairesse, Chikashi Moriguchi, Michio Morishima, Kuramitsu Muramatsu, Stephen Nickell, Konusuke Odaka, Isao Ohashi, Andrew J. Oswald, Sherwin Rosen, Kinzo Saito, Robert H. Topel, and Hirofumi Uzawa. Their comments and advice have been very useful, and I am grateful to them all.

It is my pleasure to thank Andrew Schuller and Enid Barker of the Oxford University Press for their editorial help, Sarah Barrett for copy-editing, and an anonymous referee for his penetrating and useful comments on earlier versions of this book. The manuscript was typed and handled cheerfully by Tomoko Inagaki and Kyoko Yanagida for whose skilful word-processor techniques I am much indebted.

I am solely responsible for any errors which remain, and for the opinions expressed in this book, although my thanks are offered to numerous people.

Finally, I am happy to dedicate this book to my wife, Yasuko, for her continued support.

T.T.

Kyoto University
July 1995

CONTENTS

1. Introduction — 1
2. Theoretical and Empirical Overview of Wage Determination — 13
3. How Have Wage Differentials Changed? — 24
4. The Employer Size Effect on Wage Differentials — 50
5. Wage Differentials by Industry and Labour Market — 79
6. Education, Occupation, and Earnings — 113
7. The Importance of Education, Occupation, and Hierarchy in Organizations and in Earnings Differentials — 126
8. A Theoretical and Empirical Model of Wage Determination — 149
9. The Effect of Discrimination and of Industry Segmentation on Wage Differentials — 170
10. Earnings Distribution and Inequality Over Time: Education versus Relative Position and Cohort — 200
11. Labour Market Flexibility and Wage Determination — 219
12. Conclusions — 239

References — 252

Index — 269

1

Introduction

1.1. INTRODUCTION

Wages are very influential on the determination of employment and thus of the working of the labour market in general. They also form the principal source of income for nearly all employees. This book intends to investigate wage determinations and wage differentials in Japan for the post-war period with emphasis on the recent development. An effort is made to investigate not only theoretical and empirical issues of wage determination and wage differentials but also the influence of wages on the mechanisms of the labour market such as employment and unemployment.

It may be useful to set out the reasons why it is interesting to investigate wages and earnings in Japan. First, Japan has experienced a dynamic movement of her economy. The period of destruction and confusion following the Second World War gave way to a period of strong industrialization and rapid economic growth, which began in the 1950s and 1960s and continued until the early 1970s. During this period Japan reached a high level of per capita GNP or per capita income. After the two oil crises the growth rate of her economy declined, and its level stabilized. One important characteristic during this stable period is that Japan's macroeconomic performance, in particular the level of unemployment, was considerably better than those of other industrialized countries. Such a dynamic movement and better performance in macroeconomy are likely to provide us with useful information with which to evaluate the role of wages and thus of the labour market.

Second, Japan has several institutional particularities—including the *nenko* (i.e. seniority) system, 'life-long employment', 'enterprise unionism', *shunto* ('spring offensive') system, decentralized wage bargaining, and the co-operative employer–employee relationship—which are likely to affect the determination of wages, and employment and unemployment. Particular attention is paid to investigating the effect of these institutional particularities, theoretically and empirically, based on both efficiency and equity grounds.

Third, Japan produces very fruitful data on not only macroeconomy in general but also on labour fields. The public authority, which is famous (or notorious) internationally as an agency which regulates the economy and society, conducts a large number of data collections. It is not an exaggeration to say that data exist everywhere in Japan, although their availability for public use is considerably limited.

Labour data, in particular, are fruitful. The Ministry of Labour's *Wage Structure Survey*, used at various places in this book, is an astonishing data source for the following reasons. First, it contains very useful information on wage figures cross-classified by a large number of demographic variables and firm characteristics. Second, the number of observations (i.e. employees) is over 1 million, and they are collected *every year*—an extraordinary feature of a data source. In sum, it is natural—or may even be an obligation—that economists should attempt to use these fruitful data sources for their empirical studies. This book applies econometric and statistical techniques to the data from various sources. Individual observations, which are in general better in quality than published sources, are used in various chapters.

1.2. LABOUR MARKET, INDUSTRIAL RELATIONS, AND WAGES IN JAPAN

It should be useful to describe several important characteristics of the labour market, industrial relations system, and wage structure in Japan, as an introduction to the subsequent analyses. It will be easier to understand them if the examination is made in comparison with other industrialized countries (mainly Euro-American countries).

Table 1.1 indicates very broadly the general features of the labour markets in Europe, Japan, and the USA, and Table 1.2 presents three primary institutional particularities which separate Japan from Euro-American countries. Table 1.1 gives the nine features; Of these, four refer to average levels and five refer to the

TABLE 1.1. *Key features of the labour markets in Europe, Japan, and the USA*

	Europe	Japan	USA
Level			
Unemployment rate	High	Low	Average
Working hours	Short	Long	Average
Productivity growth	Low	High	Average
Unionization	High	Low	Low
Variability			
Unemployment rate	High	Low	High
Production	Average	High	High
Employment	Average	Low	High
Working hours	Average	High	Low
Real wages	Low	High	Low

TABLE 1.2. *Labour market features: Japan and Euro-American countries*

	Japan	Euro-American countries
Labour mobility	Less mobile	More mobile
Wages and promotion	Seniority	Free competition
Union	Enterprise unionism	Crafts or industry unionism

feature's variability. Table 1.2 combines Europe and the USA because they have common particularities as a whole which are different from those of Japan. These two tables are based on Tachibanaki (1994*a*).

Since it is easy to obtain an intuitive impression of the general features of the labour markets in Japan, by contrast with Europe and the USA, based on Table 1.1, no detailed interpretation of this table is necessary. It is possible to summarize it as follows. Japan performs relatively better in terms of the rate of unemployment, in both its level and its variability, despite a large fluctuation in output. People in Japan, nevertheless, work longer hours. The three distinctions in Table 1.2, however, require some explanation, because they represent institutional particularities which govern the behaviour of both employers and employees in Japan in detail.

Three key terms—life-long employment, *nenko-joretsu* (seniority system) in wages and promotion, and enterprise unionism—are used frequently to represent the Japanese institutional particularities in the field of labour. The OECD once called them the 'Three Sacred Treasures of the Imperial Houses' of Japan, and evaluated them positively as one of the reasons for rapid economic growth. Regarding labour mobility, Japanese workers tend to stay with one employer; average job tenure in Japan is longer than that in Euro-American countries. Regarding wages and promotion, employers pay wages and determine the promotion possibilities of employees largely by workers' seniority, i.e. job tenure (internal experience or length of service) and, marginally, by age, rather than on the basis of employees' productivity and performance, as in Euro-American countries. This characteristic will be examined carefully later in this book. Nearly all unions in Japan are organized at the enterprise level, while the organization of unions in Euro-American nations are based on workers' occupation and/or the industry in which a particular firm operates.

Several reservations apply to the above three distinctions. First, it is simplistic to conclude that there is a clear distinction between Japan and Euro-American nations in reality. Seniority, for example, is also valued in Euro-American nations to a certain extent in determining employees' wages and promotion, as can be seen from several empirical studies, while competition among employees, and thus productivity and performance, are also significant even in Japan, as will be shown later. It is thus a matter of degree of difference rather than dichotomy.

Second, the above features and particularities in Japan are applicable only to male full-time employees who work in larger firms. In other words, only a limited proportion of employees and Japanese firms fit the above profile; the majority of employees and firms— female workers, part-time employees, and workers in smaller firms—have separate characteristics. Also, the rate of union participations is only just over 20 per cent: employees who are not union members form the majority, and union members the minority. These reservations are crucial to understanding the general characteristics of the labour market in Japan, as will be discussed in various later chapters.

Several important features must be added to the three previously mentioned. Fourth, long-term contractual relationships and commitments are preferred by both Japanese people and firms because they believe that such long-term relations are beneficial in the long run. Long-term contractual relationships can minimize transaction costs and establish mutual trust. Since both employers and employees recognize, explicitly or implicitly, the benefit of long-term relationships, employers try to keep employees and employees try to stay longer in one company. On-the-job training and firm-specific capital, of course, can also be argued to be benefits of long-term contractual relationships. Tachibanaki (1994a) offers several additional hypotheses to justify the reasons why long-term contractual relationships prevail in Japan: first, Japanese people are fairly risk-averse; second, coherence within a group is highly appreciated; third, strong leadership is not highly regarded (see Tachibanaki, 1994a for further detail).

Fifth, industrial relations are 'organization-oriented' in Japan rather than 'market-oriented,' as Dore (1993) emphasizes. Supply and demand forces play a less direct role in the determination of wages and employment. Thus, the role of market mechanism, or the neoclassical type of price mechanism, works only secondarily; instead, 'organization-oriented force', such as loyalty to the firm, group-oriented decision rather than individual-oriented decisions, and dominance of a group's interest over an individual person's benefit, applies to a certain extent.

Sixth, equality is highly regarded within members who belong to a group. The seniority system can be assessed on this ground because it treats equally all members who have common qualifications Wage distribution among members who have the same qualifications tends to be equal, as will be shown in subsequent chapters. This feature is likely to provide all members with higher incentive and a hard-working ethic.

Several reservations must be added. First, the importance of equality was not accepted as a prevailing principle during the pre-war period. Various studies of economic history in Japan reveal that pre-war wage distribution was more unequal than current distribution: Japan was a country of inequality in many dimensions. Modernization and democratization, which occurred after the post-war reform initiated by the American occupation force, oriented Japanese society more towards equality. Second, to emphasize the importance of equality in Japan does not imply that other industrialized countries do not stress it. The difference remains only in the concept of equality. Equality in opportunity is the most valuable equality in many Euro-American nations where individualism is highly regarded, while equality in consequence, or in actual status, is the most respected equality in Japan. This difference is likely to produce different outcomes in the working of the labour markets in the two regions. Third, a new inequality, in wealth distribution, has appeared recently in Japan (Tachibanaki 1992*b*). Also, Tachibanaki and Yagi (1985) showed a new trend of more unequal distribution in income.

Seventh, it is useful to describe briefly several institutional settings of wage determinations. Wages are determined by the following three major elements. The first element comprises factors associated with employees' demographic characteristics such as sex, age, education, and job tenure; the second element is the consideration of employees' job (or occupation); the third element is the evaluation of performance of each employee. The first may be called simply 'pay based on personal characteristics', the second, 'pay based on job and occupation', and the third, 'pay based on performance'.

Each firm has its own wage policy; thus each firm gives particular importance to each of the above three elements: one firm may stress the first element, while another may give more importance to the second element. It is risky to attempt to provide an average picture of the relative importance of the three elements, which can represent the institutional setting of wage determination in Japan, without discussing the subject extensively: wage policies differ greatly from firm to firm, and the difference in size of firm and industry is very influential.

It may be worthwhile, nevertheless, to offer several representative, stylized facts as a very rough introduction. First, the second element, pay based on job and occupation, was debated seriously during the post-war period; in particular, the employers were anxious to introducing it and to intensify its relative importance. They were not, however, successful. (Incidentally, this element plays a major role in Euro-American nations.) Second, the most important element among the above three had been the first, pay based on personal characteristics, although its relative importance is decreasing. Third, the question of what variable is important among several characteristics such as sex, age, education, and job tenure in the second element depends upon what firm, industry, and size of firm we consider. Fourth, the third element, pay based on performance, was fairly weak at the outset, although its relative importance is increasing.

Several other features related to industrial relations, wages, and labour in Japan are presented here in addition to the previous seven features, without arguing their implications explicitly. Eighth, female labour forces are treated quite differently from male workers, with a lower degree of consent of women. Ninth, the share of self-employed workers in total labour forces, and the share of part-time employees in total employees, are both high. Tenth, the most important industry, which employs more than 50 per cent of the labour force, is not manufacturing but tertiary industries. Productivity in the manufacturing sector, however, is higher, while productivity in the tertiary sector is lower by international standards. Eleventh, there are two half-yearly bonus payments to employees. The determination of such special payments is different from the determination of regular monthly wages. Twelfth, the share of non-wage labour costs within the total labour cost is relatively small; this is related to the relatively poor social security system in Japan, at least in comparison with Europe.

I have discussed several important features of industrial relations and of institutional specificities peculiar to labour in Japan. I shall hope to use these discussions and empirical results to interpret the content of subsequent chapters, which investigate various aspects of wage determinations and wage differentials. The concluding chapter will reconsider the implications of the above features in the light of the many empirical results presented in the preceding chapters.

1.3. CHAPTER OVERVIEW

It is useful to provide a brief introduction to each chapter, before presenting a full discussion of the main content.

Chapter 2 gives a very brief survey of several important and popular theoretical results of wage determination and wage differentials. Although there are a large number of theories and theorems in economics which are valuable to explain wage behaviours and wage determinations, I have selected only several theories which are likely to be particularly useful in Japan. Since this book does not intend to argue the theoretical development on wage determinations extensively, only the implications of each theory, together with its empirical background, are presented. Finally, Chapter 2 offers several empirical stylized facts about wage determination and wage differentials in Japan. This section serves as a brief introduction to empirical evidence on wages in Japan.

Chapter 3 examines a time-series change in wage differentials, explained by the six main variables with their first-order interactions. The six main variables (i.e. effects) are sex, occupation, education, size of firm, experience (i.e. job tenure or length of service in a firm), and age. The main statistical method is the analysis of variance, although its property is not so superior in comparison with other estimation methods. The analysis-of-variance method can be applied relatively easily under severe data constraint—such as unbalanced data with missing cells. Empirical analysis in this chapter covers a very long period after the Second World War, thus enabling us to reveal a change in the relative importance or contribution of each main effect to total wage differentials in the historical context. The analysis-of-variance method is capable of deriving such a contribution.

Chapter 4 investigates wage differentials by size of firm. It was believed popularly that inter-scale (or inter-size) wage differentials were the most salient feature peculiar to Japan. Many ideas were presented by various specialists in Japan to explain the cause and implication of the inter-size wage differentials. This chapter intends to perform the following four investigations. First, whether or not a pure size effect remains, after an extremely large number of control variables are used in the estimation of wage functions. Second, what are the main determinants of a pure size effect, if it remains? Various theories of wage determinations are considered and examined. Third, not only traditional interpretations by Japanese specialists but also foreign experiences of inter-size wage differentials are compared and discussed. Fourth, stratification and distribution in wages are estimated. New insights are offered into the relationship between wage determinations and industrial relations system, and into the relationship between employees' performance and incentive.

Chapter 5 examines inter-industry wage differentials, a popular subject in many industrialized countries. Therefore, attention is paid to an international comparison. This kind of study is aimed at verifying whether or not efficiency wage theory is supported. This chapter attempts to estimate a pure industrial advantage (sometimes called industrial rent) or disadvantage after controlling for a comprehensive list of qualification variables. Chapter 4 and 5, therefore, use basically a similar statistical method; their purposes, however, are entirely different. Chapter 5 tries to discover what variables are important as control variables for reducing spurious inter-industry wage differentials. Also, the argument for compensating wage difference is examined. A by-product of the two studies—inter-size wage differentials and inter-industry wage differentials—can be used to identify which differentials are more intrinsic, and to demonstrate that one may be a main determinant of the other.

Chapter 6 presents two brief surveys. The first is the issue whether or not education raises productivity of workers: if it contributes to increasing productivity, what are the main causes of it? Various arguments by education specialists and economists are briefly surveyed. The second survey concerns the relationship among education, occupation, and earnings. Emphasis is placed upon the role of occupation in its relationship with education and earnings respectively. This chapter serves as an introduction to Chapter 7, which investigates the subject of education, occupation, and earnings.

Chapter 7 presents a model which investigates the relationship among education, occupation, hierarchy (i.e. job rank), and earnings. This model has several important features: first, both occupation and hierarchy are considered as new variables, in view of the fact that these two variables are likely to work as intermediary variables which connect education to earnings. Second, a simultaneous-equation model (more specifically a recursive model), which is formed by four endogenous variables consisting of education, occupation, hierarchy, and earnings, is used to estimate parameters in the model. Third, although the previous chapters used only two classifications for occupation, white-collar and blue-collar, this chapter uses two types of occupational classification, 7 one-digit levels and 289 three-digit levels. These detailed classifications are expected to give new findings regarding the effect of occupation. Fourth, hierarchy is classified by five job-rank classes. Since it is risky to quantify hierarchy by continuous scaling, it is classified by discrete quantification. This quantification method requires the application of a discrete estimation method. Fifth, the data source is *SSM (Social Stratification and Mobility)*, which includes useful information on various individual social and economic conditions. The whole purpose of this chapter is to investigate the effect of education on earnings in the presence of both occupation and hierarchy. It is expected that new findings, not recognized previously, will be obtained from the application of several innovative approaches in theory, estimation, and data.

Chapter 8 presents a theoretical model of wage determination and its empirical result. This theoretical model tries to incorporate many stylized facts in Japan, of which some are observed in earlier chapters—the three variables, job tenure, size of firm, and education, which were found to be important. Since only male observations are used for the empirical work, sex, although supposed to be an important, factor, can be eliminated. The principal data source is the *Employment Status Survey*, which contains much valuable information on workforce status.

A theoretical model is constructed to meet the empirical observation that the path of productivity (and thus of wages under the condition of marginal productivity) during one's career is dominated by a non-linear function of job tenure. Given the estimated initial productivity and attainable maximum level of productivity, wage growth can be predicted for various groups of workers. The empirically testable wage function is estimated based on the above three variables, (job tenure, size of firm, and education). The effect of the difference between employees who change their employers and those who never change them is investigated empirically.

Chapter 9 examines more profoundly two subjects: male/female wage differential, and wage differential between competitive industries and non-competitive (concentrated) industries. The principal purpose is to estimate the true cause of the apparently very wide differential in wages between men and women found in Chapter 3. More concretely, it estimates the degree of contribution to male/female wage differentials by the difference in qualifications such as education and job tenure, and by the different treatment of men and women (i.e. discrimination).

A similar approach is applied to the difference between competitive industries (sectors) and non-competitive sectors to decompose wage differentials into various factors. One important factor is the contribution of firm size to the degree of competitiveness of an industry, because it is possible to predict that a non-competitive industry consists mainly of larger (possibly extremely large) firms.

Chapter 10 constructs a theoretical model of lifetime earnings under the condition that wages are distributed log-logistically. Its distribution was found to be more plausible in Japan than lognormal distribution, which was commonly used. Under various assumptions concerning regression towards the mean and serial correlation, an estimation method of lifetime earnings is presented; a small-scale mobility in income class is also introduced. Although this chapter is technically oriented, the empirical result is intuitively appealing.

Two important concerns in the empirical study of the model of lifetime earnings are the effect of education and the effect of location in distribution of wages. More concretely, an attempt is made to estimate which element, educational attainment or location in distribution, is more crucial in determining the amount of lifetime earnings. By comparing lifetime earnings for various positions in distribution (say, median, first quartile, third quartile, and others) under the given educational attainment, it is possible to judge on the above question. The empirical result can be used to identify whether or not raising educational attainments is recommended to reduce inequality in lifetime earnings.

Chapter 11 discusses the relationship between wage determinations and labour market flexibility in Japan. It is widely accepted internationally that labour market flexibility helped Japan to perform better macroeconomically, in particular in relation to the rate of unemployment, both level and variability. This chapter examines a number of studies, both in Japan and elsewhere, which were concerned with labour flexibility. Labour market flexibility has many dimensions, and only a few are picked up here. In particular, the effect of wage determination on labour demand, employment, and thus unemployment is examined. Three subjects are fully dealt with in this chapter. First, what is the role of the relationship between wages and employment (and thus unemployment) among many dimensions in labour flexibility? Second, some cost may have been paid in exchange for achieving flexibility; if so, who is paying that cost? Third, an international comparison with Japan is attempted with respect to these subjects.

Chapter 12 provides several important conclusions, which are derived from the analyses performed in this book, and various comments and discussions on these conclusions.

2

Theoretical and Empirical Overview of Wage Determination

2.1. INTRODUCTION

This chapter presents a survey on wages and earnings distribution in Japan. The first part provides a very brief overview of the theory, which is useful in interpreting several empirical results in Japan. The second part presents a survey of previous studies in Japan, as a background to understanding some developments in the story of wages and earnings distribution in Japan.

2.2. THEORY OF WAGES AND EARNINGS DISTRIBUTION

This part does not intend to give a comprehensive survey of the theory of wage determination, which is already available in the literature, but instead offers an overview which should be useful in understanding wage distribution in Japan. Anyone who wishes to learn such a comprehensive theoretical development can refer to, for example, Willis (1986), Weiss (1986), Rosen (1986), and other advanced textbooks of labour economics such as Hamermesh and Reeds (1993). It may nevertheless be useful to raise several representative theories in the wage determinations: (1) marginal-productivity theory; (2) comparative-advantage theory in allocating jobs; (3) equalizing (or compensating) differences; (4) human-capital theory; (5) job-matching theory; (6) wage-deferral and effort-incentive theory (agency theory); (7) efficiency wage theory. The essence of each theory is described very briefly below, because it will help readers to understand the subsequent empirical analyses of wage distribution in Japan.

1. The marginal-productivity theory proposes that a firm minimizes the cost of production, and thus that it equates physical

marginal productivities of all factor inputs, including all kinds of labour input. This provides us with a proposition that a person who contributes much to production receives higher wages. Since this theory is one of the most fundamental theories in economics, explained in many textbooks, no further elaboration is necessary.

2. The comparative-advantage theory in allocating jobs starts from an assumption that individual workers differ in capability, and that there are various jobs which require different skills and capabilities. Coexistence of these heterogeneous workers in capability and heterogeneous jobs in difficulty can be analysed within the framework of the general equilibrium, and produces efficient job allocation among workers with tastes in common based on the comparative-advantage theory, which is common in international trade theory. This type of job allocation may yield a skewed distribution of wage payments, even if the distribution in capabilities of workers is symmetrical. In other words, a smaller number of workers receive a relatively high level of wage payments, while a larger number receive a relatively low level of wage payments (see Roy, 1951; Champernowne, 1953).

3. Compensating-difference theory. If the assumption of common tastes among workers is removed, we obtain another theory of wage determination: equalizing (or compensating) differences. This theory considers the case in which workers' tastes and satisfactions differ. For example, some workers dislike physically hard jobs, while some workers love independent rather than group-oriented work; nobody likes normally dangerous and/or dirty jobs. These negative evaluations are likely to be compensated by higher wage payments, because otherwise employers would find difficulty in employing workers willing to engage in jobs under unfavourable working conditions. This theory has an effect which allows wage differentials even under the condition that heterogeneity in capabilities of workers is observed. See a useful survey article by Rosen (1986) for details.

4. Human-capital theory. The most popular and influential theory which explains the determination of wages (or earnings) and wage differentials is, probably, the human-capital approach. The theory of human capital investigates the effect of both formal schooling and job training on various aspects of labour economies, including employment, labour mobility, and wage growth path. One of the most important contributions of this theory is to show

that human capital, both formal education and job training, accounts for the greater part of earnings differentials: persons who receive more formal education and/or job training are able to receive higher earnings. The group called the Chicago School was the main advocate of this theory; we mention only a few, such as Becker (1964), Schultz (1971), and Mincer (1974), as representative studies. A large number of empirical studies appeared for various countries to test the principal idea of human-capital theory.

The fundamental equation used for many empirical studies is given by

$$\ln W_i = \ln W_0 + rs_i \qquad (2.1)$$

where W_i is earnings of the ith person, W_0 is constant, r is the rate of interest, and s_i is the schooling level of the ith person. This equation was originally proposed by Mincer (1974) and applied to the USA, after several significant improvements were achieved to obtain a better empirical result. For example, not only the variable of job tenure (or labour market experience) but also its squared form were introduced as additional explanatory variables for an empirically testable earnings function.

The theory of human capital was extended to various directions both theoretically and empirically. Three important theoretical developments are the consideration of innate ability, which promotes the efficiency aspect of human capital or acts as a complement of human capital; the role of trainability, emphasized by Thurow (1975), signifying that a person who has received more education can be trained more easily than a person who has received no education; and the screening or signalling role of education emphasized by Spence (1973) and Arrow (1973), implying that education is used as a device which solves the difficulty associated with asymmetry in information between employers and employees regarding employees' capability and productivity. Extensive research developments have been made in the third area, because it has been found that asymmetry in information between employees and employers plays an important role in the function of the labour market and human resource management. These developments departed considerably from the original formulation of human capital theory. In particular, incentive theory and agency theory became popular to explain the determination of wages.

5. Job-matching theory emphasizes the importance of job heterogeneity in the determination of employment and job tenure. If both the supply and demand for a job is matched well, a person continues to be employed; if it is not matched well, a person leaves his current employer either voluntarily or involuntarily. Empirical studies regarding job-matching theory include Jovanovic (1979; 1984) and Devine and Kiefer (1993). This idea was applied to explain the upward-sloping curve of wages based on job tenure, proposing that the positively upward-sloping curve based on job tenure is observed simply because only well-matched employees stay with current employers; other, mismatched employees would have left current employers. Wage growth path is likely to be positive for employees who stay with current employers, on the basis of human-capital theory, such as firm-specific human-capital accumulation, or other theories. Therefore, job-matching theory is not a counter-doctrine which denies human capital theory: it supports the positive tenure–earnings profile based only on statistical data argument.

6. Wage deferral and effort–incentive theory (agency theory) is concerned with the trade-off between incentive and risk. Since monitoring employee performance is expensive, and at assessing employee performance is risky, it is preferable for a firm to avoid giving employees any incentive to shirk by using several policy tools. One tool is to pay a lower wage for a worker whose tenure is relatively short, and a higher wage for a worker whose tenure is relatively long. In other words, a junior worker's wage payment should be lower than his marginal productivity, and a senior worker's wage payment should be higher than his marginal productivity. If the relationship between wages and marginal productivities were inverse, an employee would have no incentive to work hard, because he would already have received enough payment when he was young before having to show hard-working effort to his employer. This idea, sometimes called 'bonding theory', and developed by Lazear (1979), suggests that a firm issues a 'bond' when an employee is younger, and an employee collects a fund when he is older by selling that bond. This offers one reason why the age–earnings profile is upward-sloping. Also, the retirement allowance which is common in Japanese firms can be explained by this bonding theory. An implicit assumption of this theory is that employees will not leave employers easily if the age–

earnings profile is upward-sloping. It is interesting to note that both human-capital theory and bonding theory are useful to explain the cause of the upward-sloping nature of the age–earnings profile. Alternatively, it is impossible to identify which theory is more relevant to explain such upward sloping. In other words, the empirical and statistical evidence on the upward-sloping age–earnings profile is not sufficient to support either of the two theories.

Effort–incentive theory has been extended to various fields in the theory of human resource management. One principal subject is to identify the mechanism which provides workers with the highest incentive, under the condition that it is difficult to identify who is productive among many employees. A firm attempts to maximize the utilization of potential abilities of employees by collecting limited information on their abilities, performances, and productivities. Economics of information, game theory, transaction costs, economics of uncertainty, economics of organization, and other subjects and tools are employed in this field. One of the most famous approaches is the rank-order tournaments provided by Lazear and Rosen (1981). Subsequently, many ideas and theories were proposed in this field; see, for example, Holmstrom (1982), Carmichael (1983), Shapiro and Stiglitz (1984), Tirole (1986), Macleod and Malcomson (1989), and Holmstrom and Milgrom (1991). We can see these ideas and theories in, for example, Milgrom and Roberts (1992).

7. Efficiency wage theory. One field in this effort–incentive theory which has received great attention among labour and macroeconomists is the efficiency wage hypothesis. This theory proposes that the higher the wage level of an employee, the higher is the effort level of his employer. It implies that raising the wage level of employees enables an employer to increase the productivity level, because employees make a great effort to respond to high incentives provided by their employer. See a useful survey by Katz (1986).

This theory has two implications. The first is the theoretical implication which became one of the backgrounds for explaining involuntary unemployment. The idea is that employers try to raise wage levels of current employees, which are higher than the market wage levels, to increase their effort level and to discourage them to quit. This necessarily discourages employers from hiring new employees. Thus, the rate of involuntary unemployment increases.

See Shapiro and Stiglitz (1984) and many articles in Akerlof and Yellen (1986) about it. Incidentally, the insider/outsider theory of employment and unemployment, which was developed by Lindbeck and Snower (1989), is similar to the efficiency wage hypothesis because the insider (i.e. union member) is kept employed at the expense of the outsider (i.e. non-union member), who is currently unemployed.

Second is the empirical implication; this has stimulated a large number of empirical studies which have attempted to examine whether or not the efficiency wage hypothesis is valid. Since it is difficult to obtain the direct data set which contains information on both wages and effort levels of individual employees, several indirect methods which do not use such direct data are applied. One representative method is to examine inter-industry wage differentials. The degree of such differentials, which is derived from the examination of individual wage data, provides us with a useful tool for the interpretation of the efficiency wage hypothesis. Representative of this method is Krueger and Summers (1988) for the USA. Several empirical works have been presented in various countries, such as Wadhwani and Wall (1991) for the UK and Edin and Zetterberg (1992) for Sweden. The Japanese case will be examined later in this book, and it will be shown that Japan differs considerably from other countries regarding the relationship between inter-industry wage differentials and the efficiency wage hypothesis.

The above is a very brief description of various wage theories which should be useful in interpreting subsequent studies for Japan.

2.3. WAGE DETERMINATION IN JAPAN

This section is intended to give a brief survey of what is so far known about wage determination in Japan. Unfortunately, there are not many studies of wage determination in Japan, partly because data availability of individual survey observations was quite limited and partly because other subjects were more popular in labour economics. This section presents only general features of wage determination in Japan; specific features will be discussed later, when specific subjects of wages are examined in this book.

It is no exaggeration to say that the human-capital model is the only theory to attract a large number of studies of wage determination in Japan. Since a seminal unpublished study by Kuratani (1973) appeared, Stoikov (1973), Hashimoto (1979), Shimada (1981), Hashimoto and Raisian (1985), and Mincer and Higuchi (1988) have tested the validity of the human capital model. Nearly all the studies adopted a form similar to the following for their regression analyses:

$$\ln W = \alpha_0 + \alpha_1 E + \alpha_2 E^2 + \alpha_3 X + \alpha_4 X^2 + \alpha_5 T + \alpha_6 T^2 + \alpha_7 Z \qquad (2.2)$$

where W is wage figures, E stands for formal schooling, X for work experience as a civilian labour force, T for job tenure at the current firm, and Z for a vector of exogenous variables. Some studies eliminate total civilian labour force experience, and some studies do not consider a squared from but only a linear form. Emphasis is placed upon the effect of firm-specific human capital and training on wage growth in nearly all the studies, and it is proposed that formulation (2.2), or a form similar to (2.2), is reasonably successful when the Japanese data are applied.

There is another category of research which do not necessarily depend upon the notion of human capital. This approach, which may be called the *ad hoc* statistical approach, aims to identify which factors (or variables) are important among a large number of factors (or variables) which determine wage differentials, without assuming any theories of wage determination such as human-capital theory. Representative variables include sex, education, size of firm, age, job tenure, union status, and location. Ono (1973; 1989), Tachibanaki (1975; 1982), and Kawashima and Tachibanaki (1986) are typical examples of these studies, which normally use multiple-regression analyses.

Three controversies remain in Japan between the human capital approach and the *ad hoc* statistical approach. First, statistical evidence judged by R^2 for regression equations and t-values for estimated coefficients is generally better in the *ad hoc* statistical approach than in the human capital approach. In other words, the empirical regression analyses based on the human-capital approach are not so impressive as those in the *ad hoc* statistical approach. Second, some authors believe that age is much more important than job tenure (an important variable for firm-specific human capital) as a variable which differentiates wage levels (see e.g. Ono, 1989). This reminds us of the traditional understanding that the wage level in Japan is determined by workers' necessity (living expenses) rather than by their productivity (or contribution to firms): this is a controversy in Japan regarding the importance of either age or job tenure in wage determination; see Ono (1989) and Koike (1981). The former proposes that employers pay wages to their employees on the basis of employees' living expenses, while the latter believes that employers pay wages based on employees' skills which increase with the length of tenure. We call this the 'living-expense hypothesis' versus the 'skill hypothesis'. Third, formal schooling is not an important variable in differentiating wages, unlike other developed nations; see, for example, Psachalopoulos (1975), Tachibanaki (1982), and Atoda and Tachibanaki (1991).

Combining the above three controversies, it is possible to suggest that the human-capital approach (especially the importance of firm-specific human capital) is not yet a doctrine which is accepted universally, at least in Japan. Ishikawa (1991), who provides a useful survey on income distribution, also reached a similar conclusion. This does not necessarily imply, however, that the human-capital approach is inferior.

We can raise several comments and caveats here. First, with respect to the empirical superiority of the *ad hoc* statistical approach over the human-capital approach, it should be pointed out that, since the *ad hoc* statistical approach normally uses a larger number of explanatory variables than the human-capital approach, it is natural to obtain a better explanatory power through the *ad hoc* statistical approach in regression analysis. Second, with respect to the second controversy, the age variable moves in parallel to job tenure, when there is no labour turnover. Since the Japanese degree of labour turnover is lower than the other countries as shown by, for example, Tachibanaki (1987*a*), the age variable may be regarded as one which gives the analogous implication of job tenure. Simply, age and job tenure may be a tautology. Thus, even if the age variable shows a stronger effect on the growth of wages than the job tenure effect, it may, in fact, indicate that the effect of job tenure (and thus specific human capital) is very important. This suggests that a skilful statistical technique, able to distinguish between a pure age effect and a pure tenure effect, must be invented.

In other words, special care must be given to the treatment of job-changers and of no-changers when the effect of job tenure is studied in the presence of age as an independent variable. This issue will be treated in more detail later.

One variable to which particular attention is paid in Japan is the effect of firm size on wage determination. The notion of the dual structure in terms of inter-scale differentials, which hypothesizes that wage differentials, capital intensities, productivities, profit rates and many other economic indicators are very different between smaller firms and larger firms, has been quite popular. The marxian school argued extensively the economic and social implications of the dual structure before the Second World War, and the non-marxian schools also participated in the controversy. The historical development and controversies relating to the dual structure are set out in Odaka (1984). Among a larger number of issues associated with the dual structure, inter-scale wage differentials received the highest attention.

It is somewhat curious to notice that the American literature, which has the largest number of studies on wages and earnings differentials, has paid no attention to this variable. Three exceptions are Mellow (1982), Garen (1985), and Brown and Medoff (1989), to our knowledge. Two reasons for this scarcity may be suggested. First, there may be a common belief that there is no substantial difference in wage payments by the size of firms in the USA. Second, data availability with respect to inter-scale wage differentials may be limited. In any case, there is a marked contrast with the Japanese case with respect to inter-scale wage differentials.

It should be useful to summarize the stylized facts about Japanese inter-scale wage differentials. First, the degree of inter-scale wage differentials is not so great as had been believed. Very roughly speaking, about 5–20 per cent of the variance in wage figures was explained by the difference in firm sizes, after the influence of other variables is controlled for. The recent story, which will be examined in Chapter 3, is different from the above statement, which is relevant for the period of rapid economic growth. The main reason for higher payments in larger firms is that their ability to pay is normally higher for various reasons such as higher capital intensities, oligopoly, and efficient management; this subject is fully analysed in Chapters 4 and 5.

Secondly, the influence of the difference in firm size has declined constantly after the Second World War. It is, however, affected strongly by the movement in business cycles. When the economy is experiencing a boom, wage differential by firm size declines because smaller firms are able to pay higher wages. When the economy is in recession, the differential increases for the opposite reason (see Tachibanaki, 1982).

Thirdly, non-wage payments such as fringe benefits are much higher in larger firms than those in smaller firms. Since the amount of various fringe benefits is not available for each person, it is hard to examine the total compensations, consisting of wage payments and non-wage payments, for empirical research; we are thus obliged to stick to the wage figures.

In summarizing the above, although the inter-scale wage differential was not so great as was believed in the past, it is still a prevailing phenomenon in Japan, and its main cause is the difference by firm size in ability to pay. Wage differentials by size of firm will be investigated in Chapter 3.

In summarizing the empirical evidence on wage determinations and wage distributions in Japan, it would be useful to offer statistical evidence given by the analysis of variance on wage differentials. Tachibanaki (1975; 1982) estimated the relative contribution of each effect to wage differentials among six representative variables (effects) by using the analysis of variances. The six representative variables, which were used to explain hourly wage differentials, are sex, occupation, size of firm, education, job tenure, and age. It should be emphasized that occupational difference is due only to white-collars and blue-collars. Two important conclusions were obtained. First, the relative importance of each variable which contributes to overall wage differentials without paying any attention to a particular group of workers, is as follows: sex, job tenure, age, size of firm, education, and occupation. More specifically, male/female wage differentials are the much more important than any other wage differential. Age and job tenure are secondarily important for explaining overall wage differentials, with a somewhat more important effect for job tenure than for age. The next important variable is the size of firm. Neither education nor occupation was important. Second, when we investigate wage differentials for male white-collar workers, it appears that education is an important variable to explain wage differentials.

It should be emphasized that the above two conclusions were derived from a simple analysis of variance method. This analysis did not pay any attention to inter-correlations among those six variables, but noted only the independent effect of each variable among only six variables in wage differentials. It is quite natural that more complicated causality relationships must be observed among those variables. Considering these causality relationships, we would obtain the different picture of the relative contribution of each variable to wage differentials. Also, there must be some other important variables which were not taken into account in Tachibanaki (1975; 1982)—industry, job position (i.e. hierarchy in a firm), and some others. These two ignored subjects—intercorrelations among explanatory variables some variables other than the commonly used ones—are investigated fully in this book.

3

How Have Wage Differentials Changed?

3.1. INTRODUCTION

The last section of the previous chapter presented very briefly the relative importance of each variable among the six explanatory variables (or factors) which contribute to total wage differentials. This chapter investigates the change in the relative contribution of each variable during the post-war period, and at the same time demonstrates the method for investigating the relative contribution to wage differentials.

3.2. ANALYSIS OF VARIANCE

Several statistical methods enable us to investigate the issue of wage differentials quantitatively; this study adopts a regression analysis. More specifically, the analysis-of-variance method, which is a special case of regression analysis, is applied to study the issue of wage differentials. There are two main reasons for adopting the analysis of variance. The first is that the data source is relatively rich and nearly perfect, in other words, personal characteristics of each employee such as sex or age is given for all observations, and thus there is no missing information. Therefore, the analysis of variance enables us relatively easily to give not only the main effect but also the interaction effects among many variables. The second reason is that the analysis-of-variance method is well fitted for revealing the relative contribution, and thus the importance, of each independent variable to the variance of a dependent variable.

It is, however, necessary to describe several other reasons for adopting the analysis-of-variance method rather than regression analysis. The most important reason lies in the fact that 1958 is the starting-year for the observations of this study, which used the *Wage Structure Survey* in Japan. Since wage figures of individual employees in the *Survey* are not available in any data input forms such as a tape or a disk for these early years, it was impossible to use the regression analysis for individual wage figures; a taped form for individual observations has been made available only recently, on a restricted basis. Since the number of observations, however, is over 1 million every year, it is nearly impossible to apply regression analysis, since this is beyond the capability of any computers. In others words, even if individual observations had been available for the 1950s and 1960s, it would have been impossible to apply the regression analysis to these years within the capability of any computers. In summarizing the above arguments, the principal reason for applying the analysis of variance is its simplicity of calculation, and easy interpretation of the estimated result.

3.2.1. The Variables and the Data

The major variables investigated in this study are: sex; occupation; size of firm; education; worker experience, i.e. job tenure; age; working hours; bonuses (or special payments). Particular meanings of these variables will be mentioned later. The consensus among the many studies for the US economy and other industrialized countries indicates the principal determinants of wage differentials to be: differentials in education; racial and sexual discrimination; age; and trade unions.

These factors, with the exception of trade unions, are fully investigated, and eventually provide the sources of comparative studies between the USA and Japan. Since there is no major racial heterogeneity in Japan, the racial aspect is also ignored. There are no reliable data on union membership in Japan by category of labour. As Table 3.1 shows, however, the ratio of participation in trade unions is related to the size of the firm in which the workers have their jobs. More specifically, the participation ratio increases as the firm becomes bigger. See Tachibanaki (1993*a*) for details regarding the effect of unions on wage determination. It is noted that movement in the participation ratio has been fairly stable after the massive emergence of trade unions in the immediate post-Second World War period, and that the participation ratio has much weaker relationship with differences in education or sex than with

TABLE 3.1. *Number of workers in trade unions and estimated participation ratio in trade unions*

Size[a]	No. (000)		Ratio (%)	
	All firms	Manufacturing industries	All firms	Manufacturing industries
500<	4,135	2,402	60.5	69.0
100–499	1,180	729	38.4	42.9
30–99	372	202	10.6	12.4
20>	292	53	3.4	1.9
TOTAL	5,979	3,386	17.8	35.9

[a] Classified by the number of workers in a firm.
Source: Ministry of Labour, *Fundamental Survey of Trade Unions* (1963).

the size of firm. Accordingly, the exclusion of trade unions from explicit consideration in this investigation does not imply complete disregard for the effect of trade unions on wage differentials.

Now each variable mentioned in the first part of this section is explained.

1. *Sex*. Male or female.
2. *Occupation*. Two types of worker are examined: manual and non-manual. In the official terminology of the source statistics, manual and non-manual workers are called 'wage-earners' and 'salaried employees' respectively. However, since 'wage-earners' denotes workers who perform production duties of a physical nature, and since 'salaried employees' denotes workers who are engaged in tasks which are largely administrative, technical, or clerical in nature, the former terminologies have been adopted in this study. They are roughly consistent with the distinction between 'blue-collar' and 'white-collar' in many sociological studies.
3. *Size of firm*. This factor intends to clarify the inter-scale differential which has been suggested as characterizing the Japanese labour market. Three classifications are considered by means of the number of workers in the firm where they are employed. It is noted that three classifications are given for published sources. Individual observations used in Chapters 4 and 5 have more detailed classifi-

cations. A large firm is defined as one with 1,000 or more employees, a medium one by 100–999, and a small one by 10–99. Unfortunately, the data source does not give consistent classifications in time-series; in some years five classifications are given, in others three, and so. Consequently, the raw data were reduced to three classifications in order to obtain consistent measures in time series.

4. *Education.* Four types of educational level are considered. Table 3.2 shows a brief summary of educational attainment; the number in this table denotes the years of schooling corresponding to the graduation level. The level of education is expressed in terms of the new system for our purposes.

Several remarks are necessary with regard to educational attainment. First, educational attainment is not indicated by the length of schooling but by the graduation level. The fact that dropping out from school before graduation seldom occurs in Japan justifies this particular indicator. Second, there is a minor inconsistency between the new system and the old system, connected with the length of schooling. Firms, however, do not emphasize the length of schooling when they recruit their employees, but rather consider the graduation level. More concretely, even though there are three years' difference of schooling at the lowest level between the new system and the old one, firms regard this group as the lowest class of achievement in education, with the feeling that three years do not make that much difference. Third, female workers (both manual and non-manual) and male manual workers are classified only by two categories in educational attainment in the later analysis:

TABLE 3.2. *Educational attainment*

New system (post-war)	Age (years)	Old system (pre-war)	Age (years)
Junior high school	9	Elementary school	6
Senior high school	12	Middle school	11
Junior college	14	High school and technical college	14
College or university	16	University	17

Source: Ministry of Labour, *Advanced Report on Employment Activity* (1970).

junior high school and senior high school and above. This implies that the second education group included in the figures has a higher educational attainment than that of senior high school. This situation, however, does not affect the figures (mainly wage figures) in the class, because there are actually very few workers who are either female (both manuals and non-manuals) or male manuals with degrees at junior college or college. Table 3.3 indicates this explanation.

The small proportion of female workers with junior college or college degrees is usually explained by two reasons in Japan; first, there is considerable discrimination against the educated female in the process of hiring in any field; second, a number of educated women do not have strong incentives to enter the labour market. These subjects will be examined carefully in Chapter 7. For male manual workers, it is understandable that there are few male manuals who hold junior college or college degrees.

5. *Experience*. 'Duration of service' of workers with their present employer is the measure used for this variable. Of course, it is risky to state that experience, in the economic sense, is measured only by duration of service. At the moment, however, it is enough to understand that duration of service simply called 'experience' is one important variable to be used in the later analysis on wage differentials. *Nenko-joretsu*, which is a controversial system peculiar to Japan, is related to this variable, and will be discussed later. This variable is equivalent to 'job tenure', a term used frequently in the literature.

6. *Age*. Little explanation is required for this variable. Japanese firms pay particular wages on the basis of need in cost of living to

TABLE 3.3. *Newly hired females employed in manufacturing (000), 1968*

	New Graduates	%	Other Employees	%
Junior high	118.5	42.9	538.2	73.7
Senior high	144.9	52.6	183.0	26.0
Junior college, college	12.5	4.5	9.2	1.3
TOTAL	275.9	100.0	730.4	100.0

Source: Ministry of Labour, *Advanced Report on Employment Activity*.

their employees, because they feel that as the employees become older they need to spend more on housing, dependants (spouse and children), education, social necessities, etc. This kind of remuneration is usually paid in proportion to the worker's age, and is called the 'living wage' see Taira, 1970: (ch. 6, for its evolution and meaning; also Ono, 1989). This reflects the traditional or paternalistic nature of Japanese society.

7. *Working hours.* Elementary microeconomic theory teaches us that wage earnings and working hours have different dimensions. It is important to distinguish between the gross wage earning and the wage earnings *per hour* (see Hall, 1970). It is noted, however, that workers in Japan usually do not seriously consider the wage earnings *per hour* when they look for employment, but instead pay attention to the gross values (or lump-sum basis) per month. In other words, the concept of the wage per hour is not necessarily important for employees and employers as a decision-making variable. Nevertheless, as far as working hours differ between workers (see Table 3.8 below), it is much more reasonable to adopt the wage earnings per hour for a study on wage differentials. Consequently, wage earnings are adjusted by working hours of workers.

8. *Bonuses (or special payments).* The bonus system is unique in Japan, and is usually paid twice a year. This remuneration has been often neglected in the history of wages. I believe that the bonus is one of the most important regular payments to workers in Japan. The reasoning is as follows: first, the employers usually regard the bonus payment as one of the regular wage costs. Second, there are no payments to particular workers who performed very well in the particular year, though it true that the bonus in Japan is paid on the basis of workers' performance in a limited way, i.e. the bonus figures are often negotiated at collective-bargaining sessions between representatives of employers and trade unions in deciding what multiple of monthly wages should be paid as a bonus. This multiple is usually applied to all employees in the company. Third, the bonus is not thought of as a windfall by workers: they often earmark earnings from the bonus for monthly expenditure, since they expect to receive it periodically. These considerations, and the fact that the bonus makes up around 10–20 per cent, maybe more, of the total earnings, led me to conclude that the bonus should be included in wage figures. Concretely, the bonus (transformed into

an equivalent monthly figure) is added to the monthly regular contracted wage.

To sum up, (1) sex, (2) occupation, (3) education, (4) size, (5) experience (or job tenure), and (6) age are regarded as the factors which explain wage differentials. (7) Working hours and (8) bonus are considered as adjustment factors to the final wage figures.

3.2.2. Estimation Method

The estimation procedure is an application of the idea of the Analysis of Variance (ANOVA). A simple statement of the equation form for the six-way layout is given in (3.1).

$$\begin{aligned}
W_{ijklmn,h} = &\, u + a_i + b_j + c_k + d_l + e_m + f_n \\
&+ (ab)_{ij} + (ac)_{ik} + \ldots + (df)_{ln} + (ef)_{mn} \\
&+ (abc)_{ijk} + (abd)_{ijl} + \ldots + (cef)_{kmn} + (def)_{lmn} \\
&+ (abcd)_{ijkl} + \ldots + (cdef)_{klmn} \\
&+ (abcde)_{ijklm} + \ldots + (bcdef)_{jklmn} \\
&+ (abcdef)_{ijklmn} + \ldots + V_{ijklmn,h}
\end{aligned} \quad (3.1)$$

The subscripts i,j,k,l,m,n denote the level of each factor, $a,b,c,d,e,f,$ and $(ab), (ac),$ etc. indicate the parameters. Table 3.4 summarizes the meaning of the subscripts and the parameters.

The left-hand variable, $W_{ijklmn,h}$, denotes the wage earnings per hour of the hth person of the i,j,k,l,m,n 'cell'. $a_i, b_j, c_k, d_l, e_m, f_n$ refer to the effect of each level of the factor. Effects of this nature that pertain to a single level of a factor are called 'main effects'. The effects called 'interaction effects' represent the manner in which each level of one main effect interacts with each level of the other main effect: $(ab)_{ij}, (ac)_{ik}, \ldots (ef)_{mn}$ are called 'first-order interactions', and interaction between three factors is called 'second-order-interaction'. Third-, fourth-, and higher-order interactions follow in like manner. u denotes the grand mean, and $V_{ijklmn,h}$ is an error term peculiar to $W_{ijklmn,h}$.

When the data are 'unbalanced' (following the terminology in Searle, 1987), great difficulty arises in computation and statistical testing, and the standard technique (e.g. Scheffé, 1959: ch. 4 for the

TABLE 3.4. *Variables*

Sex	
$i = 1$	Female
$i = 2$	Male
Occupation	
$j = 1$	Manual
$j = 2$	Non-manual
Size	
$k = 1$	Small
$k = 2$	Medium
$k = 3$	Large
Education	
$l = 1$	Junior high school
$l = 2$	Senior high school
$l = 3$	Junior college
$l = 4$	College or university
Experience (job tenure)	
$m = 1$	0–1 year
$m = 2$	1–2 years
$m = 3$	2–3
$m = 4$	3–5
$m = 5$	6–9
$m = 6$	10–14
$m = 7$	15–19
$m = 8$	20–9
Age	
$n = 1$	18–19 years
$n = 2$	20–4
$n = 3$	25–9
$n = 4$	30–9
$n = 5$	35–9
$n = 6$	40–9
$n = 7$	50–9

higher-way layouts) is not easily applicable. 'Balanced data' means equal numbers of observation in the cells; 'unbalanced data' means unequal numbers of observations in the cells, including perhaps some that contain no observations at all (empty cells). In most cases of experimental design, unbalanced data is more common than balanced data.

There are several difficulties in this investigation. First, the figures (the wage earnings per hour) are not given individually, but are given by the sample means of the cells, although the number of workers who belong to the particular cell is given. Second, there are some empty cells because certain combinations of experience and age are not logically observable. An example is given by the case of 30-year-old workers who cannot have twenty years of experience (or job tenure) after graduation from school. The percentage of no observations to the potential (or possible) number of cells is 18 per cent. Errors may arise from neglecting this problem.

These two circumstances, together with the fact that the model itself is already higher-way layout ANOVA (which imposes a heavy computational burden even in balanced data), make several compromises inevitable. First, higher-order interactions (namely, second-order interaction and higher orders) have been ignored. This compromise is not very restrictive: even if the results of higher-order interactions were obtained, economic interpretations would be difficult. Searle (1971) actually suggests consideration of the 'main-effects-only models' in the higher-way layout for unbalanced data. In this study, first-order interaction is examined, since it is possible to interpret such interactions. Second, it is noted that several interactions even in the first order, where the factors are associated with empty cells (i.e. experience and age), are excluded from the estimation, because if included they are not estimable (see Kempthorne, 1951). Third, this compromise, albeit the most harmful, is unavoidable; the number of observations in each cell is regarded as 1 when there is the mean value there (in other words, the mean value is treated as if the observation were 1), and regarded as 0 when there is no observation. When unequal numbers of observations occur, with some empty cells, in higher-way layout, the situation becomes worse; unfortunately, this is our case. However, there is one way to overcome the non-observation problem in certain cells by way of single observation for the other cells (see Kempthorne, 1951: ch. 6). The third compromise was made with this in mind. Note that the third compromise is only an approximation to reality; the empirical results presented subsequently are approximations to the true stories.

Barger (1971) proposed an interesting procedure for the case of unequal numbers of observations in the cells without empty cells, which is primarily intended for the purpose of a statistical test (χ^2 test). His conclusion seems to indicate that if the number of observations in each cell is sufficiently large (this condition, of course, is satisfied by our data), each level of each factor together with its interaction is highly statistically significant for the explanation of wage differentials. Keeping in mind this strong significance, the third compromise is partly justified, since our number of observations in each cell is sufficiently large.

Recent years have seen several technical developments which are likely to overcome the severe difficulties described above; See, for example, Dallal (1992) and Searle (1987; 1994). The present work in this chapter has not taken into account such new developments, simply because it is impossible to recalculate parameters for the early periods of the 1950s and 1960s. In other words, it is important to keep a common statistical technique for the entire period to obtain empirical results which can be used for time-series interpretation.

After preliminary investigations of the technical difficulties, a least-squares estimate is obtained on the parameterization in equation (3.1) with neglect of second and higher interactions and certain first-order interactions.

The usual side conditions are imposed to permit estimation. The forms are slightly modified in order to implement an easy method for the solution to the normal equations

$$\sum_{i=1}^{2} p_i a_i = 0$$

$$\sum_{j=1}^{2} q_j b_j = 0$$

$$\sum_{k=1}^{3} r_k c_k = 0$$

$$\sum_{l=1}^{2} s_l d_l = 0$$

$$\sum_{m=1}^{8} t_m e_m = 0$$

$$\sum_{n=1}^{7} u_n f_n = 0$$

$$\sum_{i=1}^{2}(pq)_{ij}(ab)_{ij} = \sum_{j=1}^{2}(pq)_{ij}(ab)_{ij} = 0$$

$$\vdots$$

$$\sum_{i=1}^{2}(pu)_{in}(af)_{in} = \sum_{n=1}^{7}(pu)_{in}(af)_{in} = 0$$

$$\vdots$$

$$\sum_{l=1}^{2}(st)_{lm}(de)_{lm} = \sum_{m=1}^{8}(st)_{lm}(de)_{lm} = 0 \qquad (3.2)$$

$p, q, \ldots, (pq), (pr), \ldots, (pt), \ldots$, show the number of levels in certain factors. It is noted that the weighted factors associated with non-zero observations such as p_i, q_j, r_k, s_l, $(pq)_{ij}$, etc., give same numbers. Therefore, (3.2) reduces to the usual side conditions (3.3).

i.e. $$\sum_{i} a_i = \sum_{j} b_j = \sum_{k} c_k \sum_{l} d_l = 0$$

$$\sum_{j}(ab)_{ij} = \sum_{j}(ab)_{ij} = \ldots \sum(cd)_{kl} = 0$$

$$\ldots \qquad (3.3)$$

Two types of calculation have been performed. Table 3.5 summarizes the adopted variables for the calculations. The figures in Table 3.5 indicate the number of levels of each factor. The distinction between the two models appears mainly in education. As previously noted, male non-manuals are classified into four levels in education, and all females and male manuals are classified into two levels. The second model is intended for investigating the effect of education more clearly, particularly for male non-manuals who are supposed to be highly dispersed by education.

The actual calculation has been carried out for the two models every year to provide the bases for the study of the impact of structural change in certain variables on wage differentials. Since the estimated coefficients are too cumbersome, only the result based on the main effects is presented and discussed. Interested readers can refer to Tachibanaki (1975; 1982).

Generally speaking, there are several criteria by which to evaluate the importance of the effect of a factor on wage differentials derived from the ANOVA result:

TABLE 3.5. *Variables and the number of levels*

Factors	First model (Male and Female)	Second model (Male non-manual)
Sex	2	0
Occupation	2	0
Size	3	3
Education	2 (JH, SH)	4 (JH, SH, JC, C)
Experience	8	8
Age	7	6

1. The relative magnitudes of the estimated coefficients.
2. The comparison of the *estimated* wage earnings holding other characteristics constant.
3. The relative contribution of a particular effect measured by the ratio of the sum of squares by the coefficient to the total sum of squares by coefficients. (This method is called the 'marginal sum of squares method' for convenience in this study.)

None of these criteria is definitely better than the other; this study tries to evaluate the result using all three. Their adoption has been largely decided by the feasibility of the actual calculation or comparison. It is too cumbersome, practically speaking, to use the first two criteria in evaluating the time trend of the effect, because there are so many coefficients to be compared for criterion (1), and because there are also so many *estimated* wage earnings to be compared for criterion (2). More specifically, it is not so easy to compare six factors simultaneously when the number of levels in the factors is different from criterion (1). It is possible, however, to compare only a pair of factors. For criterion (2), there are 552 *estimated* wage earnings, for example, to show how sex affects wage earnings if other characteristics are equal between male and female.

The first two criteria are used to evaluate the effect of the factor, and to evaluate how one factor differs from other factors. The last criterion (namely, the marginal sum of squares method) is used to evaluate the time trend of the relative importance of a factor compared with other factors.

3.2.3. Empirical Result

This section is devoted to the first two criteria, particularly for main effects.

(i) The first model is discussed initially. Table 3.6 shows the estimated coefficients only for 1958, 1970, and 1985 to save space. The difference within a factor such as sex or occupation (i.e. the evaluation of the effect of the level) appeared to coincide with a priori knowledge: male receives higher wage earnings than female, and non-manuals receive higher than manuals, etc.

As to the differing importance of factors, the major effects on wage differentials are sex, experience, and age because the estimated coefficients are relatively larger than others; moderate factors are occupation and size; education shows a very weak effect because the coefficients are the smallest.

Each main effect is explained in order.

3.2.3.1. Sex. To be female in Japan implies a far lower wage, as shown in the Table 3.6: for example, the estimated wage differential due to the main effect of sex is 57.4 yen per hour in 1958 and 155.6 yen per hour in 1970. The *estimated* wage earnings per hour by sex, holding other characteristics constant (namely, manual workers who are 25–9 years old, in a medium-sized firm, with senior high school degree and three to five years' experience), are given in Table 3.7.

Since the pure sex effect on wages appears in these figures, it is possible to state that there has been considerable discrimination against women in the determination of wages in Japan. This phenomenon exists not only in wages but also in the process of hiring and promotion.

3.2.3.2. Experience. Experience is of great interest in this study. As the theory of human capital teaches, on-the job training is an important element of human capital as well as education (Mincer, 1962; 74). Long-term employment in a firm gives the opportunity to gain more job skills from 'learning by doing' and from formal and informal training. The firms are aware of the fact that the skills

TABLE 3.6. *Estimated parameters of the main effects (10 yen)*[a]

	1958	1970	1985
Grand mean	+9.39	+31.53	+100.77
Sex			
Female	−2.87	−7.78	−24.95
Male	+2.87	+7.78	+24.95
Occupation			
Manual	−1.55	−2.62	−6.50
Non-manual	+1.55	+2.62	+6.50
Size			
Small	−1.77	−4.46	−9.29
Medium	−0.77	−0.88	−3.58
Large	+1.84	+5.34	+12.87
Education			
Junior high	−0.51	−1.18	−4.80
Senior high	+0.51	+1.18	+4.80
Experience			
0–1	−1.91	−5.47	−23.77
1–2	−1.99	−4.38	−16.72
2–3	−1.57	−3.94	−13.51
3–5	−1.12	−2.54	−2.87
6–9	+0.48	+1.35	+8.93
10–14	+2.25	+6.11	+20.20
15–19	+3.96	+9.10	+32.61
20–9	+5.40	+13.10	+40.54
Age			
18–19	−4.58	−10.40	−41.12
20–4	−3.29	−6.85	−26.62
25–9	−1.47	−2.15	−18.03
30–4	+0.05	+1.00	−6.03
35–9	+1.32	+3.58	+3.22
40–9	+2.53	+4.15	+13.21 (40–4)
			+12.67 (45–9)
50–9	+1.56	+2.50	+10.75 (50–4)
			+5.08 (55–9)

[a] The first model for 1958, 1970, and 1985.

TABLE 3.7. *Estimated wage earnings*

	Female (yen)	Male (yen)	Ratio, male:female
1958	37.1	67.7	1.82
1962	64.3	111.3	1.73
1966	105.7	161.3	1.53
1970	184.3	294.5	1.60

of labour increase in proportion to workers' length of service, and respond to this benefit by offering an automatic increase in wages. In the Japanese economy, this system in called *nenko-joretsu*. There are several disputes about *nenko-joretsu*. One important controversy concerns its cause and appraisal: whether *nenko-joretsu* coincides with economic rationality, or whether it is mainly connected with the paternalistic nature of the Japanese social system, because *nenko-joretsu* is often accompanied by life-long employment at one firm. I tend to believe the former. The fact that only permanent regular workers (*Honko*) can receive the full benefit of *nenko-joretsu* in Japan is one reason; other classes of workers, such as temporary regulars (*Rinjiko*), non-committed temporary regulars, day-labourers, and extra workers (*Shagaiko*), rarely enjoy *nenko-joretsu*. Firms try to attract permanent regular workers with *nenko-joretsu* in other to keep them, while temporary workers are taken on at lower wages to meet short-run and cyclical variations in labour requirements and are laid off more frequently than permanent regular workers. Trade unions organized mainly by permanent regular workers have consistently demanded that *nenko-joretsu* be maintained. The above description clearly meets with the mutual economic interests of employees and employers.

The result shows that wage differentials are monotonically increasing functions of experience: this justifies the view that longer experience provides more skills, or that post-school investment in terms of Mincer (1970) is important.

3.2.3.3. *Occupation.* As expected, white-collar workers earn higher wages than blue-collar workers, though the effect is not so strong as that of sex, experience, and age.

How Have Wage Differentials Changed?

3.2.3.4. Size. There has been wide recognition that the inter-scale differential represents the nature of the labour market in Japan. Odaka (1984) is a comprehensive study of inter-scale wage differentials, including its historical development. Paine (1971) surveys the problem, claiming that bigger firms can pay higher wages by citing four reasons:

Bigger firms are more likely to know the advanced imported technology than are smaller ones.
A productivity difference due mainly to the differences in capital intensity causes the inter-scale difference.
The oligopolistic situations of the bigger firms allow extra profits.
Institutional factors like *nenko-joretsu* and the difference in the unionization rate depend on firm size.

The results indicate that inter-scale difference exists to a certain extent; for example, the difference between large and small firms due to the main effect is 36.1 yen in 1958 and 98.0 yen in 1970—roughly two-thirds of the difference due to main effect of sex in respective years. Two studies, Blumenthal (1966) and Stoikov (1973), dealing with inter-scale differentials in wages have shown weak effects of scale. I suspect that the difference between these studies and the present one is due to the fact that they failed to include the bonus payment which I regard as one of the regular payments, and that they did not deflate the wage earnings by working hours. Table 3.8 shows the ratio of bonus to the regular monthly contracted wages, and the working-hours difference by sex, occupation, size, and education. This table indicates that the bonus and the working hours are considerably different in size—in other words, the bonus increases and the working hours decrease as size increases—and that sex, occupation, and education do not give any sizeable changes in bonus and working hours, except for occupation on the bonus and sex on the working hours. The first assertion means that the wage earnings per hour, including the bonus, are much more dispersed by size than those unadjusted. The result of this study seems to confirm the above statement. It is noted, however, that even though the wage earnings adjusted by bonus and working hours are used, size is a weaker factor than sex, experience, and age. (Table 3.9 indicates this fact in a different way.)

TABLE 3.8. *Ratio of bonuses (on a monthly basis) to the regular monthly contracted wages (1965) and the working hours (per month)*

	Bonus/monthly wage						Working hours per month					
	JH			SH			JH			SH		
	S	M	L	S	M	L	S	M	L	S	M	L
Female manual	0.112	0.178	0.227	0.108	0.195	0.253	203	198	190	202	197	186
Female non-manual	0.138	0.228	0.308	0.151	0.220	0.268	205	197	188	204	198	188
Male manual	0.121	0.204	0.250	0.142	0.223	0.257	222	216	204	223	216	203
Male non-manual	0.202	0.290	0.330	0.204	0.278	0.338	215	209	202	214	209	200

JH: junior high graduates; SH: senior high graduates. S: small; M: medium; L: large.

TABLE 3.9. *Effects of six factors on wage differentials 1958–1970, 1975–1978, 1981–1985: partitions of the sum of squares (percentage)*

	1958	1959	1960	1961	1962	1963	1964	1965	1966	1967	1968	1969	1970
Sex	36.0	27.1	31.7	34.8	32.7	34.7	37.1	37.2	41.6	44.2	43.5	46.6	41.6
Occupation	10.5	10.0	7.9	8.8	8.6	7.9	8.5	7.3	6.8	4.1	5.1	5.7	4.7
Size	10.1	17.4	13.2	10.1	11.8	10.8	7.2	7.5	5.1	5.5	7.6	7.2	11.3
Education	1.1	0.9	0.9	1.2	1.1	0.9	1.3	1.8	1.4	1.9	0.9	1.0	1.0
Experience	24.3	25.0	26.2	25.7	26.6	23.5	25.5	27.7	26.4	28.6	26.9	24.3	23.0
Age	18.1	19.7	20.0	19.4	19.2	20.4	20.5	18.8	18.8	15.8	16.1	15.3	18.5
TOTAL	100	100	100	100	100	100	100	100	100	100	100	100	100

	1975	1976	1977	1978	1981	1982	1983	1984	1985
Sex	43.8	41.1	41.4	44.7	34.4	32.8	32.3	37.9	37.4
Occupation	4.8	4.9	6.0	5.0	4.0	4.2	4.0	3.6	2.5
Size	16.7	17.0	14.6	15.6	12.1	11.4	11.1	5.0	5.3
Education	1.1	2.0	1.6	1.4	1.0	1.1	1.4	1.2	1.4
Experience	20.0	21.1	21.7	20.1	24.9	27.1	26.6	31.9	31.7
Age	13.7	13.9	14.7	13.3	23.7	23.4	24.7	20.3	21.7
TOTAL	100	100	100	100	100	100	100	100	100

3.2.3.5. Education. This factor has the weakest effect on wage differentials when the analysis is concerned with the two-level classifications in education (junior high and senior high), because the estimated coefficients are the smallest. This implies that the difference in education between junior high graduates and senior high does not have a large influence on wage differentials.

3.2.3.6. Age. Age shows an increasing effect on wage differentials except for the oldest group (55–9 years old). The retirement age in Japan was around 60 in these years. Therefore, this group has shown a downward effect on wages.

It is important to note here the difference between experience and age. While experience reflects the economic rationality of wage determinations as described above, age reflects the paternalistic nature of the Japanese society. An important result is that experience shows a somewhat stronger effect than age, indicating that economic rationality dominates paternalism.

(ii) The second model (male non-manuals) is briefly discussed without showing the estimated coefficients to save space. One notable difference between the first model and the second is seen in the influence of education, because the estimated coefficients are relatively large. The first model revealed education to be a negligible factor in determining wage differentials. The second, however, discloses an important effect of education as far as male non-manuals are concerned. To be educated in the male non-manual category (namely, junior college graduates and college graduates) provides considerable benefits in wage earnings. It is especially disadvantageous to be a junior high graduate in the male non-manuals. These phenomena have been brought out not only by the fact that male non-manuals are highly dispersed by education but also by the fact that male non-manual workers are usually engaged in skilled tasks. Another important feature is that education is an equally powerful effect as size, which was not the case in the first model. Experience and age also have an influence, with a slightly stronger effect for age than for experience, which implies that for male non-manuals paternalism is more important than economic rationality.

3.3. TIME-SERIES CHANGE IN MAIN EFFECTS

This section discusses the change in the relative importance of each variable in explaining wage differentials in the time-series context. The basic tool for this analysis is the third of the three criteria listed above. More concretely, analysis uses the ratio of marginal sum of squares by each 'main effect (variable)' to the total sum of squares by the main effect. Although it is possible to incorporate marginal sum of squares by each interaction, including higher-order interactions, this was not attempted, because the ratio of marginal sum of squares by interactions to total sum of squares is about 10 per cent, as shown by Tachibanaki (1975). In other words, it is enough to take account of only marginal sum of squares by main effects, by ignoring the contribution of interactions, to draw the contribution of each variable to total wage differentials. The ratio of marginal sum of squares by each main effect may be called roughly 'the relative contribution of each variable to total wage differentials', because it indicates partition of sum of squares.

Table 3.9 shows the ratio of marginal sum of squares by each main effect to total sum of squares by main effects. Technically speaking, the ratio is calculated in the following way (percentage figures). Example is given for the sex variable.

$$\frac{JKLMN\sum_i (\hat{a}_i)^2}{JKLMN\sum_j (\hat{a}_i)^2 + IKLMN\sum_j (\hat{b}_j)^2 + \ldots ILKJM\sum_n (\hat{f}_n)^2} \times 100$$

where I, J, K, L, M, N denote the numbers of levels for the factors. Note that the actual calculation was slightly modified from the above formulation, because systematic adjustment due to non-existing levels in certain factors is necessary.

Some explanation is required concerning the sample period. The starting-year of the analysis is 1958, and 1970 is the end of the first period; this covers thirteen years, and corresponds to the period of rapid growth in the Japanese economy. The starting-year of the second period is 1975, and 1985 is the end; of this covers eleven years, although two years (1979 and 1980) are missing for technical reasons. This period corresponds to the period following the oil crisis, during which the country was no longer experiencing rapid economic growth. A period of low-growth economy ensued; in addition, the economy shifted from a state of nearly full employment to one with a substantial number of unemployed workers. Finally, it would be ideal if recent years were included in this time-series calculation to complete the story of the post-war wage differentials. It was not done for the following two reasons. First, the published source, the *Wage Structure Survey*, recently abandoned perfect layout of variables; in other words, complete cross-classification based on six variables is not available, at least in the published source, and thus the ANOVA is not easily applicable. Second, the author happened to be able to use individual observations of the *Wage Structure Survey* in 1988. This enables him to provide a more profound analysis, and to give a more comprehensive answer than an analysis based on the published source. The analysis based on individual observations will be presented later in this book.

Table 3.9 shows the time-series change in the relative importance of each variable to total wage differentials, which is given by the ratio of marginal sum of squares by each main effect to the total sum of squares by main effects. Some of the important observations based on this table are as follows. First, it is striking to note that sex (i.e. male/female wage differentials) accounted for over one-third of the sum of squares by main effects; the dominance of male/female difference is quite remarkable during the whole period. A surprising thing is that the percentage of marginal sum of squares by sex had increased from the beginning of the period to the late 1960s and the middle 1970s; the wage differential due to sex had been increasing during that period.

Why did this occur in Japan despite the fact that the influence of male/female wage difference had been reduced in most civilized countries owing to social pressure? Japan, however, gives the opposite result during the period. A possible explanation may be that immediately after the war, Japan became a democratic society; equal rights for men and women were proclaimed, even though it was a fairly imperfect system. Hence, wage differential due to sex was eliminated to a considerable extent. This equality was short-lived, however: as society emerged from the confusion of the post-war period, the traditional structure reappeared. It is noted, however, that the effect of sex had declined slightly in the 1980s; this is due mainly to the fact that equal employment and treatment of men and women was decreed by law in the mid-1980s; therefore, male/female wage differentials declined recently. It is impressive, nevertheless, to note that sex is still the most important factor to explain total age differentials. This aspect will be investigated more carefully in Chapter 7.

Second, occupation showed a long-run decreasing importance during the entire period, although there are several minor fluctuations. Wage differentials between white-collar and blue-collar workers in general have decreased almost constantly. It is possible to state that no apparent wage differential between them can be observed in recent years. This is a remarkable feature in comparison with other industrialized countries, where inter-occupational or inter-professional wage differentials are substantial. Three notes must be added regarding the absence of any significant effect of occupation on wage differentials in Japan. First, one would probably obtain a slightly more significant effect of occupation, even in Japan, if more detailed occupational classifications rather than just two were applied—i.e. non-manual workers versus manual workers, or white-collar versus blue-collar. Second, it is very likely that the effects of education and of occupation are interrelated. Thus, it is somewhat misleading to judge the effect of occupation as almost negligible. Third, it would be interesting to enquire into the cause of the extremely minor effect of occupation on wage differentials in Japan, since other industrialized counties have strong effects. It is not an overstatement to say that occupational and professional wage differentials are one of the most important issues in wage determination in many Euro-American countries. One obvious answer to this mystery is that the Japanese industrial relations system emphasized the importance of personal characteristics of age and job tenure in the determination of wages, and to a great extent ignored the difference in difficulties associated with jobs and assignments. There must be some other important reasons peculiar to both Japan and the Euro-American countries. (Tachibanaki 1996*b* offers a new international study of occupational wage differentials.)

Third, education maintained an almost negligible effect on wage differentials. Again, this applies only to the difference between junior high school graduates and senior high school graduates. If university graduates were included, we would obtain a different feature, as was shown by the case of male white-collar workers in this chapter and will be shown in Chapter 7 of this book.

Fourth, the most interesting result regarding the time-series change appears in the effect of inter-scale wage differentials. The effect of the size of firm fluctuates considerably. Such fluctuations correspond largely to business cycle fluctuations. In the late 1950s and the entire 1960s the Japanese economy was in a period of rapid growth with minor recessions; after the oil crises the economy entered into a serious recession, and the period of rapid economic growth ended. This continued until the early 1980s; the economy again experienced a boom, the 'bubble economy', in the middle and late 1980s. The effect of the size of firm on wage differentials is nearly counter-cyclical to the movement of business cycles. The inter-scale wage differential declined constantly during the period of rapid economic growth, while it increased significantly after the period of oil crises. The former period signifies the transformation from a labour surplus economy to a labour shortage economy (see e.g. Minami, 1972). During the period, smaller-size enterprises were obliged to offer higher wages to attract workers facing a labour shortage; this apparently narrowed the gap between wages in smaller firms and larger firms.

The serious recession in the 1970s changed the course of the Japanese economy because employers, in particular smaller-sized firms, found difficulty in keeping their employees. Also, there were again a large number of job-seekers caused by the recession. Therefore, employers in smaller firms could lower the wage level of their employees. Naturally, the inter-scale difference reappeard during the recession.

Another boom occurred in the mid-1980s. The effect of size had declined again, for the almost same reasons as described for the period of rapid economic growth in the 1960s, although there was a pressure of higher labour supply of females in the 1980s. The boom continued until the late 1980s. In facing a serious labour shortage during the period, even the introduction of foreign 'guest workers' was to consideration; in fact, a considerable number of foreign workers were employed, legally and illegally. It is not surprising, therefore, that the inter-scale wage differentials declined to their lowest in the middle 1980s.

How Have Wage Differentials Changed?

A new, serious recession, the 'post-bubble economy recession', occurred in the late 1980s and the early 1990s. This recession, caused largely by internal financial factors, is the longest and deepest in the post-war period. As was pointed out previously, the ratio of marginal sum of squares to the total sum of squares is not provided for technical reasons; figures of the size of firm in this table would be larger in these years, if calculated. Chapter 4, which deals with inter-scale wage differentials by using individual observations, in fact presents a wider wage differential by size of firm, thus confirming the fact that a recession raises the degree of inter-scale wage differentials.

In summarizing the effect of the size of firm, we conclude that there is a considerable negative correlation between the inter-scale wage differential and the business cycle. When the economy is booming, the inter-scale wage differential is narrower, while the opposite is true in a recession. The condition of the economy, a boom or a recession, affects firms' ability to pay. The inter-scale wage differential is influenced both by the ability to pay, to a considerable extent, and by general labour market conditions, such as tightness of the labour market or rate of unemployment.

Fifth, two variables—experience (i.e. job tenure) and age—have been constant influences over the period, unlike sex, occupation, and firm size. This phenomenon may be attributed to the peculiar characteristics in the Japanese labour market: economic rationality in the form of *nenko-joretsu*, and the paternalistic social system. It is important to note that experience was always somewhat stronger than age regarding the effect on wage differential during the entire period.

Finally, one question asked by many specialists is whether the above findings will apply over coming years. Before considering the matter in detail, it is necessary to discuss the changes that took place in the Japanese economy and will take place in future. On the macroeconomic level, the growth rate in Japan's gross national product decreased sharply, from its previous strong, rapid rates of over 10 per cent per year to much slower ones, of the order of 2–4 per cent annually. In addition, the economy shifted from a state of nearly full employment to one with a substantial number of unemployed workers. At that time, some labour economists conjectured that the Japanese industrial relations system had been drastically altered, as managers responded to the poor business conditions. It was reported that managers stopped observing lifetime employment relations and the *nenko* wage determination principles; this made it possible for them to hire relatively lowpaid and young workers, and to cut the high wages of older and experienced employees. It was also reported that policies on promotions, early voluntary retirement, and bonus payments were reformulated.

Those who contend that the Japanese industrial relations system changed radically during this period argue that, because of the severe recession, the economic conditions that formerly enabled employers to guarantee permanent employment to regular workers no longer existed. Temporary and female workers, who had been discharged and laid off in past, milder recessions, had to leave the labour force completely and could no longer be used to protect the jobs and salaries of regular workers. At the same time, managers were forced to deal with a growing population of elderly workers who normally received higher wages according to the *nenko* system. This problem was further aggravated because the policy of mandatory retirement at the age of 55 was being virtually ignored, owing to recent increases in average life expectancy. It was argued that the natural reaction of managers was to disregard the basic *nenko* principles and cut the wages of older and more experienced workers, thereby reducing expenses.

Some economists, including this author, disagree with this proposition. They believe that the basic *nenko* principles are essentially rules for distributing jobs and rewards among employees. These rules are economically rational for both employers and employees and, therefore, resistant to changes in external economic conditions. Arguments for the rationality and strengths of the *nenko* wage system have been made by Taira (1970) and the present author previously, and thus will not be repeated here.

The result in Table 3.9 supports the above conclusion. Recent studies, nevertheless (e.g. Tachibanaki, 1992), proposed that a merit pay system based on performance evaluation of employees should be applied more broadly and solidly than in the current system, in addition to the two main determinants of wages, namely, experience (i.e. job tenure) and age, to raise incentive and productivity of employees. Also, both employers and employees are in an agreement regarding the importance of a merit pay system. Therefore, it is likely that the two main determinants of wages in the Japanese economy will decline somewhat in importance in the future.

3.4. CONCLUDING REMARKS

The main conclusion based on the time-series analysis of the variance method can be summarized as follows. First, sex appeared to be the most important factor in the determination of wage differentials, and its role increased in the earlier period and decreased in the latter period. Second, experience (i.e. job tenure) and, to a lesser extent, age appeared relatively significant throughout, indicating that employers tended to abide by the basic *nenko* principle in determining wages. A merit pay system, however, in addition to the *nenko* system, is certainly a future determinant. Third, the dual structure, in terms of inter-scale differences in wage determination, appeared to be fluctuating according to the movement of business cycles. Fourth, education and occupation appeared to be of little importance in explaining wage differentials, except for male non-manual (i.e., white-collar) workers, at face values on the basis of the analysis of variance. The effect of education and occupation will be examined in Chapter 7 by using the different statistical method and data source.

4

The Employer Size Effect on Wage Differentials

4.1. INTRODUCTION

There is a strong tradition of studies on inter-size wage differentials in Japan both before and after the Second World War. It is no exaggeration to say that the most important subject in labour economics was to study the employer size effect not only on wage differentials but also on productivity differentials, and some other related subjects. Some economists in the marxian tradition, predominant before and even after the Second World War, attributed the effect to exploitation by capitalists or to exploitation by large firms of small firms which are administered in the *keiretsu* group. Some economists attempted to explain inter-size wage differentials by relying on the non-marxian tradition, which became more influential only after the war. Although popular in Japan, this subject is less popular in the Euro-American countries, although interest has been growing recently. It should be emphasized, however, that there is a significant difference between Japan and the Euro-American countries with respect to the reasons for the positive relationship between employer size and wages.

It was believed in Japan that the rapid economic growth of the 1950s, 1960s and early 1970s eliminated the famous inter-size or inter-scale wage differentials, because Japan's economy shifted from an economy of excess labour supply to an economy of labour shortage during the period—as emphasized in Chapter 3 below, Odaka (1984), Tachibanaki (1982), and Yasuba (1976). An economy of excess labour encourages small firms to raise their wage levels to attract new employees; otherwise, they are unable to employ more workers. This economy of excess labour ended again during and after the oil crisis. One of the purposes of this chapter is to show that Japan is experiencing a re-emergence of the dual structure which is symbolized by the inter-size wage differentials which prevailed in the past; in other words, the dual structure re-emerged during the twenty years following the end of the growth economy. Chapter 3 predicted its sign in the time-series context. The present chapter confirms it by using individual observations of wage data.

Another purpose of this chapter is to analyse the wage data more skilfully, by employing useful information on wages and other matters, and several econometric techniques. It is quite likely that there was a spurious positive correlation between employer size and wages, because large firms have several advantages over small firms—for example, large firms employ higher-quality workers, and large firms are more internal labour market-oriented. In other words, it is necessary to identify the pure effect of sizes and the spurious effect. This subject is related to the problem of endogeneity or selectivity of both employers and employees, which is the issue of non-random sorting across different-size employers and heterogeneity among jobs and workers.

Another aim of this chapter is to analyse wage distribution within a certain group of employer sizes, and the relationship between stratification and wage dispersion. Wage dispersion is concerned to examine whether larger firms have greater wage dispersion than smaller firms, or *vice versa*. This subject has never been investigated in Japan, and it provides us with a new and useful insight into the effect of employer size on wages. Stratification has also received no attention in many countries. It is concerned with the examination on the extent to which population subgroups (a group of firms of a certain size) occupy distinct strata within an overall wage distribution. In sum, the first subject investigates inequality in wage distribution within a certain size-group of firms, while the second subject examines the degree of overlap between a certain size-group of firms and other groups. The latter is called 'stratification' for simplicity, and special attention is paid to it.

The data are briefly explained: we use the *Wage Structure Survey* carried out by the Ministry of Labour. Chapter 3 used the published wage data, which provide average wages per cells classified by many personal qualifications, while this chapter uses their individual observations in both 1978 and 1988.

The organization of the chapter is as follows. Section 4.2

examines the problem of selection bias in wage determination. Section 4.3 estimates the pure effect of the size of firm on wage differentials after the influence of many control variables is removed. Section 4.4 discusses the reasons why there are substantial wage differentials between larger firms and smaller firms. Section 4.5 presents the estimated result of stratification and dispersion in wage distribution by the size of firm. Section 4.6 gives concluding remarks.

4.2. SELECTION BIAS AND WAGE EQUATIONS

This section investigates the influence of the endogeneity problem and selection bias on wage differentials by size of firm. Some Euro-American authors are concerned with non-random selection (i.e. a non-zero correlation between the unobservable factors, or error terms), when heterogeneity among workers with respect to measured and unmeasured characteristics can be assumed. Workers will normally attempt to match different-size employers on the basis of both observable and unobservable qualifications. If those qualifications have a direct effect on wages, we obtain the biased estimator of wage equations, provided that we estimate simply wage equations on a random sample of workers classified by the size of firm for which they are employed. In such a case it is necessary to derive unbiased estimates.

We follow the procedure used by Marshall and Zarkin (1987) and Idson and Feaster (1990), which applied a two-step estimation method like those of Heckman (1979) and Lee (1978) to remove the bias. Since the procedure is fairly popular, we explain the estimation method only briefly: we predict the size of firm by which individuals are employed, and then include this information in the estimation of wage functions by employer size. The first stage is to estimate β by the probit, and compute the doubly truncated means for each individual,

$$S_i = \beta' Y_i + u_i \qquad (4.1)$$

where S_i is a latent variable, β is a vector of parameters, Y_i is a vector of the individuals characteristics, and u_i is a random term which is assumed to be normally distributed. Since S_i is not observed, we use the variable Z_{ij}:

$Z_{ij} = 1$ if S_i is observed in jth firm size
$Z_{ij} = 0$ otherwise (4.2)

where Z_{ij} is defined by zero or unity. This enables us to use the probit estimation by maximum likelihood method. The second stage is to estimate wage equations by ordinary least squares for individuals who work in different firm sizes separately, including various explanatory variables and the individual predicted truncated means. The latter is frequently called the inverse Mills ratio.

Table 4.1 shows the second-stage wage equations which were estimated by employer size separately. They are corrected for selectivity bias or sorting bias because a regressor includes the selection term λ, explained above. The result for the first-stage probit estimation is not shown for the following reasons. First, the result is not so interesting; also, it is necessary to save space in this study. Second, our main concern is the employer-size effect on wage differentials. Third, it should nevertheless be noted that all explanatory variables such as education, tenure, age, and industry dummies are statistically significant in the estimated probit results. Thus the first-stage probit is fairly successful.

We observe the following results based on Table 4.1. Table 4.1(a) reports the case in which squared forms of both tenure and age are added, while Table 4.1(b) does not include them. First, nearly all explanatory variables such as education, tenure, age, industry dummies, and some squared forms are statistically significant, and their signs are correct, even though wage equations are estimated separately by size of firm. The result suggests that the standard type of wage equations can be used even for each firm-size class. Second, the great majority of the selection terms are statistically significant; the only exception is the largest employers, firms employing 5,000 and more workers, in Table 4.1(a). Thus, it is legitimate to take into account selection bias except for the largest employers, and it suggests the existence of unobservables common to both selection and wage determination.

How can we evaluate the positive and negative coefficients of the selection terms in Table 4.1? A positive coefficient of smaller firms employing fewer than 500 workers would imply negative selection, showing a predicted wage conditional on knowing employer size that is lower than the predicted wage conditional on not knowing

TABLE 4.1(a). Estimated male wage functions with a selection term (λ)

Independent variables	No. of variables						
	10–30	30–100	100–300	300–500	500–1,000	1,000–5,000	5,000–
Education	0.066*	0.063*	0.066*	0.043*	0.124*	0.054*	0.062
	(22.322)	(25.107)	(30.689)	(4.382)	(11.676)	(9.021)	(20.733)
Tenure	0.019*	0.020*	0.018*	0.015*	0.036*	0.026*	0.037
	(8.623)	(10.723)	(8.720)	(6.589)	(10.547)	(12.446)	(15.203)
(Tenure)^2	−0.0001*	−0.0001	0.000	0.000	−0.000*	−0.000*	−0.000*
	(−2.290)	(−1.524)	(0.717)	(0.223)	(−2.318)	(−5.592)	(−9.479)
Age	−0.065*	0.065*	0.068*	0.067*	0.056*	0.071*	0.054*
	(−23.679)	(26.142)	(22.685)	(19.449)	(14.007)	(39.568)	(14.295)
(Age)^2	−0.001*	−0.001*	−0.001*	−0.001*	−0.001*	−0.001*	−0.001*
	(−27.103)	(−26.947)	(−21.015)	(−13.777)	(−13.856)	(−29.526)	(−12.750)
λ	0.381*	0.508*	1.541*	8.042*	−7.483*	0.511*	0.084
	(4.020)	(4.623)	(3.631)	(2.635)	(−5.814)	(1.980)	(0.843)
Industry dummies							
Adjusted R^2	0.315	0.426	0.504	0.582	0.600	0.644	0.670
Standard deviation	0.406	0.398	0.425	0.443	0.470	0.452	0.435

Notes. Figures in parentheses are the estimated ratios of coefficients over standard errors. * signifies that the coefficient is statistically significant at the 5% level.

TABLE 4.1(b). *Estimated male wage functions with a selection term (λ) with no squared forms of ages and tenures*

Independent variables	No. of employees					
	>50	50–100	100–300	300–500	500–1,000	1,000–5,000	>5,000–

Independent variables	>50	50–100	100–300	300–500	500–1,000	1,000–5,000	>5,000–
Education	0.132*	0.119*	0.097*	−0.031*	0.215*	0.064*	0.076*
	(68.43)[a]	(73.394)	(57.330)	(−3.491)	(22.648)	(9.630)	(24.663)
Tenure	0.038*	0.038*	0.004*	0.008*	0.048*	0.014*	0.031*
	(34.39)	(42.477)	(39.101)	(6.389)	(22.564)	(6.752)	(17.606)
Age	−0.006*	0.0002	0.006*	0.021*	0.003*	0.023*	0.006*
	(−7.493)	(0.294)	(10.608)	(29.916)	(2.369)	(24.542)	(5.283)
λ	2.118*	2.570*	7.691*	36.435*	−16.315*	1.609*	−2.253*
	(27.730)	(30.229)	(23.358)	(15.033)	(−13.449)	(5.718)	(−2.421)
Industry dummies							
Adjusted R^2	0.189	0.344	0.450	0.538	0.553	0.551	0.626
Standard deviation	0.406	0.398	0.425	0.443	0.470	0.452	0.435

Notes. Figures in parentheses are the estimated ratios of coefficients over standard errors. * signifies that the coefficient is statistically significant at the 5% level.

employer size. In other words, employees in smaller firms would be earning less than would be the case for average smaller firms' wages if there were a random sorting of employees. A positive coefficient for firms employing 1,000 and more workers would imply positive selection in larger firms, showing a predicted wage conditional on knowing employer size that is higher than the unconditional predicted wage. In other words, average wages for the observed (sorted) larger firms would be higher than we would observe for a random sorting.

A special case must be mentioned: firms of 500–1,000 employees, in the case of Table 4.1(a), and 500–1,000 employees and 5,000 employees, in the case of Table 4.1(b). These classes may be judged as firm sizes which are larger than the average firm size. The selection terms are negatively significant. Economic interpretation of these coefficients would be as follows. A negative coefficient for these classes would imply negative selection, indicating that average wages for the observed (sorted) employees in these classes would be lower than those for a random sorting.

The overall result suggests that selectivity bias is marginally important and cannot be ignored in the determination of the effect of the size of firms on wages. It is possible to understand that these selectivity biases are generated by the factor which is largely unobservable, or individual taste and motivation. It might be desirable to estimate a wage figure for each individual which is corrected for such unobservable factors in order to obtain a more robust result on wage differentials by size in the subsequent sections. That task was not attempted for the following reasons. First, the estimated wage equations in Table 4.1 are somewhat unstable in view of slightly unsystematic signs of the selection term and of a smaller number of explanatory variables for an endogenous choice. Thus, it is somewhat risky to use these equations to produce an unbiased estimator of wages which treats the size of the firm at which a worker is employed as endogenous. Second, the purpose of this section was to estimate only the direction of bias due to a selectivity problem, not to estimate the magnitude of bias. Wage figures which are corrected for selectivity bias must be estimated more carefully. Third, the current state of the art regarding wage differentials by size of firm in Japan does not necessarily encourage us to be occupied seriously with selectivity bias and *unobservable* factors, but does encourage us to investigate the contribution of *observable* factors more carefully. Therefore, the task in this study for Japan is comparable with Brown and Medoff (1989), who ignored the issue of selectivity bias for the U.S. This does not necessarily imply, however, that the issue of selectivity bias and unobservable factors is unimportant for Japan; the preliminary analysis in this section can be regarded as a starting-point for more serious investigations in this field.

4.3. PURE SIZE EFFECT

This section attempts to estimate the pure size effect on wage differentials after controlling for various observable variables. Motivations for this exercise come from the anticipation that several observable variables would also contribute to the wage differentials by size of firm. Let us consider an example. It is widely believed that employees with longer job tenures receive higher wages than those with shorter tenures in Japan because of the famous seniority system. Chapters 2 and 3 showed the meaning of the *nenko joretsu*, or seniority system. It is also true that larger firms retain a higher proportion of employees with longer job tenures than smaller firms because the labour turnover rate is lower in larger firms than in smaller firms (see statistical evidence in e.g. Tachibanaki, 1975; 1982; 1984*a*). Under these conditions we would observe a wider wage differential between larger firms and smaller firms, which may be called a spurious positive correlation between employer size and wages. Brown and Medoff (1989) judge this effect as a cause of wage differentials by firm size, and call it the labour quality hypothesis. Although this hypothesis is acceptable, I find that a stricter cause for the employer size–wage effect after controlling for the difference in labour quality would be desirable: I call it the 'pure' effect. The labour quality hypothesis would be responsible for uncontrolled wage differentials by size.

Several observable variables, which are used for control, are explained in addition to job tenure described above. Age, industry, education, sex, occupation, and region are the control variables. Age is important in Japan because older workers receive higher wages than younger workers, as stated previously. Industry is also important, as shown by Tachibanaki and Ohta (1994). If many larger firms were located in highly paid industries, some of the employer-size wage differentials would be due to the industry effect, and thus it would be necessary to remove this effect. It is not necessary to explain about education, sex, and occupation, because these variables are the important factors which determine wages in many countries. Educated employees, male workers, and white-collar workers earn higher wages than less-educated employees, female workers, and blue-collar workers, respectively. See, for example, Tachibanaki (1975) or Kawashima and Tachibanaki (1986) on the implication of these variables for Japan. Region is less obvious: this was chosen as a control variable simply because wage differentials by region are observed in Japan.

The pure size effect on wage differentials would be obtained after we estimated the wage equation which is explained by the control variables described above, namely: (1) sex, (2) age, (3) job tenure, (4) industry, (5) education (6) occupation, and (7) region. Some variables have not only a linear term but also a quadratic term; also, some variables are interacted with other variables. Readers who would like to know more about the meaning of these control variables can refer to Chapter 5, which uses a more comprehensive list of control variables and explains more in detail.

The pure size effect is obtained in the following way:

$$\ln\left(W_{ij}\right) = \text{const} + \left(\text{size dummies with respect to i-th firm size}\right) + \left(\text{many control variables}\right) \quad (4.3)$$

where W_{ij} stands for hourly wage figure for jth individual in ith firm size. There is an argument whether hourly wages or total wage payments should be adopted. We used hourly wages figures simply because wages should be free from working hours, which is one quality variable; Chapter 3 also adopted hourly wage figures. There is a common understanding that the size effect is stronger for hourly wages than for total wage payments. We consider seven classes of size of firm in this study, employing respectively: 5,000 and more, 1,000–4,999, 500–999, 300–499, 100–299, 30–99, and 10–24. The pure size effect (or premium) is given by

$$P_i = \frac{\hat{W}_i - \overline{W}}{\overline{W}} \quad (4.4)$$

where p_i is the premium for ith size class, $\hat{W}_i$ is the average estimated wage for ith size class after the control, and $\bar{W}$ is the overall average wage before the control. The estimated result for the wage equation is not reported simply because it takes up too much space. There are about 80 explanatory variables. Therefore, it is a comprehensive wage equation which considers so many variables. It should be emphasized, nevertheless, that nearly all variables are statistically significant, and the estimated R^2 is about 0.60. The estimated wage equation is fairly successful despite the individual cross-section data. Normally, individual cross-section data give a smaller number of statistically significant variables and a lower R^2; thus the estimated wage equation can be used for the control. Interested readers can see the result in Chapter 5, which presents similar wage equations to those adopted here.

Table 4.2 shows the estimated wage premiums (advantages) and

TABLE 4.2. *Advantages and disadvantages in wage payment by firm size (%)*

No. of employees	1978		1988	
	Before[a]	After[a]	Before	After
5,000–	28.61	23.11	32.10	27.16
	(7,448)[b]		(8,647)	
1,000–4,999	20.49	17.03	21.86	15.96
	(7,356)		(7,091)	
500–999	9.95	5.61	9.24	2.68
	(3,552)		(3,667)	
300–499	1.01	–3.31	–1.55	5.60
	(3,235)		(3,038)	
100–299	–7.54[c]	–12.10	–11.93	15.37
	(8,215)		(7,271)	
30–99	–15.71	–19.90	–20.29	23.36
	(10,382)		(9,330)	
10–29	–21.24	–25.34	–25.34	28.78
	(8,355)		(7,329)	

[a] 'Before' means before controls, and 'After' means after controls by a large number of quality variables.
[b] Figures in parentheses are sample nos.
[c] Minus signs signify disadvantages.

disadvantages for each firm size both before controls and after controls in both 1978 and 1988. We can describe several noteworthy findings based on this table. First, both before-controls and after-controls show that there are substantial differentials between extremely large firms and extremely small firms. The degree of advantage in working in larger firms is over 20 per cent in comparison with the overall average wages, and the disadvantage is again over 20 per cent. These large figures are startling, because economists in Japan have not hitherto thought that such wide wage differentials by the size of firm existed. One reason for such wide wage differentials is the fact that this study considered extremely large firms (5,000 and more employees) and extremely small firms (10–29 employees) separately. The usual size of firm was defined by only three categories. 1,000 and more employees, 100–999 employees, and 10–99 employees. Note that the inter-scale wage differential estimated in Chapter 3 adopted these three classifications; we considered seven classes in this chapter, including both extremely large and extremely small firms. Thus, one cause for the wider wage difference is a statistical data problem which was not taken into account previously. We have to understand, now, that wage differential by size of firm is much more serious than commonly assumed on the basis of more appropriate data sources.

Second, controls for various quality variables such as education, job tenure, sex, and many other variables do not contribute to any significant reduction in the advantages and disadvantages by the size of firms: we observe reductions by only 4–6 percentage points by including the control variables. It may be useful to mention the work of Green, Machin, and Manning (1992), who proposed no necessity for controls by job tenure and industry in the UK. In other words, we can conclude that a pure size effect is substantial as far as the inter-size wage differential is concerned. This is a big contrast with the substantial contribution of the controls when inter-industry wage differentials are estimated (See Chapter 5). Larger firms in Japan are able to offer substantially higher wages than smaller firms, and their higher wages are not explained by higher qualifications of employees and other advantageous factors peculiar to larger firms. This may be called an intrinsic effect of firm size.

Third, the result for both 1978 and 1988 suggests that the increase in wage differentials by size of firm is observed because figures, both positive and negative, in 1988 are larger than those in

1978. The employer size wage effect has increased in the past ten years. It was pointed out previously that the inter-size wage differential (called 'dual structure' in Japan) became weaker during the period of rapid economic growth. Nowadays, the dual structure is reviving: wage differential by size of firm is reappearing. We can suggest two principal reasons for that: first, the latest recession is responsible for a wider wage differential by size because of the negative correlation with the business cycle, as shown in Chapter 3; second, there is a significant change in wage payment system, as will be argued later.

Fourth, it might be interesting to enquire into the important variables which reduce the degree of wage differential by size after the controls. In other words, which variables are relevant and important as controls? This exercise is not performed simply because we found a much less substantial contribution of the control or of quality variables. Instead, it would be more attractive if we could explain the reasons why the pure wage differential by the size of firm even after controlling for quality variables is so large. This task is performed next.

4.4. WHY DO LARGER FIRMS PAY HIGHER WAGES?

The controversy over the dual structure has a long tradition in Japan; Chapter 3 provided a very brief survey. It would be useful to provide a historical survey of its development, and the explanations of Japanese economists, before presenting the discussion of this section.

According to Odaka (1984), there are three socioeconomic backgrounds which produced the so-called dual structure in either the late 1920s or the late 1950s. First, new technologies imported from abroad promoted rapid industrialization, and raised labour productivity in larger firms. These firms also provided extensive training for their employees. Second, there was an unlimited labour supply in these periods. Those workers were absorbed largely in smaller firms, and their wages were kept lower because of the unlimited labour supply; the reason is that employees in these firms could not demand higher wages. On the other hand, employers of small firms could hire employees easily, because there were many job applicants to their firms owing to excess supply. Third, new management techniques and efficient industrial organization such as *Keiretsu* were introduced in larger firms.

These three socioeconomic backgrounds in industries and firms enabled economists to propose various explanations for the dual structure; we can summarize these explanations briefly. First, several marxian economists, of whom Yamada (1934) is representative, proposed the exploitation theory, which asserts that workers in general are simply exploited by capital or capitalists. Also, Yamada suggested the emergence of the dual structure: the modern sector and the traditional sector. Arisawa (1957) gave a clear definition of these sectors. The modern sector, which consists of larger firms, has a monopolistic or non-competitive power in the market, and dominates the traditional sector, which consists of largely *Keiretsu* smaller firms. There is an implicit understanding that larger firms which have larger capitals exploit smaller firms.

Second, labour quality is very different between larger firms and smaller firms. Odaka (1984) finds this explanation very plausible: larger firms can employ better workers with excellent qualifications in terms of morale, discipline, work ethic, education, and skills. Also, they are able to provide efficient training, and thus their skill level is raised naturally after training. If the skill difference were plausible, it would be necessary to control employees by their skill level, which is indicated largely by job tenure. It is true that the average job tenure in larger firms is much longer than that in smaller firms (see e.g. Tachibanaki, 1984*a*; 1987*a*). Note our previous section controlled inter-size wage differentials by job tenure. Despite this control, it did not reduce the differential substantially; therefore, I doubt whether skill difference caused by job training is a convincing hypothesis for inter-size wage differentials. This does not necessarily imply, however, that there is no unmeasured ability difference between larger firms and smaller ones: no studies are available in Japan which estimate the contribution of unmeasured ability. It may be useful to point to a rigorous study by Gibbons and Katz (1992), which concluded that the contribution of unmeasured ability was not significant in explaining inter-industry wage differentials in the USA, and the survey by Brown and Medoff (1989), who are also sceptical about the measured size/labour quality differential in the USA. Thus, it is possible that the contribution of unmeasured ability is minor in Japan.

Third, there is a school which emphasizes the particular Japanese type of paternalism. Industrial relations, including seniority system, lifetime employment, and enterprise unionism, in Japan is explained by its particularity, in contrast to industrial relations in Euro-American countries, which emphasize the importance of individual contracts between firms and employees. In Japan, paternalism and collectivism underlie the whole system. Inter-size wage differentials can be explained by this cultural factor according to this school. Since I do not share the ideas of this school (although I do not reject it entirely), I add no further explanation.

Fourth, there is a school which stresses the importance of the segmented labour market hypothesis (e.g. Ishikawa, 1989). There has always been rationing in the labour market in Japan: there has been an excess labour supply for employment in larger firms, and thus, rationing was necessary for the working of the labour market. Privileged workers who were employed by larger firms could enjoy better working conditions, including higher wages. It is important to investigate who are the privileged workers among many suppliers. Also, the segmented labour market school does not explain why larger firms are able to pay higher wages in comparison with smaller firms. I feel some sympathy with this hypothesis, because it is quite likely that the labour market in Japan is segmented. In the USA there is a school which believes in the labour market segmentation theory (see e.g. Dickens and Lang, 1992a; 1992b). Since the Japanese version of labour segmentation is distinction by size of firm, it is necessary to reconcile this with the American version. In sum, labour market segmentation is a useful concept, but one requiring further work.

Fifth, larger firms normally have greater capital equipment because they enjoy advantages in financing activities (see Shinohara 1961; Miyazawa, 1976). Therefore, larger firms normally have higher capital:labour ratios which are likely to raise labour productivity in these firms. Firms which have a product market advantage, or are in other ways more profitable, are normally larger in size because they are able to exercise their market power in the industry (see Chapter 9). If employees in these firms can capture a share of these rents, the effect of profitability will be positive on wage payments. This assumes that the rents are also shared by employees, and strong union power may be required to acquire such rents. In Japan the unionization rate is positively correlated with the size of firm; thus the rents in larger firms could in principle be shared by employees in these firms. The fifth explanation described here may be called the 'ability to pay' theorem, or 'rent-sharing' theorem, and is supported in several countries.

Several causes have been offered to explain inter-size wage differentials in Japan. I would like to discuss later my judgement on which causes are more appropriate, or to offer other hypotheses. Before presenting them, it will be useful and interesting to compare these explanations with other countries.

Brown and Medoff (1989) considered six explanations for the positive relationship between employer size and wages for the USA. Large firms hire higher-quality workers, offer inferior working conditions, make more use of high wages to forestall unionization, have more ability to pay high wages, face smaller pools of applicants, and are less able to monitor their workers. Green *et al.* (1992) offered a dynamic monopoly model based on the theory of job matching for the UK.

Many European labour market studies seem to support the 'ability to pay' theorem, as shown by Blanchflower, Oswald, and Garrett (1990), Carruth and Oswald (1989), Holmlund and Zetterberg (1991), Denny and Machin (1991), Nickell and Wadhwani (1990), and others, although they do not always investigate the effect of firm size, but largely the effect of industries. A similar observation on wage differentials by industry was made for the USA by Dickens and Katz (1987), Krueger and Summers (1988), and Katz and Summers (1989). In Canada, Christofides and Oswald (1992) obtained a similar result, which supported the rent-sharing hypothesis. Many American and European studies support the importance of 'ability to pay' in wage determinations.

How can we evaluate the Japanese explanations in comparison with American and European evidence? Is the explanation for wage differentials by industry applicable to wage differentials by size of firm? Among the US explanations, only two were mentioned for Japan: quality difference in labour, and ability to pay. The other four explanations and a dynamic monopoly model have not so far been considered in Japan; it would be useful to spell out why these explanations are not so important in Japan.

First, it is believed that working conditions in larger firms are superior to those in smaller firms in various fields, unlike the US case. For example, jobs are more secure, working hours are shorter, dangerous and unhealthy conditions are less common, and job tasks are easier and more pleasant because better equipment and machines are available. Most importantly, wages are higher. This may be, however, a chicken-and-egg problem, and suggests a source of compensating wage differentials if other working conditions are inferior. It is, nevertheless, noted that Tachibanaki (1992*a*) and Tachibanaki and Ohta (1994) find no evidence of compensating wage differentials in Japan. The only two possible inferior working conditions are impersonal working atmosphere and less freedom, and frequent, forced inter-establishment mobility within a firm for white-collar workers in larger firms; and these were not so serious, since workers found that other superior conditions compensated for them. I believe that the majority of the Japanese workers find that working conditions in larger firms on average are more favourable than those in smaller firms. If fringe benefits or non-wage payments are included, there is no question that working conditions in larger firms are superior to those in smaller firms.

Second, since the unionization rate is highly correlated with employer size, as shown by Tachibanaki (1993*a*), there is no necessity to consider the effect of union avoidance, unlike the case of the USA. Conversely, employers in larger firms regard unions as a smooth communication device (see Morishima, 1991; Tachibanaki and Noda, 1994).

Third, large Japanese employers can draw on more pools of applicants relative to vacancies. This is confirmed by looking at figures on unemployment–vacancy data, and by accepting the previous statement that there has been a rationing in the labour market for larger employers because of the excess labour supply for them. Consequently, the Japanese experience runs counter to that of the USA because larger employers face more applications.

Fourth, the most controversial explanation for Japan would be the question whether large employers are less able to monitor their workers. Brown and Medoff (1989) examined this issue comprehensively for the USA, and they are sceptical whether monitoring is the correct explanation for the positive relationship between employer size and wages. Although the next section will examine wage dispersion for each firm size, and will provide my judgement on this issue for Japan, this section merely suggests that Japanese evidence is too scarce for us to propose any conclusive answer to this question.

Fifth, there are several convincing pieces of evidence in Japan (as shown later) that a rent-sharing model is useful to explain the positive effect of firm size on wages. Thus, I judge that this idea must be working well.

I have presented a brief evaluation of the explanations for the positive relationship between employer size and wages, discussed not only in Japan but also in Euro-American countries. We can conclude that only three explanations—quality difference in labour, ability to pay, and the rent-sharing model—are candidates for explanations in Japan, because it was found, on the basis of casual observations, that the other explanations could not be supported. I would like to examine these three effects more carefully, and to argue whether they are truly important or whether other alternative explanations must be prepared.

The labour quality argument has already been handled previously, since we controlled for various quality variables such as age, tenure, education, and occupation in estimating wage equations. We found that these quality variables, as well as other variables, did not reduce the wage differentials substantially. Therefore, it was tentatively concluded that the hypothesis of difference in labour quality would not be supported, at least for Japan. This does not necessarily imply, however, that we took into consideration the contribution of unmeasured quality. It is widely believed in Japan that the great majority of graduates in several prestigious universities seek jobs in large firms, in particular in gigantic firms, by reason of the favourable labour conditions described previously. This is the explanation for white-collar workers; even for blue-collar employees, talented and motivated graduates in high schools aspire to work in larger firms, and thus those employers are able to hire the best workers. Therefore, it is plausible that unmeasured labour quality in larger firms is high, although it is hard to show strict empirical evidence. Better working conditions described previously in larger firms indirectly support the above conclusion. We need another new data set to test the contribution of unmeasured quality. It is, nevertheless, noted again that the US case does not support this interpretation.

The 'ability to pay' hypothesis is examined here. There is no consensus about which variable is most plausible among many which indicate the power or ability to pay. Some emphasize a monopoly power in the industry, which enables a large firm to gain extra profit. Some say that higher capital equipment per employee enables a large firm to achieve higher labour productivity. A higher unionization rate leads a firm to pay higher wages because rents can be shared by the strong voice of the labour side. We consider various variables which are supposed to indicate some degree of ability to pay and rent-sharing: profit rate, labour productivity, capital labour ratio, and unionization rate. Labour separation rate is added in order to examine whether a lower labour separation rate in large firms raises the possibility that experienced workers stay longer in these firms. A simple regression analysis, in which the after-control wage premium in Table 4.2 is the dependent variable and the variables described above are the independent variables, is performed in Table 4.3. Since the sample has two years, 1978 and

TABLE 4.3. *Regressions for wage premiums*

Independent variable	Dependent Variable		
	Wage premium by size	Wage premium by size	Wage premium by size
Constant	−50.805	−50.095	−29.639
Profit rate	183.73*[a]	190.94*	132.06
	(2.441)[b]	(2.749)	(1.04)
Labour productivity	−0.316		2.217*
	(0.423)		(3.154)
Capital: labour ratio	6.824*	6.228*	
	(4.056)	(7.116)	
Unionization rate	27.486*	27.521*	38.851*
	(4.118)	(4.552)	(3.746)
Separation rate (labour)	−0.287	−0.385	−1.094
	(0.596)	(0.96)	(1.456)
1988 dummy	−12.669*	−12.967*	−10.471*
	(5.187)	(5.852)	(2.568)
Adjusted R^2	0.995	0.995	0.983

[a] *implies statistical significance at 5%.
[b] Figures in parentheses are the estimated t-values.

1988, a dummy variable for 1988 is included. The Appendix to this chapter explains the method for obtaining the data for Table 4.3.

The following observations are based on Table 4.3. First, the first column in the table suggests that the three variables, profit rate, labour productivity, and capital labour ratio, are correlated with each other because they all show some degree of efficient management or productivity. Thus it is necessary to delete at least one variable from the list of the independent variables. Second, profit rate, labour productivity, and/or capital:labour ratio are all statistically significant, and the signs are all positive, deleting one variable in the second and third columns. The 'ability to pay' hypothesis is rigorously accepted because a higher profit rate, a higher labour productivity, and/or a higher capital:labour ratio contributes to higher wage payments. Third, since 'rent-sharing' is a variant of the 'ability to pay' hypothesis, it is also supported in view of the positive coefficient of profit rate. The statistically significant positive coefficient of unionization rate provides more evidence to support the 'rent-sharing' hypothesis. Fourth, the labour separation rate is negative, but statistically insignificant. Thus, the degree of labour turnover does not contribute to the determination of the wage premium.

We conclude, on the basis of regression analysis, that the 'ability to pay' hypothesis and/or the 'rent-sharing' hypothesis are supported in Japan in the determination of wage premiums, where larger firms are able to pay higher wages than smaller firms, even after controls for many labour quality variables and other variables in wage equations. It is now necessary to discuss the reasons why the 'ability to pay' hypothesis and/or the 'rent-sharing' hypothesis are plausible in addition to the arguments described previously in various places.

These reasons, which are described here, are not so quantitative, but fairly descriptive and speculative in nature. A separate work is required to perform a more quantitative analysis; this part provides only several hypotheses and speculations.

First, higher capital:labour ratios in larger firms are, probably, the most intrinsic cause of higher labour productivities and profit rates in these firms. These firms enjoy the benefit of better capital equipment, which can be financed easily for various reasons. I would like to emphasize capital–skill complementarity in these firms because they employ high-quality workers. Good machines and tools are utilized more efficiently by skilled and talented workers. This capital–skill complementarity must be crucial for larger firms: Hamermesh (1980) suggested it for the USA; Hashimoto and Suruga (1990) obtained a higher degree of capital–skill complementarity than capital–skill substitutability for Japan. It is now desirable to investigate whether capital–skill complementarity contributes to the 'ability to pay' hypothesis.

Second, a large firm, in particular an extremely large firm, has many *keiretsu* firms, or subcontracting firms. These firms have long-run 'customer relations' with a parent company, and they sell parts continuously, with sometimes cheaper prices and better quality, to a parent company. A parent company transfers new technologies and occasionally human resources to these *keiretsu* firms. These long-run relationship enables a parent company to enjoy a higher profit. Normally, a parent company is very larger in size; therefore, it is possible to state that the *keiretsu* relationship can be a source of the 'ability to pay' hypothesis for larger firms. Although there several studies emphasize the importance of *keiretsu* group—Aoki (1988), Asanuma (1989), Kawasaki and McMillan (1987), and some others—no direct test has examined whether the *keiretsu* relationship raised the wage level of employees in a parent company. The above understanding with respect to the *keiretsu* is a highly neoclassical interpretation; it was stated previously in this chapter that the marxian school in Japan regarded it as an exploitation of subcontracting firms by a parent company.

Third, several economists (e.g. Komiya, 1989) understand that large firms in Japan are characterized by the so-called 'labour-managed firms.' Managers, longer-tenured employees, or core workers in these firms are able to receive higher wages because they share rents produced by 'labour-managed firms.' As long as Japanese firms, in particular larger firms, can be regarded as 'labour-managed firms', it is quite reasonable to assert that the 'ability to pay' hypothesis and/or 'rent-sharing' hypothesis are accepted. Incidentally, the 'profit-sharing' hypothesis *à la* Weitzman (1984) is believed to prevail in Japan, as shown by Freeman and Weitzman (1987). Although it is not possible to proclaim that the implication of 'labour-managed firms' and that of the 'profit-sharing' hypothesis are the same, the above description tends to support the 'ability to pay' and/or 'rent-sharing' hypothesis are supported for Japan.

Fourth, many large firms, in particular extremely large firms, are in monopolistic or non-competitive industries. These industries can enjoy higher revenues, and are thus able to pay higher wages than competitive industries (see the statistical evidence of the comparison between competitive and non-competitive industries with respect to wage payments in Kawashima and Tachibanaki, 1986). Tachibanaki (1992c) reported the reasons why wages in the financial industry are so high. The financial industry is largely non-competitive, and stringent regulation has been applied to the industry. These results suggest that many larger firms are able to offer higher wages to their employees simply because they can enjoy the benefit of non-competitive industries. It is noted, however, that the non-competitive industries hypothesis must be tested carefully because we used industries as one of the control variables. Therefore, the 'ability to pay' theory has to be examined within a common industry in order to perform a strict test. Another appealing idea, that of input–market differences, may be more promising in the examination of industrial wage differentials.

Summarized above are several reasons why the 'ability to pay' and/or 'rent-sharing' hypothesis can be supported in Japan; and we presented a näive empirical test. Some other explanations are largely intuitive and speculative, or are based on the findings proposed by other studies. The next task would be to perform a more rigorous study in order to examine whether the above hypotheses are plausible.

4.5. STRATIFICATION AND DISPERSION IN WAGES BY FIRM SIZE

We investigate these two issues to examine the argument of monitoring the performance of employees and ability to judge worker quality; see a useful survey by Brown (1994). Also, both stratification and dispersion are interesting because they give us a useful insight into distribution in wage payments by firm size both within and between groups where groups are classified by the size of firm; in particular, stratification has never been studied in the field of wage distribution in any country. Finally, it is possible to guess about how abilities and productivities of employees are distributed within a particular group of sizes by examining stratification and dispersion in wages.

Stratification is a useful concept in sociology, which is concerned with the division of a society or a status into a number of strata, or hierarchically arranged groupings. In this study, status represents wages and strata (or groupings) represent the size of firm. A sound index of stratification should indicate the degree of *overlap* between group members and others. Suppose we consider two groups of firms, a large firm and a small firm. If no employees of another firm are in the range of wage payments in one firm, they are called perfect strata. That is, there is no overlap in wage payments for employees in two firms. At the other extreme, we can conceive of the case in which the two firms have identical distributions (or perfect overlap in wage payments). Therefore, stratification means a group's isolation from members of other groups; we gave the example of two firms. Stratification is extended to many groups: in this study we take seven groups of firms which are classified by the number of employees. The classification is the same as in Table 4.2.

We adopt the index of stratification of group i (i = size class) which was developed by Yitzhaki and Lerman (1991),

$$Q_i = \frac{\text{Cov}_i\left[(F_i - F_{ni}), y\right]}{\text{Cov}_i(F_i, y)} \quad (4.5)$$

where y (i.e., y_{ij}) is the wage-level of member j of group i, F_i (y_{ij}) is the value of the cumulative distribution at ij within group i, and F_{ni} (y_{ij}) is the value of the cumulative distribution at ij excluding group i. ni signifies 'not in group i'. All F_i and F_{ni} are defined by ranks. The index Q_i may be interpreted as follows: the numerator of Q_i is the covariance over group i between the wage and the difference between the ranking of a member of group i in his own group and the ranking he would have in the rest of the population. The denominator is used as a normalizing factor.

The index Q_i has the following property.

1. $Q_i = 1$: group *i* forms a perfect strata (i.e. there is no overlap), and no members of other groups are in the range of the wages of group *i*.
2. $Q = -1$: group *i* is composed of two groups, and all members

of the other group lie inside the range of the wages. In other words, group i is not a group at all, but is composed of two perfect strata.

The real and empirical value of Q_i lies between -1 and 1, and the estimated Q_i can provide us with useful information on wage differentials by the size of firm. This section estimates Q_i by using the same data source as the one used previously, and discusses the various issues based on the estimated Q_i. Dispersion in wages within a particular size class is estimated by the Gini coefficient. Since the Gini coefficient is commonly used, no explanation is required.

Table 4.4 gives the estimated result of both stratifications and dispersions for each class of firm size. Wage figures are examined for particular groups such as 35 and 45-year-old employees who are either blue-collar or white-collar workers, and who are either high school or college graduates. The reason why we fix the qualification of employees is that stratification and dispersion should be free from the influence of other factors such as education, occupation, and age. We use mainly the stratification index to interpret wage distribution by the size of firm, and the Gini coefficient is used as a supplementary source. The following are the empirical findings derived from this table.

First, the estimated Q is an increasing function of the size of firm. For smaller firms, some of the coefficients are negative, while those for middle-size firms and larger firms are all positive. The result implies that the larger the size of firm, the more strong stratification is. In other words, the degree of stratification in wage payments increases as the size of firm becomes larger. The wage levels in larger firms tend to form separate groups (i.e. there is no overlap with other groups) whose members' wage levels are concentrated in the higher range in the overall distribution. It should be noted that stratification in extremely large firms, i.e. 5,000 employees and more, is quite distinctive, because its value is much higher than other groups. To put it more simply, the result implies that the great majority of employees in larger firms receive higher wages with small variations, and very few employees in these firms receive lower wages. The estimated Gini coefficients support this statement. An interesting observation is found for smaller firms: the negative coefficients in Q for firms with 10–29, 30–99, and/or

TABLE 4.4. Stratification and dispersion in male wages by firm size

Age (years)			Size of firm (no. of employees)							Total
			10–29	30–99	100–299	300–499	500–999	1,000–4,999	5,000–	
25										
	HS[a] (b)[b]	Q[c]	−0.140	−0.050	−0.004	0.055	0.083	0.162	0.207	
		D[c]	0.151	0.119	0.108	0.091	0.090	0.084	0.096	0.111
	HS (w)	Q	−0.142	−0.068	−0.029	0.038	0.087	0.162	0.190	
		D	0.159	0.116	0.106	0.089	0.082	0.076	0.074	0.106
	C (w)	Q	−0.192	−0.092	−0.044	0.000	0.006	0.075	0.235	
		D	0.151	0.098	0.079	0.063	0.068	0.064	0.070	0.076
35										
	HS (b)	Q	−0.076	0.002	0.083	0.044	0.074	0.228	0.282	
		D	0.161	0.137	0.117	0.114	0.111	0.092	0.093	0.128
	HS (w)	Q	−0.108	−0.098	0.004	0.061	0.087	0.168	0.237	
		D	0.172	0.151	0.122	0.105	0.101	0.093	0.094	0.125
	C (w)	Q	−0.117	−0.080	−0.010	0.046	0.068	0.140	0.240	
		D	0.156	0.131	0.117	0.107	0.102	0.096	0.097	0.118
45										
	HS (b)	Q	−0.034	0.083	0.075	0.030	0.116	0.201	0.362	
		D	0.188	0.154	0.138	0.143	0.126	0.116	0.095	0.154
	HS (w)	Q	−0.039	−0.009	0.010	0.062	0.141	0.154	0.204	
		D	0.184	0.149	0.140	0.125	0.100	0.116	0.120	0.142
	C (w)	Q	−0.074	−0.003	0.073	0.102	0.152	0.164	0.362	
		D	0.178	0.154	0.126	0.109	0.102	0.105	0.087	0.130

[a] HS and C stand for high school graduates and college graduates respectively.
[b] (b) and (w) stand for blue-collar and white-collar employees respectively.
[c] Q is the stratification index, and D is the dispersion index. Q is given in Yitzhaki and Lerman (1991), and D is given by the Gini coefficient.

100–299 employees imply that the divergence within the ranking of employees of these firms in the overall population is greater than the divergence in these firms. In other words, these small firms are not homogeneous groups but are composed of several different groups: the *majority* of employees in these firms receive lower wages, while *some* employees in these firms receive distinctively higher wages whose levels are comparable with wage levels in larger firms and even in extremely large firms.

The above finding leads us to suggest the following economic interpretations. First of all, qualified employees, although they are not measured, tend to work in larger firms. Also, variations in quality in these firms are small. It is not true, however, for smaller firms. Some talented and motivated workers wish to work in smaller firms, and are able to receive higher wages comparable to the level in larger firms; such workers probably dislike undesirable working conditions in larger firms, such as greater reliance on rules, less freedom of action, and a more impersonal work atmosphere, which were emphasized by Masters (1969), Stafford (1980), and Lester (1967) for the USA. Their higher marginal productivities were assessed properly in smaller firms, and it is possible that they might not be so productive if they worked in larger firms. Unfortunately, the ratio of these employees who can receive higher wages is relatively small in smaller firms. The higher Gini coefficients for smaller firms support it indirectly. The great majority of employees in smaller firms have to accept lower wages.

Is it possible to draw any implication for the difficulty associated with monitoring the performance of employees? Many studies in the USA suggested that the larger firm would face difficulties in monitoring employees and implementing judgemental rating schemes, as given by Stigler's (1962) classical analysis, and subsequently by Stafford (1980) and Garen (1985). The consensus suggests that the monitoring difficulty produced greater wage dispersion in larger firms. The recent study by Brown and Medoff (1989), however, is sceptical. How about Japan?

Figures in Table 4.4 based on the Gini coefficients show that wage dispersions decline constantly as the size of firm becomes larger. Extremely large firms, of more than 5,000 employees, show a very marginal increase in dispersion in several cases. The general finding, nevertheless, is summarized by the constant decrease in dispersion within a group when the size of firm is larger. Figures based on stratification also tell a similar story. This finding is inconsistent with the usual assumption in the USA, and consistent with Brown and Medoff (1989), who estimated the difficulty associated with monitoring controlled data by occupation. The Japanese wage data suggest a constant decrease in dispersion, even for controlled data. It is noted that age, education, and occupation are controlled in Table 4.4, therefore it is concluded tentatively that the role of monitoring difficulties is minor for explaining the general relationship between size and wage. We need, however, to conduct more careful analyses in order to obtain a more convincing result. Our tentative conclusion is only a speculation.

Going back to the economic interpretations of Table 4.4, we can point to several findings based on both stratification and dispersion in wages by the size of firm. The degree of stratification is stronger for blue-collar than for white-collar workers because the estimated indexes are larger in many cases for the former than for the latter, if other conditions such as age and education are kept constant. Blue-collar workers tend to form separate groups in the overall distribution more strongly than white-collar workers. The extent of overlap between a particular firm size and the rest of firm sizes is smaller for blue-collar workers than for white-collar workers. This is consistent with the general understanding that wages for blue-collar workers are determined by single-rate wage schemes or piece-rate systems within job categories, and are less likely to be determined by judgemental evaluation in comparison with those for white-collar workers. It must be emphasized, however, that the influence of merit on pay is stronger in Japan than in Euro-American nations, even for blue-collar workers, as pointed out by Ishida (1990) and Tachibanaki (1992a; 1995b).

Education also has an impact on stratification: the degree of stratification for college graduates is somewhat higher than for high school graduates. We can see this by noticing somewhat higher coefficients for college graduates than for high-school graduates in the case of white-collar workers. Age is also a factor which affects the degree of stratification by the size of firm. An interesting effect of age is observed in increasing dispersion by age. Although the effect of education, occupation, and age on stratification are interesting in understanding the role of education in the determination of occupation and earnings, no further interpretations are provided in this study because its main concern is to study the relationship between the size of firms and wages. Interested readers can refer to Tachibanaki (1993*b*) on the role of education in stratification, and Chapters 5 and 6 below, which investigate the relationship among education, occupation, hierarchy, and earnings.

4.6. CONCLUDING REMARKS

This chapter has investigated various issues of wage differentials by size of firm in Japan—one of the most popular subjects in labour economics. An effort was made to compare with past studies in Japan; and a serious comparison with several foreign countries, in particular the USA, was attempted in order to reveal the common and uncommon explanations for the relationship between size of firm and wages. The paper by Brown and Medoff (1989) for the USA was selected for a particular comparison.

The following observations were obtained. First, the wage differentials by the size of firm in recent years are more apparent than those commonly believed in the past. This is true even for the wage data after many explanatory variables have been used to control for wage figures.

Second, several reasons, in addition to a pure statistical data problem, were suggested in order to explain why the traditional dual structure reappeared. Among many reasons, this chapter emphasized the importance of the 'ability to pay' and/or 'rent-sharing' hypotheses. Large firms are able to offer higher wages for various reasons, but their ability to pay and/or rent-sharing are probably the most salient reasons; this was supported by a simple wage premium function. Several specific reasons for supporting these hypotheses were also suggested. Incidentally, it should be emphasized that Japan and the USA offer very different reasons for explaining wage differentials by size.

Third, the issue of stratification and dispersion in wages by size of firm was examined. It was found that stratification and dispersion were very different between larger firms and smaller firms. This suggests that the role of monitoring difficulties is minor in explaining the general relationship between size and wage, unlike many American studies. Stratification and dispersion in wages are likely to provide us with a new insight into the understanding of industrial relations as shown by Lazear (1989) because incentives and performances can be evaluated by them. I hope that the current work is a starting-point for more works in this appealing area.

This chapter is probably the first econometric attempt in Japan to estimate the pure effect of the size of firm on wage differentials. It has many deficiencies; for example, a possible selectivity bias was presented in the determination of the effect of size on wages. Therefore, it would be desirable to take into account more seriously the contribution of unobserved factors. Another drawback is the joint determination of wages and employments; alternatively, it is feasible to suppose that higher wages in larger firms can attract qualified employees. The present study took into consideration only the effect of labour quality on wages, when the control was made to estimate the pure effect of size on wage differentials. This inverse causality should not be ignored: although it is not an easy subject, it is a challenging one in the future. Finally, it is desirable to consider the contribution of fringe benefits to overall differences in working conditions between larger firms and smaller ones in Japan.

Data Appendix

The principal data source is the *Wage Structure Survey* conducted by the Ministry of Labour. The survey is distributed to employers, who are responsible for answering many questions on their employees; it is said that the data are fairly accurate. Many questions concern monthly wage payments, working hours of each employee, and various qualifications of each employee such as sex, occupation, age, job tenure, educational attainment, and some others. Also, information on employers, such as size of firm, size of establishment, industry, region, and some others, is available. The most astonishing thing about the *Wage Structure Survey* is its number of samples, over 1 million employees—a number beyond computational feasibility. I selected samples purely randomly. The number of samples is about 50,000; exact numbers are given in the Tables.

The other data sources are briefly described. Data on productivity, sales, profits, and some related variables are available in the *Industry Survey* by the Ministry of International Trade and Industry. One difficulty concerns the definition of the size of firm by the *Wage Structure Survey* on one hand and the *Industry Survey* on the other, because the former uses the number of employees while the latter uses the figures of capitalization. By assuming that there is a correlation between the number of employees and the figure of capitalization for each industry, we converted the latter to the former to indicate the size of firm.

The rate of union participation is available in the *Survey of Basic Trade Unions* by the Ministry of Labour, and the rate of separation of employees is available in the *Employment Trend Survey* by the Ministry of Labour.

5
Wage Differentials by Industry and Labour Market

5.1. INTRODUCTION

Wage differential by industry is an old issue and a revivified one. It has in the past been fairly popular to investigate inter-industry wage differentials; these studies used data which reported only the average wage figures for various groups of workers, and derived implications from these figures. Recently, individual survey data on wages and other personal characteristics have become available. Economists attempt to standardize individual wage figures, by controlling for various quality variables of individual employees such as education, sex, and many others. These works derive a pure effect of industrial differences on the wage differential, after controlling for the contribution of quality variables. Past studies typically used average figures, and it was not easy to derive a pure effect; the new type of study typically uses individual observations, and thus it is easy to derive a pure effect.

There are various studies on the inter-industry wage structure in Japan. Sano (1969) and Mizuno (1973) belong to the old type, while the present work belongs to the new type. It would be useful to summarize studies on wage differentials in Japan as a rough introduction to the literature. Theoretically speaking, the human-capital theory was a dominant and possibly sole theory which attracted economists in Japan, according to Tachibanaki and Taki (1990); an example of such work is Mincer and Higuchi (1988). Empirically speaking, various studies such as Ono (1989) and Tachibanaki (1975; 1982) quantitatively investigated the contribution to wage differentials of individual characteristics and firm effects, without necessarily relying on the human-capital theory.

The neoclassical theory of wage determination suggests that the wage rate is equal to the marginal value product of labour in the ideal market, and thus employees who have common qualifications normally receive identical wages. In the real economy, various wage levels are paid to individual employees. The above studies in Japan estimated the difference in wage payments caused by various qualifications, and found that the wage is not determined by neoclassical economic theory. The present study examines another aspect of wage differentials: the inter-industry wage differentials, and a pure effect of differences in industries.

This chapter examines inter-industry wage differentials and derives a pure effect of industries after a comprehensive control of various factors and qualifications, and estimates the effect of economic factors which are responsible for explaining the pure difference in industrial wages. At the same time, we are concerned with some empirical tests of the compensating wage differences. Section 5.2 presents the pure effect of industries on wage differentials, after controlling for qualifications, and the method of the control. Section 5.3 estimates dispersion of wage differentials by industries, and attempts to investigate the relative importance of various qualifications to such dispersions. Section 5.4 presents various economic factors capable of explaining the pure industry effect on wage differentials, and discusses them. Section 5.5 presents the result, under the assumption that returns to various labour qualifications are not identical for all industries. Section 5.6 summarizes the result, and discusses implications for further studies.

Finally, the data used in this chapter are briefly explained. The principal data source is the *Wage Structure Survey* (popularly called the *Census of Wages*) collected by the Ministry of Labour; we use individual observations from this survey. Since Chapter 4 has explained this data source, no explanation is necessary here.

5.2. ESTIMATION OF A PURE EFFECT OF INDUSTRY

Wages are differentiated by the characteristics and quality of both employees and employers. It is essential to eliminate these contributions in order to investigate inter-industry wage differentials. In other words, it is necessary to estimate them under the condition of equal qualifications of employees and common firm specificities, after controlling for human-capital variables and a variety of job characteristics. It is natural that an industry in which the majority of employees are male, educated, and longer-tenured and work in larger firms pays a higher average wage than another industry in which the majority of employees are female, less educated, and shorter-tenured and work in smaller firms. It is necessary to control for these effects in order to derive a pure effect of industry on wage differentials by industry. The inter-industry wage differentials which are estimated without such controls may be a spurious effect of industry. This pure effect may be called an industrial rent, which indicates a capability of paying higher wages in one industry even though the qualities of the employees and characteristics of firms in this industry are the same as in others.

The compensating wage differential is a popular theory among labour economists, which suggests that inferior work conditions such as longer working hours, dangerous jobs, and physically hard jobs have to be compensated to attract workers, because otherwise firms would find difficulty in employing them. A higher wage payment is a representative compensation. Conversely, an industry or a firm which provides superior work conditions may keep the wage level lower for this reason. It is interesting to examine whether this theory of compensating wage differential is supported in Japan, because the confirmation of this theory would induce a departure from neoclassical wage determination. The popular term '3K industries', specifying industries which have many *kitsui* (physically hard), *kitanai* (dirty), and *kiken* (dangerous) jobs, implies that these industries are not preferred by people, in particular by the youth in contemporary Japan. Thus, the examination of compensating wage differentials is worthwhile.

What kind of variables should be used for controls is the next subject. Fortunately, we know quite a lot about the wage differentials by various factors in Japan, as given for example by Ono (1989), and Tachibanaki (1975; 1982). We thus adopt variables which are supposed to be influential in the determination of wages. The method of controls for such variables is performed through the estimation of the following wage function,

$$\ln(W_{ij}) = \text{constant} + (\text{industry dummies}) + (\text{various variables})$$
(5.1)

where W_{ij} stands for hourly wage figures for jth employee in the ith industry, and industry dummies signify two kinds of industry classification. The first is the one-digit broad industry classification such as mining, manufacturing, construction, and others. There are nine industries in total in this classification. The second is the two-digit industry classifications, which consists of fifty-five industries. Bonuses are excluded in wage figures, but working hours are taken into consideration.

The pure industry effect can be estimated by the following formulation:

$$p_i = \frac{\hat{W}_i - \overline{W}}{\overline{W}} \qquad (5.2)$$

where p_i is the ith industry's pure effect, $\hat{W}_i$ is the estimated average wage for the ith industry on the basis of the above wage function, and $\overline{W}$ is the overall average wage before the control.

We estimate the data for two years, 1978 and 1988, to study a time-series change in wage differentials. It is noted that the following categories of employees are eliminated from the sample: public employees, part-time employees, employees whose working hours are zero; employees whose wages are zero.

The control variables adopted are briefly explained. Appendices 5.1 and 5.2 show a list of variables and their statistical sources. Note that the control variables in Chapter 4 and in this chapter are different for the following reasons. First, the list of control variables in this chapter is more comprehensive. Second, many control variables are dummy variables rather than continuous variables.

1. Regular employee dummies; a regular permanent employee is unity, and a fixed-duration employee is zero. This variable is important in view of so-called implicit 'lifetime employment' in Japan, because employees with fixed-duration contracts are not guaranteed implicit lifetime employment.
2. White-collar and blue-collar dummies: a white-collar is unity and a blue-collar is zero.
3. Six firm-size dummy variables, i.e. number of employees, is classified by the following seven classes: (i) 5,000 and more, (ii) 1,000–4,999, (iii) 500–999, (iv) 300–499, (v) 100–299, (vi) 30–99 and (vii) 10–24 in 1988. Classes (i)–(vi) take unity, and class (vii) takes zero for these dummies. In 1978

an additional size, 15,000 and more, is added. These dummies are crucial in view of the fact that inter-scale wage differentials have been believed to be important in Japan (see Chapter 4).
4. The establishment variable is scaled by the number of workers in one establishment.
5. Sex dummy: a male is unity and a female is zero.
6. Two regional dummies are defined as follows. One group consists of the following prefectures which show the highest wages: Tokyo, Kanagawa, Saitama, Chiba, Osaka, Kyoto, Hyogo, and Aichi. The remaining prefectures are subdivided into two groups: one which shows higher wage payments and the other which shows lower wage payments.
7. Fixed regular working hours.
8. Overtime hours.
9. Ages.
10. Job durations at the current employers.
11. Three education dummies: one in which university graduate is unity, and another one in which Junior college graduate is unity, while senior high school graduate is zero.

Several comments should be made with respect to the above explanatory variables. First, it may be somewhat redundant to include both firm-size variables and establishment-size variables, because they may be slightly co-linear. They were included, nevertheless, to meet our preference to take account of as large a number of control variables as possible. Incidentally, establishment variables were not included in Tachibanaki (1975; 1982) and Chapter 4, but Ono (1989) included them. See Brown and Medoff (1989) for the treatment of firm size and establishment size for the USA. Second, the inclusion of working hours, both fixed regular hours and overtime, may be somewhat strange in view of the fact that the dependent variable is already standardized by fixed regular hours. They were included for the purpose of examining compensating wage differentials related to working hours. A simple idea may be suggested: jobs with longer working hours may be compensated by higher per-hour wages. Another reason is that in many cases wages in Japan are determined on monthly figures rather than per-hour figures. Thus, with the inclusion of working hours as one independent variable we are able to investigate the effect of working hours on wages. Third, regional dummies are a new addition to the knowledge of past studies; higher living expenses in urban areas are likely to offer higher wages in these areas. This variable has been totally ignored in Japan. Fourth, we considered a square form for all continuous variables in addition to a linear form, and all possible interaction terms among independent variables. The consideration of squared variables and interactions is highly desirable because the effect of one variable is normally non-linear and also highly interacted with other variables. This is probably the most important contribution to the wage function here, because no other studies have adopted such comprehensive square forms and interaction terms. In sum, the total number of control variables is 112 for one-digit industries and 158 for two-digit industries. Therefore, the controls are nearly comprehensive and thorough, and thus a pure effect of industry is derived after the comprehensive control. Table 5.1 shows the estimated wage function for the one-digit industry level in 1988. Other estimated functions are not shown, to save space.

It is impossible to interpret the empirical results of the estimated wage functions, partly because they have so many explanatory variables and partly because our main concern is to derive a pure effect of industry after the controls. The estimated wage functions are fairly robust because of both the calculated R^2 (over 0.70) and the statistical significance of the majority of the estimated coefficients. We have rarely seen studies of individual wage functions whose R^2 are higher than 0.50; thus this function is fairly successful as a wage function. This is due largely to an extremely large number of explanatory variables. Moreover, it should be emphasized that the null hypothesis, such that all industry dummy variables are equal to zero, is rejected at the 1 per cent significance level; so we can safely estimate a pure effect of industry on wage differentials based on the estimated wage functions.

Table 5.2 shows the figures of industry effect before and after the controls. Figures in the first column are industrial advantages (and disadvantages) compared to the average wage of total observations, while figures in the second column are industrial advantages (and disadvantages) after the controls. The former may be called a spurious advantage (or disadvantage) of an industry, while the

TABLE 5.1. *Estimated wage function, one-digit industry level, 1988*

Dependent variable	ln W Coefficient	T Standard error
INTERCEPT	0.99779710**	0.09652899
PRO[a]	−0.21296776**	0.02491041
PRO*T[b]	−0.00082827**	0.00040450
PRO*A	−0.00167548**	0.00030556
PRO*ESZ	5.40994E-06	0.00000370
PRO*HR	0.00089407**	0.00012498
PRO*EHR	0.00159893**	0.00013922
SX	−0.22331547**	0.02356294
T*SX	−0.00469097**	0.00045526
A*SX	0.00976419**	0.00029726
ESZ*SX	−1.76474E-05**	0.00000488
HR*SX	0.00137010**	0.00011939
EHR*SX	−0.00152505**	0.00022685
PER	0.50553926**	0.06970156
T*PER	0.00855983**	0.00179829
A*PER	−0.00148486*[c]	0.00084729
ESZ*PER	3.72223E-06	0.00002116
HR*PER	−0.00228296**	0.00032618
EHR*PER	0.00037447	0.00051403
PRF1	0.03868837	0.03266555
T*PRF1	0.00183436**	0.00054921
A*PRF1	−0.00094809**	0.00041935
ESZ*PRF1	6.90310E-05**	0.00001516
HR*PRF1	−0.00079056**	0.00015991
EHR*PRF1	7.39328E-05	0.00020239
PRF2	−0.04314644*	0.02207358
T*PRF2	−0.00185466**	0.00036469
A*PRF2	0.00255435**	0.00028875
ESZ*PRF2	−1.29766E-05**	0.00000305
HR*PRF2	0.00056130**	0.00011545
EHR*PRF2	−0.00069715**	0.00012977
T	0.02975502**	0.00260156
T*T	−0.00037258**	0.00002077
T*A	0.00029697**	0.00002664
A	0.04536628**	0.00178074
A*A	−0.00061161**	0.00001290
ED1	0.17357611**	0.02875426
T*ED1	0.00182208**	0.00039547
A*ED1	0.00042278	0.00034891

Wage Differentials by Industry and Labour Market

TABLE 5.1. Continued

Dependent variable	ln W Coefficient	T Standard error
ESZ*ED1	−3.15111E-06	0.00000450
HR*ED1	−0.00067679**	0.00013422
EHR*ED1[a]	−0.00114715**	0.00015326
ED2	0.11183046**	0.05021893
T*ED2	−0.00222366**	0.00098245
A*ED2	0.00753524**	0.00072208
ESZ*ED2	−1.50091E-05*	0.00000831
HR*ED2	−0.00100197**	0.00025162
EHR*ED2	−0.00129193**	0.00030981
ED3	0.34436756**	0.04145866
T*ED3	−0.00615863**	0.00071707
A*ED3	0.01456672**	0.00062797
ESZ*ED3	1.29507E-05**	0.00000631
HR*ED3	−0.00324393**	0.00019277
EHR*ED3	−0.00207503**	0.00023129
FSZ1	0.54613188**	0.04336746
T*FSZ1	0.00265162**	0.00075235
A*FSZ1	0.00341879**	0.00062618
ESZ*FSZ1	−0.00221116**	0.00055457
HR*FSZ1	−0.00267904**	0.00021200
EHR*FSZ1	−0.00024088	0.00026178
FSZ2	0.57553105	0.04443052
T*FSZ2	0.00507726**	0.00074619
A*FSZ2	−0.00028101	0.00059710
ESZ*FSZ2	−0.00219736**	0.00055458
HR*FSZ2	−0.00252868**	0.00022273
EHR*FSZ2	−0.00036608	0.00024701
FSZ3	0.63218921**	0.05062316
T*FSZ3	0.0049362**	0.00082557
A*FSZ3	−0.00135322**	0.00063817
ESZ*FSZ3	−0.00212980**	0.00055481
HR*FSZ3	−0.00286697**	0.00024865
EHR*FSZ3	−0.00046819**	0.00026955
FSZ4	0.56609994**	0.05076716
T*FSZ4	0.00393203**	0.00081251
A*FSZ4	−0.00051674	0.00060604
ESZ*FSZ4	−0.00212329**	0.00055548
HR*FSZ4	−0.00258134**	0.00024804
EHR*FSZ4	−0.00075563**	0.00028072

TABLE 5.1. Continued

Dependent variable	ln W Coefficient	T Standard error
FSZ5	0.45087864**	0.03959155
T*FSZ5	0.00263093**	0.00061192
A*FSZ5	−0.00020054	0.00042434
ESZ*FSZ5	−0.00216124**	0.00055626
HR*FSZ5	−0.00197145**	0.00018396
EHR*FSZ5	−0.00035716**	0.00021202
FSZ6	0.19623953**	0.03645808
T*FSZ6	0.00214806**	0.00056488
A*FSZ6	−0.00016766	0.00037472
ESZ*FSZ6	−0.00213152**	0.00056907
HR*FSZ6	−0.00067227**	0.00016231
EHR*FSZ6	−0.00059634**	0.00019486
ESZ	0.00232565**	0.00055552
T*ESZ	−2.56593E−07	0.00000041
A*ESZ	−1.46211E−07	0.00000038
ESZ*ESZ	−4.61942E−11	0.00000000
ESZ*HR	−5.23403E−07**	0.00000010
ESZ*EHR	−3.15792E−08	0.00000008
HR	−7.51269E−05	0.00053511
T*HR	−0.00012162**	0.00000724
A*HR	−3.01457E−07	0.00000529
HR*HR	9.74912E−07	0.00000096
HR*EHR	−2.56117E−05**	0.00000287
EHR	0.00600783**	0.00085630
A*EHR	−1.27197E−05*	0.00000743
T*EHR	−9.25798E−05**	0.00000922
EHR*EHR	1.74390E−05**	0.00000162
D1	−0.01944335	0.01285998
D2	−0.08428975**	0.01146452
D3	−0.02068015	0.01549764
D4	−0.14140039**	0.01229343
D5	−0.07262488**	0.01225233
D6	0.05398482**	0.01274532
D7	−0.02783857**	0.01640771
D8	−0.04132546**	0.01199761

R-square: 0.764616
Sample: 35,977

[a] Explanation of the independent variables appears in Appendix 5.1.
[b] * means cross term.
[c] ** = 5% significant; * = 10% significant.

TABLE 5.2(a). *Spurious and pure industrial advantages (or rents) before control and after control, for various qualifications in employees and firms: one-digit industrial classification*

	Before control	After control	SE[a]
1988			
Mining	0.0022642	0.0688731	0.0965289
Construction	0.0332822	0.0482913	0.0128599
Manufacturing	−0.075479	−0.017529	0.0114645
Electricity, gas, heat supply and water	0.4233582	0.0469956	0.0154976
Transport and communication	0.0974100	−0.072066	0.0122934
Wholesale and retail trade, eating and drinking places	−0.094351	−0.006001	0.0122523
Financing and insurance	0.3717543	0.1281620	0.0127453
Real estate	0.0013904	0.0395275	0.0164077
Services	−0.029218	0.0256017	0.0119976
1978			
Mining	0.0657732	0.0779355	0.670855
Construction	0.0127176	0.0315322	0.0120081
Manufacturing	−0.048808	−0.024461	0.0103942
Electricity, gas, heat supply, and water	0.4105111	0.0270313	0.0147992
Transport and communication	0.0274655	−0.030584	0.0115914
Wholesale and retail trade, eating and drinking places	−0.066326	−0.011391	0.0113104
Financing and insurance	0.2938798	0.1413137	0.0117937
Real estate	0.1038490	0.0250128	0.0162508
Services	−0.037510	0.0138866	0.0112348
1988 R-square: 0.764616 Sample: 35,977	1978 R-square: 0.729380 Sample: 35,952		

[a] SE: standard error of the coefficient of the industry dummy variables (SE of mining is that of the constant term).

TABLE 5.2(b). *Pure industrial advantages (or rents), after control for various qualifications in employees and firms: two-digit industrial classification*

	1988		1978	
	After control	SE[a]	After control	SE[a]
Mining	0.0630820	0.0965866	0.0773383	0.0671347
Construction works, general	0.0420218	0.0136066	0.0320689	0.012543
Construction works, by occupation	0.1047455	0.0196002	0.0901645	0.0256065
Equipment installation works	0.0199896	0.0158291	0.0036186	0.0152269
Food	−0.048762	0.0134045	−0.049537	0.0120622
Beverage, food, tobacco	0.0247300	0.0182095	0.0098796	0.0215465
Textile mill products	−0.0081299	0.0139650	−0.095620	0.0128092
Clothing	−0.119869	0.0144577	−0.124767	0.0135315
Lumber and wood products	−0.074478	0.0151229	−0.074824	0.0136986
Furniture and fixtures	−0.045157	0.0155176	−0.044422	0.0150593
Pulp, paper, and paper products	−0.011029	0.0145457	−0.030183	0.0134151
Publishing and printing	0.0375836	0.0139563	0.0038484	0.0126630
Chemical products	0.0469377	0.0132674	0.0279523	0.0123302
Plastic products	−0.013052	0.0148065	−0.040215	0.0161776
Rubber products	−0.036864	0.0152747	−0.019782	0.0144918
Ceramic, stone, and clay products	−0.005803	0.0136362	0.0014246	0.0123943
Iron and steel	0.0069158	0.0140705	0.0239815	0.0134544
Non-ferrous metal and products	−0.008703	0.0148532	−0.005370	0.0142208
Fabricated metal products	−0.000430	0.0136508	0.0011418	0.0129889
General machinery	0.0106363	0.0131682	0.0055347	0.0122905
Electrical machinery	−0.038717	0.0125663	−0.052968	0.0116956
Transportation equipment	−0.027709	0.0128400	−0.016294	0.0118202
Precision instruments	0.0018323	0.0145074	−0.008199	0.0137137
Electricity	0.0494885	0.0172018	0.0436140	0.0163697
Gas	0.0476073	0.0204269	0.0160781	0.0197327
Railways	−0.162059	0.0142224	−0.141886	0.0165318
Road passenger transport	−0.120455	0.0137067	−0.049389	0.0128420
Road freight transport	0.0019792	0.0138340	−0.003010	0.0130759
Transport services	−0.019801	0.0169754	0.0086445	0.0163498
Communication	−0.028858	0.0155688	0.0087671	0.0520756
Wholesale trade	0.0116925	0.0129443	0.0174983	0.0119778

TABLE 5.2(b). Continued

	1988		1978	
	After control	SE[a]	After control	SE[a]
Retail trade: general merchandise	−0.016637	0.0155914	−0.005666	0.0144512
Retail trade: dry goods, clothing, and accessory stores	0.0237663	0.0207473	−0.009725	0.0210873
Retail trade: food and beverage stores	−0.060776	0.0174092	−0.052895	0.0175541
Retail trade: motor vehicles, bicycles, carts	−0.005588	0.0161425	−0.037863	0.0161538
Retail trade: furniture, store fittings, and household utensil	−0.009814	0.0194091	−0.038717	0.0231030
Miscellaneous retail trade	−0.008561	0.0212494	−0.031446	0.0175167
Eating and drinking places	0.0039983	0.0168264	−0.049909	0.0149906
Banks and trust companies	0.2190921	0.0157661	0.1270166	0.0137199
Financial institutions for small enterprises, etc.	0.0279219	0.0144734	0.0344601	0.0138189
Securities and commodity brokers, dealers, and exchanges	0.2354562	0.0172531	0.1231129	0.0165879
Insurance trade	0.2351779	0.0157494	0.3318523	0.0139754
Real estate	0.0436456	0.0160327	0.0339615	0.0158224
Goods rental and leasing	0.1164276	0.0202444	0.0441111	0.0420159

latter may be called a pure advantage (or disadvantage) of an industry, or a pure industrial rent (or a pure negative rent).

Spurious advantages (or disadvantages) are discussed first. The highest wage payment is by the electricity, gas, and water supply industries in 1988, and its advantage is very high, 42.3 per cent above the average. The next highest wage is paid to the finance and insurance industries, and its advantage is 37.1 per cent. Conversely, the lowest wage payment is made to the wholesale, retail trade, and restaurant industries, and its disadvantage is 9.4 per cent below the average. Thus we observe a wide difference in wage payments by industries. This is also true for 1978.

TABLE 5.2(b). Continued

	1988		1978	
	After control	SE[a]	After control	SE[a]
Hotels, boarding houses, and other lodging-places	−0.000758	0.0149435	−0.056230	0.0138880
Laundry, beauty, and bath service	−0.087610	0.0188912	−0.098729	0.0162623
Amusement and recreation services except cinema	0.0328151	0.0160465	−0.039253	0.0151600
Miscellaneous repair services	−0.038774	0.0198148	−0.027264	0.0309762
Co-operative associations	−0.090116	0.0187414	−0.060035	0.0160755
Information services, research, and advertising	0.0733508	0.0151927	0.0795933	0.0268062
Miscellaneous business services	−0.137943	0.0160191	−0.123456	0.0177577
Professional services	0.0433529	0.0170664	0.0659924	0.0207185
Medical services	0.1307453	0.0137501	0.2122353	0.0137048
Education services	0.0985617	0.0147242	0.1143864	0.0146006
Social insurance and social welfare	0.0950856	0.0181598	0.1668690	0.0234047
1988 R-square: 0.774971 Sample: 34227 WASD[b] 0.0781719			1978 R-square: 0.743496 Sample: 34072 WASD[b] 0.0764758	

[a] SE: standard error of the coefficient of the industry dummy variables (SE of mining is that of the constant term).
[b] WASD: Weighted Adjusted Standard Deviation.

What happened to pure industrial advantages (or disadvantages) or rents after the very comprehensive controls? Some authors use the term 'industrial rent'. Since 'rent' must be defined fairly rigorously, we use the word 'advantages' (or 'disadvantages'); we have used 'rent-sharing' in Chapter 4. The pure advantage of the electricity, gas, and water supply industries has reduced to 4.7 per cent, and of the finance and insurance industries to 12.8 per cent. The highest industrial advantage is given to finance and insurance industries. The change is from 42.3 per cent to 4.7 per cent, and from 37.1 per cent to 12.8 per cent, respectively: these decreases are drastic. Incidentally, three effects—a greater number of larger firms, a greater number of male employees, and a greater number of longer-tenured workers—are responsible for the drastic decrease in advantages from before-control to after-control for the gas, electricity, and water supply industries. A similar explanation is also possible for the finance and insurance industries; see Tachibanaki (1992c). It is interesting to observe that the lowest spurious disadvantage for wholesale, retail trade, and restaurant industries disappears, while the lowest pure industrial disadvantage is observed for the transportation and communication industries. The service industry turned out to show a pure positive advantage after the control, while it showed a disadvantage before the control. The above observations are largely applicable for 1978 as well.

We can derive three implications from the above results. First, it is crucial to control for employees' qualifications and firms' specificities to derive a pure industry effect on wage differentials by industries, because spurious wage differentials by industries were reduced substantially. In other words, it is quite risky to analyse the inter-industry wage differentials on the basis only of the wage figures before controls.

Second, the ranking of industries due to industrial advantages is subtly different before and after the controls, as explained previously. This again suggests the necessity of controls. We found that the finance and insurance industries showed the highest advantage, 12.8 per cent in 1988 and 14.1 per cent in 1978, and that the transportation and communication industries showed the highest negative advantage, 7.2 per cent in 1988 and 3.1 per cent in 1978 (see e.g. Tachibanaki (1992c) on the finance industries). We need a subjective judgement to evaluate whether the pure advantage is too high, and/or the pure disadvantage is too low. The comparable figures for the USA are about 22 per cent advantage (mining) and 12 per cent disadvantage (wholesale and retail trade). See these numbers in Kruger and Summers (1988), which concludes that the difference is substantial. It is possible to conclude that the Japanese difference is considerably smaller than the US one.

Third, somewhat related to the above, there is a substantial difference between Japan and the USA with respect to ranks of industries due to pure effects. Japan ranks as follows: (1) finance and insurance, (2) mining, (3) construction, (4) electricity, gas, and water supply, (5) real estate, (6) services, (7) wholesale, retail trade, and restaurant, (8) manufacturing, and (9) transportation and communication. The USA ranks as follows: (1) mining, (2) transportation and public utilities, (3) construction, (4) manufacturing, (5) finance, insurance, and real estate, (6) services, and (7) wholesale and retail trade. Since one-digit-level industrial classifications are not identical for the two countries, it is somewhat risky to draw a firm conclusion; it is obvious, nevertheless, that ranking differs considerably. This contradicts the proposition by Katz and Summers (1989), which claimed a fairly similar pattern in spurious wage differentials by industry in the international context. When we use wage figures after controls, the inter-industry wage differentials are different, at least between Japan and the USA, for one-digit-level industries. It may be too hasty to predict that all countries have an identical structure of industrial advantages. The examination of two-digit-level industries between Japan and the USA confirms the finding more rigorously, although lack of space prevents its presentation here.

Next, we examine the pure industrial effect of two-digit industries in 1978 and 1988. The highest advantage was given to securities and commodity transactions industries, and insurance industries (both 23.5 per cent) in 1988, and to insurance industries (33.1 per cent advantage) in 1978, while the highest disadvantage was given to railroad industries (16.2 per cent) and 1978 (14.2 per cent). Within manufacturing industries, the highest advantage was given to chemical industries in both 1988 and 1978, while the highest disadvantage was given to apparel and other textile industries in both 1988 and 1978. A similar pattern was observed also for the USA, when we pay attention to two extremes—highest positive and negative effects. The above results suggest a fairly stable inter-industry wage structure across time. The very high correlation coefficient between 1978 and 1988 with respect to pure industrial advantages, 0.893, confirms the stability of the inter-industry wage structure over time in Japan.

5.3. DISPERSION IN WAGE DIFFERENTIALS BY INDUSTRY

This section examines what kind of employee qualifications and firm specificities are crucial controls in the determination of pure

TABLE 5.3. *Contribution of explanatory variables to wage differentials estimated by WASD after elimination of variables*

Eliminated variables	1988	1978
Working hours	0.110	0.091
Education dummies	0.099	0.088
Tenure	0.095	0.083
Blue-collar dummy	0.093	0.088
Firm-size dummies	0.089	0.083
Male dummy	0.088	0.089
Age	0.088	0.076
Regular-worker dummy	0.086	0.078
No elimination	0.086	0.076
No control	0.211	0.179

industrial advantages. In other words, we seek the important variables among many control variables, using weighted deviation for analysis. The weight is the number of employees in industries; the standard deviation is an upwardly biased estimate. We follow the method used by Kruger and Summers (1988) to correct this bias.

We use somewhat simplified versions of wage functions compared with those in the previous section, in the sense that a somewhat smaller number of control variables are used. This is due only to the technical reasons associated with computations; it raises weighted adjusted standard deviations very marginally, but does not give any significantly different result. One justification for this statement is provided by the extremely high correlation coefficient, 0.973, between the inter-industry wage differentials estimated in the previous section and those estimated by the present method.

Table 5.3 shows 'various' weighted adjusted standard deviations (WASD) in pure industrial advantages. This is calculated for log-wage figures. 'Various' means that one, two, or more explanatory variables are eliminated from the list of the control variables, and the resulting WASD is presented. The result suggests that the largest increase in WASD is obtained when the variable of working hours is eliminated in 1988; the next is education; job tenure, occupation dummy (white-collar and blue-collar), firm size, and establishment

TABLE 5.4. *Contribution of explanatory variables to wage differentials estimated by WASD after addition of variables*

Added variables	1988	1978
(1) No control	0.211	0.179
(2) Added except tenure, education, and firm size	0.117	0.113
(3) (2) + tenure control	0.103	0.095
(4) (3) + education control	0.089	0.083
(5) (4) + Firm-size control	0.086	0.076

size follow. In 1978 working hours is again the largest increase; the rank of other variables is fairly different in 1978 compared to 1988: the next one in 1978 is sex, and education, occupation, job tenure, firm size, and establishment size follow. The fact that the contribution of both sex and occupation had declined from 1978 to 1988 signifies that wage differentials by sex and occupation probably declined during the period. It is useful to mention that the law of equal treatment of men and women was implemented during the period, and also that a move toward more white-collar than blue-collar jobs in industry was initiated; these are probably responsible for the above trends.

Next, we examine the impact of adding control variables such as human-capital variables and firm-size variable on WASD. Each variable is added successively, and the results are presented in Table 5.4. We obtain the following observations. An addition of job tenure reduced WASD by 12.5 per cent; education reduced it by 13.5 per cent, and firm size by 3.6 per cent in 1988. The corresponding figures in 1978 were 15.1 per cent, 13.2 per cent, and 8.2 per cent. These results, together with the ones in the previous section, suggest that job tenure, education, and firm size are responsible for the very spurious wage differentials by industry. This is consistent with the paper by Tachibanaki and Taki (1990), who proposed that the wage function which used these three variables is fairly successful and sufficient in the estimation of wage determination in Japan.

Finally, we investigate the influence of control variables in more detail, by classifying samples in 1988 further; age, tenure, and firm

TABLE 5.5. *Comparison of WASD: subdivided samples (1988)*

	WASD		Correlation[a]
Age (years)			
15–29	0.064	a	a–b 0.673
30–50	0.097	b	b–c 0.771
51–	0.114	c	a–c 0.307
Tenure (years)			
0–4	0.069	d	d–e 0.789
5–10	0.110	e	e–f 0.879
11–	0.104	f	d–f 0.636
Size			
10–99	0.072	g	g–h 0.804
100–999	0.073	h	h–i 0.786
1,000–	0.089	i	g–i 0.488
Education			
Secondary school	0.092		0.619
University and junior college	0.066		
Sex			
Female	0.094		0.638
Male	0.073		
Type of worker			
Blue-collar	0.048		0.687
White-collar	0.026		

size are subdivided. Table 5.5 shows the result, which induces the following findings. The younger the age, the smaller the WASD; also, the shorter the tenure, the smaller the firm size. A similar finding is observed for higher education. WASD for men is smaller than for women, and is smaller for white-collar than for blue-collar workers. These results suggest that employees who are obliged to receive lower wage payments, say female, less educated, or blue-collar workers, are likely to receive more positive (or negative) industrial advantages than those who are supposed to receive higher wage payments, say male, educated, or white-collar workers. A simple example is the following: women are more advantaged in wage payments than men in advantageous industries like finance and insurance, while women are more disadvantaged than men in disadvantageous industries like manufacturing. A similar argument is also possible for less educated versus educated, and blue-collar versus white-collar.

5.4. ECONOMIC FACTORS WHICH EXPLAIN PURE INDUSTRIAL ADVANTAGES

It is appealing to investigate why pure industrial advantages appear even after controlling for various human-capital variables and firm characteristics. Since we obtained the degree of pure industrial advantages in the previous section, a natural task is to seek the cause of pure industrial advantages. There are several studies which performed a similar task including Sano (1969) and Mizuno (1973) for Japan, and Dickens and Katz (1987) for the USA. It should be noted that the Japanese studies adopted spurious industrial advantages (i.e. before controls) which are somewhat dubious as a data source for the reasons described above; Also, they did not consider a comprehensive list of causes. In sum, we would like to investigate the true causes of the appearance of pure industrial advantages, which are specific to Japanese institutional characteristics and industrial relations. The method is fairly simple: we consider a large number of economic variables, and estimate correlations between them and pure industrial advantages. Pearson correlation coefficients are estimated. It might be preferable to adopt partial correlation coefficients; but this is a future work. Pearson correlation coefficients are estimated for weighted figures, with weight being the number of employees in industries. Economic interpretations are provided for these empirical results.

Two types of data on pure industrial advantages are used. The first is two-digit industrial classifications for whole industries; two years, 1978 and 1988, are pooled. The total number of observations is 110. The second is two-digit classifications only for manufacturing industries, again pooled. The total number of observations is 38. The former is called whole industry for simplicity, and the latter is called manufacturing industry. It might be interesting to look at first differences, removing the fixed effect of individual industries, since we have two years of data; that was not attempted, however, because there were so few observations. We use a fairly large number of economic variables as candidates for explaining the causes of pure economic advantages, which are collected from various statistical sources; therefore, industrial classifications are not perfectly identical. Although there may be some errors and biases, they are not serious, since various government agencies have a policy favouring the identical definition of industries. Appendix 5.2 shows the list of variables and their statistical sources.

It is necessary to explain why variables which were used as control variables are used again as candidates for the causes of pure industrial advantages. We thought that several variables might be influential on the determination of industrial advantages. Since we use the average figures or the ratios (or shares) of these economic variables, this is not necessarily double-counting. Let us give an example by using the age variable. Suppose that there are two industries such that the average age of employees is older in one industry and younger in another. If the former industry requires knowledge and skills of older employees, average productivity in this industry may be higher. It raises the industrial advantages of this industry; therefore, average age may be a candidate for the explanation of the industrial advantage.

Table 5.6 shows the estimated correlation coefficients. Since there are so many numbers in this table, we restrict our attention to the influence of economic variables on pure industrial advantages. Let us first examine the average worker characteristics of industries. Average age has a negative influence on industrial advantages (or pure wage differentials) for whole industry, while it has no influence for manufacturing industry. Average tenure is different from average age; it has no correlation with wage differentials for whole industry, while it has a strong positive correlation for manufacturing industry. Manufacturing industry evaluates firm-specific human capital more highly than whole industry. The ratio of university graduates to total employees, which signifies a higher education level in the industry, has a strong positive influence for both whole and manufacturing industries. The ratio of blue-collar workers to total employees has a negative influence. The effect is weak for whole industry and strong for manufacturing industry. The rate of male employees has a weak positive effect for manufacturing industry.

TABLE 5.6(a). *Correlation coefficients between pure industrial advantages and economic variables: whole industry*[a] *(see also Appendix 5.2)*

	WD	A	T	ED	PRO	SZ	SX	BONUS	UNION
WD	1.00								
A	−0.20*[b]	1.00							
T	−0.12	0.25**	1.00						
ED	0.52**	−0.44**	−0.01	1.00					
PRO	−0.29**	0.30**	0.15	−0.35**	1.00				
SZ	0.35**	−0.20**	0.49**	0.17*	−0.25**	1.00			
SX	−0.22**	0.23**	0.59**	−0.03	0.09	0.09	1.00		
BONUS	0.39**	−0.41**	0.52**	0.52**	−0.26**	0.69**	0.13	1.00	
UNION	0.08	0.07	0.65**	0.03	0.01	0.70**	0.34**	0.62**	1.00
CWELF	0.36**	0.04	0.48**	0.11	−0.02	0.63**	0.30**	0.52**	0.74**
INJURY	−0.27**	0.47**	0.25**	−0.44**	0.25**	−0.06	0.35**	−0.26**	0.09
REST	−0.25**	0.35**	−0.31**	−0.30**	−0.06	−0.50**	−0.07	−0.52**	−0.48**
RED	−0.12	0.34**	−0.03	−0.16*	0.21**	−0.26**	0.17*	−0.30**	−0.08
QUIT	0.04	−0.09	−0.38**	0.12	−0.20**	−0.17**	−0.25**	−0.20**	−0.39**
HIRING	0.07	−0.18*	−0.60**	0.09	−0.33**	−0.25**	−0.48**	−0.33**	−0.59**
EMP	0.31**	−0.12	0.01	0.43**	−0.42**	0.12	−0.10	0.20**	−0.08
VACANCY	−0.36**	0.19**	−0.02	−0.25**	0.57**	−0.26**	0.14	−0.38**	−0.23**
EXPORT	−0.30**	−0.08	0.15	−0.25**	0.35**	0.11	0.28**	0.01	0.38**
CAPRET	−0.13	0.17*	0.06	−0.07	0.20**	−0.29**	0.10	−0.20**	−0.10
REGUL	0.62**	−0.26**	0.09	0.27**	−0.40**	0.60**	−0.32**	0.56**	0.36**

TABLE 5.6(a). Continued

	CWELF	INJURY	REST	RED	QUIT	HIRING	EMP	VACANCY	EXPORT
CWELF	1.00								
INJURY	0.14	1.00							
REST	-0.54**	0.43**	1.00						
RED	0.09	0.32**	0.19**	1.00					
QUIT	-0.27**	-0.21**	0.10	0.13	1.00				
HIRING	-0.46**	-0.21**	0.36**	-0.02	0.48**	1.00			
EMP	-0.09	-0.25**	-0.04	-0.51**	0.19**	0.39**	1.00		
VACANCY	-0.32**	0.29**	0.32**	0.08	-0.05	0.13	0.03	1.00	
EXPORT	0.05	-0.01	-0.35**	-0.03	-0.20**	-0.40**	-0.26**	0.23**	1.00
CAPRET	-0.17**	-0.08	-0.01	0.06	-0.14	-0.09	0.01	0.10	0.14
REGUL	0.48**	-0.21**	-0.30**	-0.35**	-0.04	-0.02	0.31**	-0.43**	-0.30**

	CAPRET	REGUL
CAPRET	1.00	
REGUL	-0.29**	1.00

[a] Weighted by the no. of workers in industries. Sample size: 110.
[b] ** = 5% significant; * = 10% significant

TABLE 5.6(b). Correlation coefficients between pure industrial advantages and economic variables: manufacturing[a]

	WD	A	T	ED	PRO	SZ	SX	BONUS	UNION
WD	1.00								
A	0.02	1.00							
T	0.64**[b]	0.44**	1.00						
ED	0.70**	-0.31*	0.54**	1.00					
PRO	-0.70**	0.40**	-0.43**	-0.95**	1.00				
SZ	0.28	0.35**	0.54**	0.34**	-0.18	1.00			
SX	0.81**	0.22	0.68**	0.45**	-0.43**	0.38**	1.00		
BONUS	0.77**	-0.31*	0.58**	0.79**	-0.84**	0.11	0.60**	1.00	
UNION	0.43**	-0.24	0.45**	0.42**	-0.43**	0.05	0.46**	0.72**	1.00
CWELF	0.62**	0.06	0.60**	0.38**	-0.43**	0.17	0.60**	0.64**	0.83**
INJURY	-0.15	0.69**	-0.07	-0.41**	0.36**	-0.03	-0.01	-0.44**	-0.56**
REST	-0.54**	0.45**	-0.49**	-0.64**	0.61**	-0.16	-0.46**	-0.77**	-0.75**
RED	0.02	0.19	0.13	-0.19	0.14	-0.18	0.18	0.06	0.25
QUIT	-0.76**	-0.20	-0.65**	-0.45**	0.44**	-0.20	-0.82**	-0.59**	-0.60**
HIRING	-0.40**	0.05	-0.30**	-0.24	0.24	-0.12	-0.43**	-0.41**	-0.50**
EMP	0.14	0.02	0.26	0.39**	-0.33**	0.64**	0.05	0.09	-0.15
VACANCY	-0.58**	-0.08	-0.49	-0.36**	0.36**	0.03	-0.45**	-0.56**	-0.47**
EXPORT	0.06	-0.60**	-0.05	0.16	-0.21	-0.11	0.17	0.37**	0.56**
CAPRET	0.19	0.29*	0.48**	0.14	0.01	0.53**	0.34**	0.02	0.14
CAPITAL	0.53**	0.17	0.58**	0.29**	-0.22	0.14	0.50**	0.52**	0.66**
HI	0.45**	-0.11	0.21	0.20	-0.28*	0.07	0.39**	0.47**	0.49**
RD	0.17	-0.61**	0.02	0.38**	-0.49**	-0.04	0.12	0.55**	0.61**
VALUE	0.72**	-0.01	0.61**	0.62**	-0.64**	0.15	0.57**	0.80**	0.72**
PROFIT	0.47**	0.14	0.35**	0.26	-0.31*	0.10	0.31*	0.48**	0.55**

TABLE 5.6(b). Continued

	CWELF	INJURY	REST	RED	QUIT	HIRING	EMP	VACANCY	EXPORT
CWELF	1.00								
INJURY	-0.32**	1.00							
REST	-0.62**	0.79**	1.00						
RED	0.40**	0.04	-0.10	1.00					
QUIT	-0.74**	0.16	0.48**	-0.28*	1.00				
HIRING	-0.47**	0.36**	0.54**	-0.28*	0.60**	1.00			
EMP	-0.21	-0.12	-0.14	-0.68**	0.10	0.08	1.00		
VACANCY	-0.61**	0.10	0.42**	-0.27*	0.59**	0.27	0.32*	1.00	
EXPORT	0.20	-0.63**	-0.59**	0.05	-0.16	-0.42**	-0.01	0.07	1.00
CAPRET	0.24	-0.14	-0.26	0.21	-0.24	-0.23	0.18	0.06	0.04
CAPITAL	0.90**	-0.23	-0.45**	0.38**	-0.68**	-0.37**	-0.24	-0.56**	-0.01
HI	0.50**	-0.25	-0.44**	0.04	-0.39**	-0.46**	0.14	-0.22	0.42**
RD	0.32**	-0.63**	-0.61**	0.05	-0.26	-0.55**	0.01	-0.15	0.78**
VALUE	0.83**	-0.27*	-0.55**	0.25	-0.70**	-0.40**	-0.08	-0.61**	0.06
PROFIT	0.73**	-0.10	-0.27	0.30*	-0.50**	-0.36**	-0.13	-0.44**	-0.04

	CAPRET	CAPITAL	HI	RD	VALUE	PROFIT
CAPRET	1.00					
CAPITAL	0.21	1.00				
HI	0.10	0.28*	1.00			
RD	-0.06	0.09	0.41**	1.00		
VALUE	0.07	0.79**	0.31*	0.34**	1.00	
PROFIT	0.05	0.70**	0.35**	0.26	0.79**	1.00

[a] Weighted by the no. of workers in industries. Sample size: 38.

Many of the above variables were used as control variables, as noted previously. What implications can be derived from the above observations obtained by the estimated correlation coefficients? The positive influences for manufacturing industry are observed by the ratio of male employees, average job tenure, the ratio of university graduates, and the ratio of white-collar employees. It is possible to conclude that these characteristics raised average productivity of the industry, which is one of the indicators of a pure industrial advantage. Incidentally, this table suggests that per capita value added (i.e. average productivity) has the strongest positive effect on pure industrial advantages. We can interpret this result in the following way. First, various variables, such as average job tenure and other variables examined above, raise the average productivity of the industry. Second, this higher productivity produces an industrial advantage. This is our interpretation of the table; it is necessary to use a simultaneous-equation model to confirm whether the interpretation is correct.

The share of bonus payments over total wage payment is highly correlated with pure industrial advantages (pure wage differentials). This reflects the fact that bonuses are an indicator of firm-specific human capital, as proposed by Hashimoto (1979). We can conceive another hypothesis for bonus payment: the profit-sharing hypothesis popularized by Weitzman (1986) and Freeman and Weitzman (1987). The present chapter does not intend to determine which hypothesis is more helpful in understanding bonus payment in Japan. The rate of union participation has no impact for whole industry, while it has a strong positive effect for manufacturing industry. Combining with a strong negative effect on quits and a strong positive effect on productivity and profit, the influence of the union participation rate may be regarded as a voice mechanism of the union movement, at least for manufacturing industry; thus, this work supports Muramatsu (1984). However, a separate careful study is required for confirmation; see, for example, Tachibanaki and Noda (1994).

Next, we investigate the effect of working conditions on pure wage differentials. Non-statutory fringe benefit per employee, the rate of labour accident, and the rate of utilization of one day's holiday per week are the variables which show the degree of working conditions. Non-statutory fringe benefit is positively correlated in ranks for both whole and manufacturing industries. The rate of labour accidents has a negative impact for whole industry, while it has no significance for manufacturing industry. The day-holiday rate is negatively correlated for both whole and manufacturing industries. These observations lead us to conclude that lower wages are paid to workers in the industry with unfavourable working conditions. It would be premature to accept the theory of compensating wage differentials; instead, I suggest that the '3K' industries argument described above is very plausible.

Variables like the rate of involuntary quit, the rate of voluntary quit, the rate of new job entry, the rate of increase in employment, and the vacancy rate indicate the degree of labour mobility. Statistically significant variables are observed only by the rate of increase in employment (positively) and vacancy rate (negatively) for whole industry. Voluntary quit rate and vacancy rate are negatively related with industrial advantages for manufacturing industry. A higher industrial advantage probably lowers the rate of voluntary quit. Higher labour demand, which is indicated by the rate of increase in employment indirectly, raises wage levels. We consider, nevertheless, that these variables related to labour mobility do not have a strong influence on industrial wage differentials on average; they are more influential on wages for newly hired employees than those for currently employed workers.

A regulation dummy variable was introduced to examine whether government regulation on competition and business activity has an impact on industrial advantages. The table indicates that this variable has quite a positive influence on industrial advantages for whole industry. Typical industries which receive higher benefits from regulation are finance and insurance, and electricity, gas, and water supply; see Tachibanaki (1992), which analyses the benefit for finance and insurance. Besides the effect of regulation on industrial wage differentials, it is interesting to observe that a regulation dummy has higher correlations with firm size, non-statutory fringe benefit, and bonus ratio. These results suggest the need to investige the effect of regulation further, as well as utilizing a more reliable measure of regulation than a dummy variable, since this is one of the most peculiar variables in Japan.

The share of exports over total production has a negative effect on industrial wages for whole industry, while it is not statistically significant for manufacturing industry. The highest rate of exports is observed by several manufacturing areas such as cars, electrical goods, chemical products, and machines. These manufacturing industries do not necessarily pay higher wages, but probably around average. A more interesting observation concerns the high positive correlation between the share of exports over total production and R&D expenditure rate, which signifies one of the causes of their success in exports.

Next, variables which indicate market concentration rate and profit rate per employee are examined. The Hirfindarl index is used to show market concentration for industries. These two variables have strong positive effects on industrial advantages; thus, firms' ability to pay is an important source of higher wage payments. Other indicators of firms' ability to pay, such as value added per employee (productivity) and capital:labour ratio, have a strong positive effect on wages. Note that the variables examined above are interrelated to each other to a greater extent. Finally, the rate of return to stocks, which shows one indicator of investment incentives like the Q-ratio, has no impact.

5.5. THE EFFECT OF DIFFERENT RETURNS TO THE LABOUR FORCE AMONG INDUSTRIES

Above we have estimated pure industrial advantages after controlling for various qualities of employees and firms, and investigated the causes of pure industrial advantages. It was assumed that differences in returns to labour forces among various industries were not observed. This assumption implies, for example, that monetary returns (i.e. wages) to university education do not differ from industry to industry. Another assumption is that the treatment of male/female wages is common for all industries. A similar argument is possible for other qualifications and characteristics, such as firm size and tenure. We have not considered the case in which industrial differences do not matter in the determination of returns (or wages) to various qualifications. This assumption may be somewhat unrealistic, as examined by Kawashima and Tachibanaki (1986), who investigated the difference in wage structures between competitive sectors and non-competitive sectors. This section examines what would happen if this assumption was removed.

It is not implausible to presume that returns to various labour qualifications do not differ greatly by industry unless the labour markets are highly segmented. In fact, a large number of studies on wage differentials by industries, including the present one in the previous sections, assumed no variations by industry. It is, however, useful to investigate the case in which this assumption is removed; therefore this section starts to re-estimate the wage functions, which were estimated for whole industries in section 5.2, for each industry separately. These wage functions obviously produce different estimated coefficients of education, firm size, tenure, and other characteristics by industry. We perform this experiment only for 19 manufacturing industries (1978 and 1988); thus we have 38 different estimated returns (i.e. coefficients) to various qualifications such as education, size, sex, and others. The specification of the wage functions was simplified to reduce a heavy burden of computation; in particular, various interaction variables adopted previously were eliminated. It should be emphasized, however, that this simplification does not affect the substance of this section.

It requires considerable space to discuss in detail the difference in the estimated returns (i.e. the coefficients) to various qualifications like education, sex, and firm size. The present section utilizes only the estimated returns, and examines the correlation between pure industrial advantages and estimated returns.

Table 5.7 shows the correlation coefficients between pure industrial advantages and estimated returns to various qualifications. Several important observations derived from the correlation coefficients are described. Since our main concern is the relationship between industrial wage differentials and differences in returns to labour qualifications by industry, we concentrate on the contribution of each quality variable to the degree of wage differentials by industry.

First, wage differentials between white-collar and blue-collar workers narrow as pure industrial advantage increases. This is confirmed by the effect of a blue-collar worker dummy, indicating that occupational advantage is smaller in highly paid industries than in low-paid ones because the correlation is significantly positive.

Second, a similar story applies to the effect of a male sex dummy. Females are treated more favourably in highly paid industries than low-paid industries because the correlation is negative significantly. These two observations suggest that 'handicapped' workers such as

TABLE 5.7. *Correlation coefficients between pure industrial advantages and estimated returns to various labour and firm qualifications*

Return to blue-collar	0.493**[a]
Return to male	−0.518**
Return to senior high school	0.480**
Return to university, college	0.537**
Return to medium-scale firm	0.327
Return to large-scale firm	−0.052**
Return to tenure (years)	
0	0.661**
5	0.679**
10	0.670**
15	0.583**
20	0.385**
Return to outside experience (years)	
0	0.780**
5	0.780**
10	0.778**
15	0.765**
20	0.707**

[a] ** = 5% significant.

blue-collar workers and females should not work in low-paid industries, because they are treated less favourably in these industries.

Third, a different outcome applies to educational attainment. The statistically significant positive correlation coefficients with both a high-school graduate dummy and a university graduate dummy suggest that the return to education is more favourably assessed in highly paid industries than in low-paid ones; in other words, educationally privileged workers should not work in low-paid industries. Katz and Revenga (1989) estimated changes in wage differentials by educational attainments in the USA and Japan since the early 1970s; their study supplements the effect of education on wage differentials in Japan, and is largely consistent with the result here.

Fourth, the effect of firm-size dummies is very minor because the correlation coefficient is either near zero or statistically insignificant. It is possible to conclude that the contribution of firm size to wage differentials by industry has no significant effect, unlike the case of occupation, sex, and education.

Fifth, the effect of job duration (i.e. job tenure) and outside experience (i.e. labour market experience prior to the current employer) is examined. The correlation coefficients between wage differentials by industry and job tenure are positive with statistical significance, and they have a minor convex nature. Thus, job tenure is evaluated more highly in highly paid industries than in low-paid industries; however, this advantage declines as job tenure becomes longer and longer. The correlation coefficients between wage differentials by industry and outside experience are also positive, and their values are slightly higher than those for job tenure. Outside experiences in the labour market are evaluated more favourably in highly paid than in low-paid industries; more importantly, the correlation coefficients do not decline as outside experiences become longer. This indicates that changing employer within highly paid industries does not affect the advantage of longer job tenure with the current employer, but retains the advantage of outside experience. This is somewhat inconsistent with our understanding of the labour market in Japan, because it was believed that returns to tenure would not decline, and that returns to outside experience would not be so large. It is necessary to investigate further the relative contribution of job tenure and outside experience to wage differentials by industry, because the statistical tool for investigating the effect of job tenure and outside experience is not so rigorous.

5.6. CONCLUDING REMARKS

This chapter investigated wage differentials by industry in Japan by using individual wage data. First, we attempted to estimate wage functions which are explained by an extremely large number of independent variables, and derived pure industrial advantages after controlling for labour qualities and firm characteristics. Second, we investigated the causes for pure industrial advantages, and tried to find what kind of economic variables are responsible for inducing them. Again, a large number of economic variables which show the condition of an industry and the labour market condition have been considered in order to estimate pure industrial advantages. Third,

Wage Differentials by Industry and Labour Market 109

we considered the case in which returns to various labour qualities differ by industry, in view of the fact that previous studies assumed no differences in returns to labour qualities across industries. We investigated the outcome, after the assumption was removed.

We have obtained the following results in this chapter. First, although there appeared to be a considerable difference in wage payments by industries before the control, controlling for labour qualities and firm characteristics substantially reduced the degree of spurious wage differentials by industry. The important variables for the control were job tenure, education, and firm size. Incidentally, this study found that Japan's industrial structure of wage payments differed considerably from that of the USA, at least for the one-digit industry level. Two-digit-level industries within manufacturing are quite similar in both countries, while two-digit-level industries in whole industries are not similar.

Second, we found that the most important economic variables for pure industrial advantages were ability-to-pay variables and variables related to productivity. These include many variables, including profit rate, concentration rate, and capital:labour ratio (see Chapter 4). The variable on regulation was also important; the variables related to labour mobility turned out to be less important.

Third, data in Japan did not support the theory of compensating wage differentials. In other words, inferior working conditions in an industry have not been compensated by higher wage payments. It is anticipated that Japan will face a more serious labour shortage in coming years, and thus the theory of compensating wage differentials may work in future there.

Fourth, a removal of the assumption of no difference in returns to various labour qualities across industries did not alter the substance of the empirical findings obtained in the former sections. In other words, the result in section 5.5 supported the empirical analyses in the former sections. It is feasible to conclude, therefore, that the results in this chapter are fairly robust, since the two different methods produced consistent findings with respect to the relationship between pure industrial advantages and economic variables.

Fifth, one important implication derived from the result in Chapters 4 and 5 is that a highly intrinsic variable for wage differentials is the size of firm for the following reasons: while a large number of control variables reduced the spurious advantages of wage payments by industries, they did not reduce the spurious advantages of wage payments by sizes. In other words, if we compare industry effect and size effect, the latter is more intrinsic and the former is more spurious regarding wage differentials.

The most serious deficiency in this chapter is probably the lack of a simultaneous consideration of the causes of pure industrial advantages. It is possible to anticipate that economic variables considered in this chapter are interrelated to each other; in other words, it is possible that several variables such as tenure, firm size, and even industry may be jointly determined variables. Future work is called for which constructs a simulataneous-equation model in investigating the influence of various economic variables on pure industrial advantages.

Another weak point in this chapter may be less frequent references to economic theories which justify wage differentials by industry. The most popular theory is probably the efficiency wage hypothesis, which supports the existence of wage differentials by industry. A useful survey was given by Akerlof and Yellen (1986), and Katz (1986). Since this theory is currently under severe scrutiny, as represented by Carmichael (1990) and Lang and Kahn (1990), we did not refer to the efficiency wage theory explicitly. In other words, since we have not obtained an apparent empirical support of wage differentials by industry, unlike the United States, in this chapter, it is risky to commit ourselves to the efficiency wage theory at least for Japan. However, the important effect of profit, capital:labour ratio, and value-added variable on pure industrial advantages may support the corollary of the efficiency wage theory. Further serious studies are required for Japan in order to test whether the efficiency wage theory is supported.

Finally, it should be useful to note that some economists propose the following interpretation regarding industrial advantages: the significance of industry dummies in wage equations demonstrates that there are omitted variables which could easily be compatible with competition theory (see Murphy and Welch, 1992; Topel, 1986: 91). The present study applied a large number of control variables, which may be regarded as omitted variables in terms of these authors. Thus, if we took account of a large number of omitted variables, the spurious industry effect would disappear. It is possible to conclude that the present study has confirmed the idea of these authors. This does not necessarily imply, however, that competitive theory is relevant, because we still have a remaining and intrinsic inter-size effect on wages at least in Japan, as shown in Chapter 4. Whether the inter-size difference is compatible with competition theory is another question which needs further scrutiny.

APPENDIX 5.1. *Notation of variables in Table 5.1*

PRO	Production-worker dummy
SX	Female-worker dummy
PER	Permanent-worker dummy
PRF1	Regional dummy (1), high-wage districts
PRF1	Regional dummy (2), low-wage districts
A	Age
T	Tenure
FSZ1	Firm-size dummy (1), 5,000–
FSZ2	Firm-size dummy (2), 1,000–4,999
FSZ3	Firm-size dummy (3), 500–999
FSZ4	Firm-size dummy (4), 300–499
FSZ5	Firm-size dummy (5), 100–299
FSZ6	Firm-size dummy (6), 30–99
ESZ	Establishment size
ED1	Senior high-school dummy
ED2	Junior-college dummy
ED3	University dummy
HR	Regular working hours
EHR	Excess working hours
D1	Industry dummy (1), construction
D2	Industry dummy (2), manufacturing
D3	Industry dummy (3), electricity, gas, heat supply, and water
D4	Industry dummy (4), transport and communication
D5	Industry dummy (5), wholesale and retail trade, eating and drinking places
D6	Industry dummy (6), financing and insurance
D7	Industry dummy (7), real estate
D8	Industry dummy (8), services

APPENDIX 5.2. *Meanings of variables and data source in Table 5.6*

A	average age
T	average tenure
ED	ratio of university graduates
PRO	ratio of blue-collar employees
SZ	ratio of firms employing over 1,000
SX	ratio of male employees
	Ministry of Labour, *Wage Structure Survery*.
UNION	union membership rate
	Ministry of Labour, *Survey of Trade Unions*.
CWELF	non-legal fringe benefit per employee
REST	ratio of employees who have only one non-working day per week
	Ministry of Labour, *Wage and Working Hours Survey*.
INJURY	frequency of labour injury
	Ministry of Labour, *Survey on Labour Injury*.
RED	separation rates initiated by employers
QUIT	separation rates caused by personal reasons
HIRING	entry rates
EMP	hiring minus separation
	Ministry of Labour, *Employment Trend Survey*.
VACANCY	vacancy over number of workers
	Ministry of Labour, *Job Vacancy Survey*.
EXPORT	ratio of export over domestic output
	Ministry Secretariat, *Input–Output Table*.
CAPRET	rate of return to stock
	Research Institute of Stocks Economy, *Annual Statistics*
CAPITAL	capital : labour ratio
	Ministry of International Trade and Industry, *Industry Survey*.
HI	hirfindahl index
	Fair Trade Commission
RD	R&D ratio over sales value
	Ministry Secretariat, *R&D Survey*.
VALUE	labour productivity (i.e. per capita value-added)
	Ministry of International Trade and Industry, *Industry Survey*.
PROFIT	Profit over employees
	Ministry of Finance, *Survey on Corporated Firms*.
REGUL	regulation dummy
	Regulated industries are electricity and gas, telecommunication, banking and insurance, and medical industries

6
Education, Occupation, and Earnings

6.1. INTRODUCTION

This chapter presents two brief surveys of the relationship between education, occupation, and earnings. The first survey deals with how education specialists interpret the reasons why education contributes to increased worker productivity; the second attempts to show various views of economists on the relationship between education, occupation, and earnings. This chapter serves as an introduction to the next, which investigates this relationship in the Japanese context. Section 6.2 depends heavily upon Carnoy (1994), and Section 6.3 is derived from Tachibanaki (1994a).

6.2. EDUCATION AND PRODUCTIVITY

It is widely believed that productivity differences among workers are so marked that education contributes to raising an individual's productivity. In fact, earnings differentials are explained by the difference in educational attainment to a large extent in many developed and developing countries—except possibly for Japan, to which special attention is paid in this book. If workers' earnings are differentiated by their productivity achievements, it is possible to predict that education raises worker productivity. We assume that workers' wages are paid according to their productivities; the marginal productivity theory, explained previously, supports this assumption. We can presume, then, that education contributes to increased productivity, as Schultz (1961) proposed. It is useful to investigate what kinds of explanation are provided to support the above proposition.

Education specialists have suggested five main reasons for

interpreting increased productivity through education. First, the human-capital argument is, again, useful. Individuals acquire skills not only through formal education but also through job training. This is the main idea of human capital.

Second, the disequilibrium explanation is advanced by several specialists. Educated people are likely to use other resources, such as machines, and to make more use of new technologies. These observations have been made for farmers who are educated and who experience higher productivity, as pointed out by Welch (1970) and Schultz (1975). This interpretation of education assumes that a person with more education makes a better and quicker decision, and it can be applied to farmers, the self-employed, employees whose role is supervising, and female employees who can decide many matters without recourse to male colleagues.

Third is the skill explanation. Formal schooling imparts fundamental skills such as mathematical calculation and reading and writing ability. Education serves as a formal training institution within which such skills are taught. Although these fundamental skills useful to explain the difference in productivity between people in advanced countries and people in developing countries, they are not so useful to explain the difference in productivity among employees in advanced countries, where nearly all workers acquire such fundamental skills in compulsory education. Thus, the human-capital approach is more useful for workers in advanced and developed countries.

Fourth is the organizational explanation. This argues that schooling can socialize young people into functioning effectively in modern society. It teaches people how to be motivated in production lines and offices, how to be co-operative and patient, how to be effective in many behaviours, etc. This explanation does not concern itself with productivity improvement through individual skill or fundamental knowledge of techniques, but instead emphasizes mental and social aspects such as motivation, leadership, and co-operative behaviour in a 'team production'. Schooling is effective in such mental and social behaviour.

Finally comes the trainability explanation. A similar explanation has already been suggested in Chapter 2. The notion of trainability is related to the human-capital approach, since a person who has received schooling is ready to go further in many directions. A company can provide employees who completed formal schooling with efficient training, and they are likely to carry out their jobs skilfully after such training; in effect, formal education is a training-ground for further training or learning. As Rosen (1977) showed, different levels of formal schooling allow different levels of future success, since schooling affects the kind of job for which people can be trained, and thus their productivity. The idea of trainability or learning ability is somewhat related to the notion of the filtering or screening role of education, which will be explained later in this chapter.

It would be useful to refer briefly to empirical findings on whether or not these theoretical explanations of why formal education contributes to higher productivity are valid. Empirical results must be clearly distinguished as between developed and developing countries. Also, the difference in industry, say agriculture versus non-agriculture, is significant in terms of the effect of education on productivity, and thus on earnings.

A large number of studies propose that literacy and primary education influence the increase in productivity and thus economic growth. This is particularly true throughout the developing world, because the increased enrolment in primary schools has contributed to rapid increases in economic development (see e.g. Bowman and Anderson, 1963). The above result is supported more strongly if we pay attention to farmers' productivity in developing countries in Asia and Latin America (see e.g. Jamison and Lau, 1982). This is true even for developed countries, as Welch (1970) skilfully verified for US agriculture. It is concluded that education contributes positively to productivity in agriculture.

Non-agricultural jobs, however, in developed counties do not support the positive correlation between education and productivity. This is explained partly by the difficulty associated with various categories of non-agricultural jobs. In other words, it is difficult to compare productivity in different non-agricultural jobs, although it may be easier to compare productivity between less-educated and educated persons within the same job. The reason is that more formal education raises the possibility that educated people may take jobs where productivity is higher. This is a dilemma: education raises the productivity of people, but educated persons tend to take jobs where productivity is higher. The present author believes the latter, however, at least for industrialized countries, as will be surveyed later. In addition to this dilemma there is a complex set of issues for the developed world proposed by the so-called radical economists' group (Bowles and Gintis, 1976). They proposed that socioeconomic background was a more important determinant than ability for earnings when years of schooling are controlled for. Chapter 7 will examine the contribution of socioeconomic background in Japan. In summarizing the above, it is less apparent to suppose the positive correlation between education and productivity in non-agricultural jobs in developed countries than in agricultural jobs. Also, the positive correlation between education and productivity (and thus earnings) in developed countries is a much more complex issue than that in developing counties.

6.3. EDUCATION, OCCUPATION, AND EARNINGS

The relationship between education, occupation, and earnings is surveyed both theoretically and empirically.

6.3.1. Occupation and Earnings

The effect of education on the determination of wages and earnings has been analysed by employing the concept of human capital, which emphasizes the importance not only of formal education but also of job training. A basic premiss of this concept is that higher levels of educational attainment increase individuals' productivity and, consequently, their earning capacity. Since formal education and job training are costly, however, it is impossible to invest in human capital endlessly. Many studies have been devoted to examining the effect of education on earnings within the framework of human-capital theory.

The relationship between occupation and earnings has been analysed extensively in many countries; it may be described as 'pay difference by occupation' or 'pay structure by occupation'. It is important to stress that occupation is the variable that has received most attention in studies investigating earnings differences. Researchers were interested in studying whether there were earnings differences between occupations by estimating the magnitudes of such differences, if any; they usually suggested social and economic reasons to explain occupational earnings differentials.

It is possible to conclude that difference of earnings by occupation can be observed in all societies in all periods of history. In modern times, the pattern of pay difference by occupation is common to many countries, particularly capitalist ones, suggesting that occupations which pay higher wages and those which pay lower wages do not differ significantly from country to country. For example, white-collar workers receive higher wages than manual workers in nearly all countries. This situation is found even when a wider range of occupations is considered. What kind of justification can be offered to explain earnings difference by occupation?

Brown (1977) provides a useful survey of the causes for pay difference by occupation. The starting-point for explaining pay difference by occupation can be found in the usual functions of supply and demand, consisting of both wage rates and the number of jobs available for any occupation. Economics asserts that the intersection of the supply and demand curves determines the equilibrium wage and the number of jobs for each occupation. When adjustments of both supply and demand for all occupations are made smoothly, nearly all occupations produce equilibrium wage rates. In some occupations, however, the effects of supply and demand are often limited for various reasons. This limitation is responsible for pay differences between occupations. Several institutional and economic factors can be suggested that prevent free and perfect adjustments of supply and demand.

1. Perfect monopoly in supply: the number of people available for a particular occupation is perfectly controlled by a group of people who engage in the same occupation. In other words, there is an entry barrier to working in a particular occupation to protect the workers already engaged in it. This is a variation of the guild system developed in medieval Europe, and continues to be commonly observed.

2. Licence: a public authority grants special privileges to a particular occupation such that only people who have received licences or other types of certification can engage in the occupation. Examples include medical doctors and airline pilots.

3. Compensating wage differentials: some types of occupations involve dangerous tasks, require special physical abilities, or are located in unfavourable environments. It is expected that higher

wages will be paid in these occupations to compensate for unfavourable or excessively demanding working conditions. This concept is called 'equalizing' or 'compensating' wage differentials. The idea goes back to Adam Smith's *The Wealth of Nations* (1776). The concept can be analysed by supply–demand relations; it suggests that jobs or occupations that offer favourable working conditions attract many workers at lower than average wages, while jobs or occupations that offer unfavourable working conditions must pay premiums (i.e. higher wages) to compensate for such unpreferred working conditions in order to attract workers. Examples of the working conditions concerned are: unsocial working hours, high risk levels, high skill levels, locations of factories and offices, unemployment risk. This kind of theory can be explained by the demand–supply relationship between a firm and a worker who has certain preferences, and between the number of firms and the number of workers. A simple economics equation can describe theoretically this idea of compensatory wage differentials, as Rosen (1986) has elegantly shown. The results of empirical observations are, however, mixed, with only some supporting the theory; and the result in Chapter 5 did not support the theory for Japan.

4. Risk: this refers to a personal trait of individuals which affects their choice of occupation. Individuals' attitudes toward risk have been included in studies by several economists, such as Friedman and Kuzunets (1954) and Weiss (1972). Friedman, for example, suggested that skewed earnings distribution arises from the fact that, while most persons are risk-averse, some persons are risk-lovers. By employing von Neumann and Morgenstern's notion of expected utility maximization, he was able to show that risk-lovers choose an occupation in which there is a small chance of success at a higher income, while risk-averse people choose an occupation in which there is a large chance of receiving a lower income. Consequently, the degree of risk determines an individual's occupation, and thus produces the observed difference in earnings. The effect of compensatory wage differentials caused by various occupations and the risk element are somewhat conflicting, because the latter is a rationale for wage differentials while the former is a rationale for equalizing wages by occupations. The actual earnings differentials by occupation may be a hybrid of the two. Discovering which of the two is dominant may be an interesting area for further empirical research.

5. Imperfect or asymmetrical information: individuals in the labour market do not have perfect access to all available information. When they seek jobs, they often lack sufficient information on both wage levels and the number of jobs available. Such imperfect information creates a distortion and causes pay difference by occupation.

6. Formal education and training costs: several occupations require higher formal education or more training to obtain them and to perform their tasks successfully. Formal education and training incurs cost; a portion of workers cannot afford the education and training when they have to bear the cost. In such cases the situation may be observed where one group of people can engage in higher-wage occupations because they were able to pay the cost, while another group of people is obliged to engage in lower-wage occupations because they are unable to bear the cost.

7. Ability: some jobs or occupations require special talent or ability, such as artistic activities and professional sport. Work in these fields cannot be gained through education and training alone; innate ability is essential. It is quite natural for extra money to be paid to talented people in such fields because the supply is very limited.

8. Regional immobility: even if information is perfect, there are significant transaction costs for both employers and employees, which restrict the movement of workers and/or offices or factories. This influences the determination of wages and produces pay difference: two identical people engaged in the same occupations but who live in different locations may receive different wages.

Other reasons may be advanced to explain pay differences by occupation. Among these is the 'occupation-matching' theory. This is influenced by the notion of 'job-matching', which emerged as an alternative explanation for several labour market phenomena explained by human-capital theory. The job-matching model arose from dissatisfaction with human-capital theory in explaining wage-tenure profiles and turnover-tenure relations. Human-capital theory predicts the positive growth of wage by length of job tenure, but job-matching theory proposes that this positive rate appears because only those workers who are well matched to their jobs stay in those jobs. If workers who changed jobs because of mismatching were included, the positive wage growth would not appear. The occupation-matching model is an extension of the job-matching model; and therefore it is likely either that it can deny the human-capital interpretation of the effect of education and job tenure on earnings, or that it can give an alternative understanding of education in relation to earnings which has not been disclosed by the human-capital model. Since these issues have not yet been exhaustively analysed, fuller analyses and examinations of the relationship between the occupation-matching model and earnings are tasks for the future (but see the pioneering work by Miller, 1984).

6.3.2 Education and Earnings

The effect of education on determining a person's occupation can be analysed from various perspectives. One approach is to examine the relationship between educational attainment and jobs obtained (or simply occupation). A second approach is to investigate the relationship between education and earnings without necessarily referring to occupation. The second approach has been applied frequently when the concept of human capital is used to investigate the economics of education. Using this approach, the internal rates of returns to various education levels are estimated. It should be emphasized, however, that the first approach actually examines the effect of education on earnings, because average earnings of each occupation are used to represent occupations quantitatively; in other words, jobs (or occupations) are ranked by their average earnings. Consequently, both the first and second approaches in fact applied the same approach: that of focusing on the relationship between education and earnings.

Apart from the relationship between education and earnings, it is important to explain the effect of 'credentialism' and the 'screening hypothesis' when the relationships between education, occupation, and earnings are investigated. They are particularly important for understanding the effect of education on determinating occupation.

The screening hypothesis is sometime referred to as 'educational signalling', a concept proposed by Arrow (1973) and Spence (1973). It argues that education serves as an informational device for distinguishing between talented and untalented people. It does not indicate any direct effect of education on a person's skill. A person who has a higher educational attainment is judged to be an able person because he or she can purchase the educational signal on more favourable terms, whereas a less able person cannot. Credentialism is a more direct form of educational signalling, which guarantees certain benefits for a person who has a higher education or who has graduated from a particular school or university. Some of the implications of these signalling and credential effects were described above, in the discussion of the relationship between occupation and earnings. It should be remembered that education or education in a particular school is made a prerequisite for certain occupations or for obtaining a higher status, since it conveys a signal to employers of the job applicant's capability.

The relationship between the signalling hypothesis and occupation can be understood easily by considering occupations such as flying and law. There are often particular schools that produce pilots and lawyers: in Japan, pilots attend an airline pilots' school; in almost every country, lawyers must attend law school or university law faculties. Those universities or schools select entrants by means of tough physical and/or intellectual examinations. Students who are admitted to and who graduate from these schools convey, through their credentials, the information that they will conduct their professional activities successfully. Of course, several further examinations have to be passed even after eligibility to become a pilot or lawyer has been secured. The great majority pass such entry examinations after they graduate from these schools. Thus, the examinations are only formal matters; graduation (i.e. education) is more important. The education of medical doctors proceeds along similar lines.

It should be emphasized, however, that the meaning of educational screening, signalling, and credentialism is much more general than is suggested by the previous paragraph: they signify a device for identifying more or less able persons. Three comments can be offered about the implications of the signalling aspect of education, following the arguments of Rosen (1987).

First, although the human-capital interpretation of education and the signalling (or screening) interpretation of education are proposed on different theoretical grounds, they have very similar implications for the rational choice of schooling. In particular, empirical studies of income and schooling cannot distinguish between the human-capital interpretation of education and the signalling interpretation of education: it is nearly impossible to identify which interpretation is more appropriate to explain empirical evidences of the relationship between education and earnings. This is due partly to the fact that a person's productivity or earnings capacity cannot be observed in the production process. Thus it is impossible to test directly the effect of education (i.e. schooling) on earnings capacity, as the theory of human capital proposes. Therefore, Rosen (1987) argues that schooling has little social value when it serves as a signal, and much social value when it produces real human capital. Second, schooling contributes only a very marginal part of earnings differentials. Other important variables, such as ability, job tenure, family background, contribute significantly to variation in earnings. The limited explanatory power of schooling in the determination of earnings obscures the value of education as a signal. Third, if people are identified and classified properly by using schooling and education as a signalling device, it may be socially productive, because such sortings of people are likely to allocate both talented and untalented people to the most relevant places in the market.

6.3.3. Education, Occupation, and Earnings

As noted previously, the relationships between education, occupation, and earnings have traditionally been examined separately. When the comprehensive relationship between these variables is investigated by applying econometric techniques to individual survey data, a recursive-type simultaneous-equation system is used. Typical examples of the endogenous variables are education, occupation, and earnings. The theory behind this system implies that education determines occupational attainment, and occupation then determines earnings. If these observations, together with other information on various exogenous variables, are available, the ordinary least-squares method or the two-stage least-squares method can be applied, depending upon the correlation among the error terms. Representative examples are shown by Griliches and Mason (1972) for the USA, Tachibanaki (1980) for France, Hübler (1984) for Germany, and Tachibanaki (1988) for Japan. Before discussing these issues, several observations should be made about this econometric approach.

First, many sociological studies strongly suggest that sociological background (such as father's or mother's educational attainment and occupational level and family income) are important determinants of an individual's educational level. Thus, it is customary to consider social background variables prior to the determination of educational attainment (see Duncan et al., 1968).

Second, occupational level is a difficult variable for quantification. Several US studies use the sociologist Duncan's socioeconomic index, which gives a weighted average of income and corresponding educational attainment for occupations in order to quantify occupations. Griliches (1976) posed a serious question concerning the introduction of occupation, claiming that it correlates with dependent variables such as earnings or education; he advocated ignor-ing occupation, if occupational attainment were quantified as in Duncan's socioeconomic index. This elimination causes an omitted-variable problem; so it would be preferable not to ignore occupation in a recursive-type simultaneous-equation system. A variable such as prestige, which was used by Tachibanaki (1980; 1988), may be an alternative idea to quantify occupation. Needless to say, prestige is measured independently of education and/or income.

Third, when an estimate is made of the earnings function which enters as part of a recursive simultaneous-equation system, ability (innate ability) of an individual cannot be ignored, because it affects not only earnings but also occupation and other variables which may raise earning capacity. This subject has received considerable attention, and has been set out in the following way.

Ignoring other variables, a simple earnings function can be written:

$$Y = \alpha + \beta S + \gamma A + u$$

where Y is income, S is education, and A is a measure of ability. When we ignore ability, we obtain a biased estimator of β as follows:

$$E b_{YS} = \beta + \gamma b_{AS} = \beta + \gamma \mathrm{cov}\,(AS) / \mathrm{var}\,A$$

where the return to education is estimated with a bias. Thus, it is necessary to include A when ability has an independent positive effect on earnings, and the relationship between the excluded ability and included schooling variable is positive. However, Griliches

(1977) proposed that the 'ability bias' caused by the excluded ability was minor; so it is not so serious even if ability is excluded. Moreover, serious problems remain for the ability variable even if it is included. First, even if a popular variable such as IQ is included, there is a question about whether this indicates a proper measure of ability: a professional baseball player has a particular ability rather than a particular IQ. Therefore the ability variable should be fairly multi-dimensional. Second, even if we assume that IQ is a relevant measure, it includes considerable measurement errors. In other words, errors in variables may be more serious than the previous omitted-variable bias. 'Ability' is a difficult subject and needs to be investigated seriously.

6.3.4. Concluding Remarks on Empirical Results

Although the above problems cannot be ignored, empirical estimates of earnings functions, together with other variables which are included in recursive-type simultaneous-equation models, suggest the following conclusions. First, the social-background variable is a very important factor and affects a student's success. Second, education determines the level of occupational attainment fairly directly: the higher the educational attainment, the higher the occupational attainment. Third, both higher educational attainment and occupational achievement contribute to providing people with higher earnings. Fourth, many exogenous variables must be included to obtain a better estimate of the earnings function, in addition to social background, education, and occupation; these include age, tenure, family status, region, religion, and working hours. Fifth, the recursive model is fairly successful in explaining the relationship between education, occupation, and earnings in Japan and in European nations such as France and Germany, judging from the estimated R^2 of earnings functions. However, the result for the USA is less impressive, because the estimated R^2 of earnings functions are fairly low (0.1–0.3). In other words, there are 'unexplained factors' or large residuals in the estimation of earnings functions in the USA (see e.g. Taubman, 1975). Jencks (1972) once attributed this residual to 'luck'. The determination of which variables are left out in explaining earnings differentials in the USA requires investigation, even though more empirical studies have been carried out there than in other countries.

Three important variables which need more attention in research are hierarchy (or position) in a firm, size of firm, and industry. The first variable is strictly related to the relationship between supervisory job and incentive; the second is related to the ability of firms to pay higher wages; and the third is related to the efficiency wage hypothesis. Representative works dealing with these variables include Lazear and Rosen (1981), Rosen (1982), Brown and Medoff (1989), Akerlof (1982), and Katz (1986). Chapter 4, 5, and 7 in this book investigate these three variables for Japan.

7

The Importance of Education, Occupation, and Hierarchy in Organizations and in Earnings Differentials

7.1. INTRODUCTION

This chapter examines the effect of education, occupation, and job rank (hierarchy) on the distribution of personal earnings in Japan, using individual data in a recursive multinomial model. Chapter 3 showed that the effect of both education and occupation was weak; this chapter attempts to investigate the issue in more depth by using a comprehensive individual survey, and taking account of a possible joint determination of education and occupation in the presence of job rank.

Empirical studies of earnings distribution in Euro-American countries based on human-capital theory assert that education is one of the most important factors in explaining earnings differentials. When post-school investment is taken into account, as emphasized by Mincer (1974), this hypothesis is reinforced. Many empirical works which are not derived from human-capital theory also support the importance of education. Psachalopoulos (1975) provided a useful survey of this work in the context of the OECD countries, but also, however, showed that education was much less important in Japan than in other countries. A similar hypothesis was proposed; at about the same time by Tachibanaki (1975; 1982), who showed that education was much less important than other factors in Japan. I examine this question from a different angle here.

Job rank (hierarchy) has a particular importance in the Japanese setting, although little attention seems to have been paid to this variable in past empirical works. One exception is Wise (1975), who measured the relationship between personal attributes and job performance for a large corporation in the USA. There are more theoretical developments in the recent literature, including Williamson (1967; 1975), Stiglitz (1975), Lazear and Rosen (1981), Calvo and Wellisz (1979), Rosen (1982), Malcomson (1984), Hart and Holmstrom (1987), Aoki (1988), and Holstrom and Milgrom (1991). Three important results were obtained in these studies. First, an enterprise assigns the better-quality workers to the higher ranks and pays them higher wages as an incentive. Secondly, optimal inter-hierarchical wage differentials are greater than the effectiveness of workers in hierarchies. Thirdly, these two propositions apply with greater force in larger than in smaller firms. A better understanding of those organizational characteristics should lead to a better explanation of the role of education in determining wage differentials. That is the purpose of the present undertaking.

7.2. DATA AND ANALYSIS

The data source is the 1975 survey on *Social Stratification and Mobility* (*SSM75*). The original sample of 4,001 males was drawn at random from all regions in Japan.[1] Table 7.1 shows the simple correlation matrix of variables.

Education, occupation, hierarchy, and earnings form the group of endogenous variables. Exogenous variables include social background, age, experience in the civilian labour force, marital status, size of organization, and aspiration. Education is measured by years of schooling. We adopt two approaches, however, for scaling of occupation and hierarchy: we measure occupation by continuous numbers (i.e. prestige value of occupations) and hierarchy by the numerical order in the hierarchy, when these two variables are used as independent and explanatory variables; and secondly, we scale

---

[1] Since each respondent was interviewed personally by a specialist, the quality or the survey is fairly high. The number or reliable observations which do not have any missing values is 2,724 (68.1%); this rate is fairly high. The number of observations which were used in this study is reduced to 2,407 (88.3% of available observations). Although it might be preferable to attempt to eliminate a sample selection bias, the present study does not do so, in view of the fact that the bias is not very serious.

TABLE 7.1. *Simple correlation coefficients among the major variables*[a]

	Father's occupation	Education	Occupation	Hierarchy	Experience	Marriage	Size of firm	Aspiration	Earnings
Father's occupation	1.000								
Education	0.332	1.000							
Occupation	0.245	0.421	1.000						
Hierarchy	0.197	0.207	0.592	1.000					
Experience	−0.038	−0.378	0.020	0.208	1.000				
Marriage	0.016	−0.117	0.128	0.242	0.406	1.000			
Size	0.100	0.262	0.183	−0.039	−0.028	0.099	1.000		
Aspiration	0.065	0.042	0.136	0.163	0.047	0.091	0.043	1.000	
Earnings	0.191	0.221	0.458	0.500	0.187	0.271	0.158	0.172	1.000

[a] Independent workers are excluded from samples. Experience is measured by job tenure.

Source: SSM (1975).

occupation and hierarchy by adopting a discrete value (namely, zero or unity). Classification is the sole criterion when these variables are used as dependent variables.

Occupation is based on seven one-digit levels, when it is entered as a dependent variable: (1) professional and managerial, (2) clerical, (3) skilled labourers, (4) semi-skilled labourers, (5) farmers, (6) sales (retail), (7) labourers. The order of the above description corresponds very roughly to the order of the prestige values of seven one-digit-level occupations in Japan. Note that, when occupations are used as independent variables, 289 occupations (continuous quantification by prestige values) are considered in order to take account fully of the effect of various occupations. See Naoi (1977) on prestige values in Japan.

Because the data on earnings are given by income classes, annual total earnings are classified into twenty groups, with an equal range of income in each group; the lowest group is equal to unity, and the highest one to twenty. The estimated coefficients for the earning function, therefore, do not indicate the measured income effect.

It is necessary to explain why earnings were not transformed into log-forms. First, since the data on earnings are quantified by the somewhat unusual method described above, the log-form of the variable cannot be easily interpreted. Secondly, it is true that the log-normal distribution is fitted better in many income data. The principal purpose of this study, however, is not to seek a better fit but to investigate the effect of hierarchy on earnings. Nevertheless, it would be highly desirable if a further study could compare this result based on untransformed earnings with the one based on log-transformed earnings.

'Hierarchy' in this work does not refer to the hierarchical distinction between capitalists and workers, but rather to the hierarchical ranks in organizations: 'hierarchical ladder' or 'hierarchical position' may be more appropriate than 'hierarchy'. Any organization forms a management order: one director supervises a number of his subordinates, and the management order spreads downward. We consider five classifications in this study. The highest rank is executives in the company and highest civil servants, called Hierarchy 5, followed by directors, division heads, and similar, Hierarchy 4; deputy division heads, section heads, and similar, Hierarchy 3; foremen and similar, Hierarchy 2; ordinary,

Hierarchy 1. The numbers 1–5 are used in the continuous scaling of hierarchies.[2]

Although the above classifications are, in general, admitted as representing the hierarchical structure of employed persons in Japan, the actual power structure may not be so simple as it looks. For example: a division head (*kacho*) in an extremely large organization may be superior to a director (*bucho*) in a small one. A division head in one organization may supervise twenty subordinates, while a section head in another organization may have thirty subordinates. The original data source has been constructed without taking account of such problems. There are no ways of modifying the power structure of the hierarchies consistently. We perform one experiment in order to obtain more acceptable terminologies which are roughly consistent with the actual power structure. Workers in organizations which employ more than 1,000 people are selected as a subsample, and some comparison will be made. It is assumed that the large organizations have a common terminology with respect to the ranks, and similar power structures.

The endogenous variables are assumed to be related according to the recursive causal ordering illustrated in Fig. 7.1. The numerical value written for each variable denotes the order of causality; this is an extension of Tachibanaki (1980).

The theory behind the causal relations is briefly explained. The influence of social background on the determination of human resources does not require any detailed explanations, since the consensus of many studies admits the importance of social background. One of the most important variables which is ignored in this study is native ability, for two reasons: first, reliable data

---

[2] There remain several difficulties and ambiguities in classifying the hierarchical ranks in this way. Firstly, independent and individual workers, for example self-employed doctors, retailers, etc., are normally excluded from the list of the classifications. Because it is nearly impossible to rank these independent workers in the above hierarchies appropriately, the exclusion is unavoidable. However, if we are interested in analysing the difference between employed workers (who could be included in any of the positions in the hierarchy) and independent workers with respect to their influence on earnings, the exclusion causes a serious problem. Secondly, there are several employed workers who do not exactly fit into the above hierarchical classification, e.g. schoolmasters and directors of hospitals. Admitting some ambiguity and arbitrariness, these posts are allocated to positions to which they are supposed to be roughly equivalent. The number of these posts is actually very small (16); So the bias due to such misallocations is negligible.

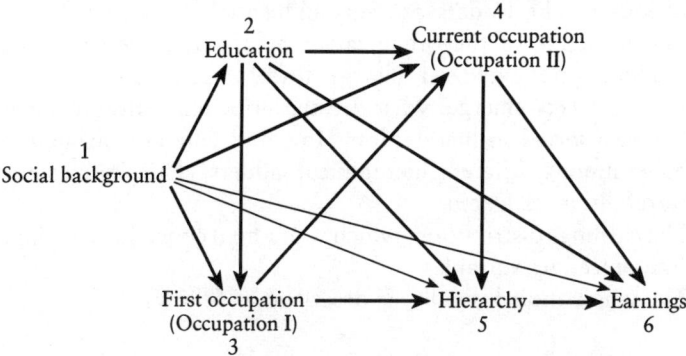

FIG. 7.1.a A recursive model of education, occupation, hierarchy, and earnings

cannot be linked legitimately to SSM75; second, as Griliches (1977) concludes, the bias due to omitting ability is negligible. The effect of education on occupational achievement is fairly simple: a large number of sociological studies accept the notion that the higher the educational attainment, the higher the occupational achievement.

Hierarchy must be clearly distinguished from occupation. While occupation characterizes the nature or the quality of a job, hierarchy is strictly related to the organizational and supervising activity. A hierarchy normally comes into existence when several people, who engage in similar occupations, form a small organization. A leader of such an organization supervises and monitors the members. The higher the position in the hierarchy and the larger the organization, the larger the number of people whom the leader is expected to supervise. Some of those supervised men engage in various occupations with various responsibilities. Obviously, supervisory work would require higher skills and strong leadership; thus it would be natural to presume that the higher the occupational achievement, the higher the hierarchical position. Since the number of superior ranks, however, is inevitably limited, higher occupations do not necessarily provide promotion to a superior position in the hierarchy. Because hierarchy exists even when all the people engage in the same occupation in one organization, the concept of hierarchy may be understood in the framework of the theory of organization which has nothing to do with occupation.

Decisions by the leaders are very influential on the productivity of the members of the organization as a whole; power and responsibility are exercised by the leaders. Here some very attractive subjects emerge: what are the principal factors by which people are sorted in hierarchies? How and why are earnings distributed among different hierarchical ladders? These subjects will be carefully investigated.

The earnings distribution, which is our final concern, is explained by the preceding variables.

The whole model, finally, is described as follows:

(A) Education $= f_A$ (background) + exogenous variables + error terms

(B) Occupation I $= f_B$ (background, education) + exogenous + error terms

(C) Occupation II $= f_C$ (background, education, occupation I) + exogenous + error terms,

(D) Hierarchy $= f_D$ (education, occupation II) + exogenous + error terms

(E) Earnings $= f_E$ (background, education, occupation II, hierarchy) + exogenous + error terms

where f_i, i = A, B, C, D, E indicates the function.

When some variables are discrete, the model needs more elaborated estimation methods, with a further consideration of identification problems. We discuss the case where hierarchy is defined in discrete mode, and where other variables are continuous, as one example. Three variables, current occupation (Z), hierarchy (X), and earning (Y), are of principal interest. The other variables are for the moment left out without loss of generality. The model could be written as:

$$X_t = f(Z_t) + U_{1t} \qquad (7.1a)$$

$$Y_t = f(X_t, Z_t) + U_{2t} \qquad (7.1b)$$

where X_t is discrete, and t is the observation. U_1 and U_2 are the error terms.

In the first case we assume that U_1 and U_2 are independent. We assume also that U_1 has the logistic distribution and that U_2 has the standard normal distribution. The maximum-likelihood estimate is equivalent to maximizing the likelihood functions for the first and second equations separately, due to the purely recursive nature of the model.

$$\log e \frac{P_r(X=i)}{P_r(X=1)}\bigg|_t = Z_t \beta_i \qquad i = 2, \ldots m \qquad (7.2a)$$

$$Y_t = \sum_{k=2}^{m} \alpha_k X_{kt}^* + Z_t \gamma + U_{2t} \quad \text{where} \qquad (7.2b)$$

$X_{kt}^* = 1$ if $X_t = k, k = 2, \ldots, m$ (m: possible discrete cases)
$\phantom{X_{kt}^*} = 0$ otherwise.

The βs and γs are coefficients for the exogenous variables Z_t, and the αs are coefficients of the dummy variables. The model expressed in equations (7.2a) and (7.2b) may be called 'a recursive multinomial logit model', which is a special case of a simultaneous logit model given by Schmidt and Strauss (1975; 1976), and an extension of a recursive model with dichotomous endogenous variables discussed by Maddala and Lee (1976). See useful survey papers by Amemiya (1975; 1985), McFadden (1974) and Maddala (1983).

When U_1 and U_2 are not independent, the *joint* ML estimator cannot be obtained easily. This case may be called 'simultaneous recursive multinomial logit model'. A modified version of Maddala and Lee (1976) may be applied to estimate this model.

7.3. EMPIRICAL RESULTS

We have basically four empirical results which are classified by (1) quantification method (continuous versus discrete) for occupation and hierarchy, and (2) estimation method (pure recursive versus simultaneous recursive). We present here three results. The first part presents the case in which quantification is made continuously. Both pure and simultaneous recursive models are applied. The results are discussed in more detail in Tachibanaki (1987b; 1988).

7.3.1. Quantification Is Continuous

This section presents principally two empirical results which are classified by estimation method (pure recursive versus simultaneous recursive).

7.3.1.1. Case 1. Errors; independent. Table 7.2 provides a summary of the results of estimation by ordinary least squares; it is presented for the purpose of comparing the Japanese results with the French ones. The table shows the estimated coefficients; the numbers written to the right of the estimated coefficients are the beta coefficients, and the numbers in parentheses are the estimated t-statistics.

It is found that educational attainment is influenced, very roughly speaking, equally by four background variables, father's education, mother's education, father's occupation, and standard of living during childhood. The educational levels of parents seem to be marginally more influential than the other two variables in view of the beta coefficients. See Tachibanaki (1981) on social mobility in Japan.

As for first occupation, education is far more important than father's occupation: Japan seems to be a meritocracy. The positive coefficient of age shows that if one wants to obtain a higher occupational status, one must enter his professional life at an older age. It is no surprising to find that first occupation is the most crucial in determining the level of current occupation. One's first occupation determines one's professional life to a considerable extent. A similar result has been obtained for France. Those properties with respect to first occupation have been accepted in many sociological works. Since the indirect effect of education via first occupation is 0.172 (the beta term), education is still fairly important. It is worth mentioning that experience in the civilian labour force affects the level of occupational achievement fairly significantly; thus, one normally increases one's occupational status during one's career. It must be pointed out, nevertheless, that the R^2's for the two occupations are considerably lower than those in

TABLE 7.2. *A simple recursive model, with all variables scaled in continuous mode*

	Education	Occupation I	Occupation II	Hierarchy	Earning
Education		1.300 (19.68) 0.394	0.914 (10.63) 0.229	0.023 (2.06) 0.045	0.111 (4.44) 0.113
Occupation I			0.532 (23.13) 0.438		
Occupation II				0.064 (26.71) 0.556	0.025 (4.81) 0.124
Hierarchy					0.586 (13.63) 0.358
Fatheduc	0.241 (11.48) 0.269				
Motheduc	0.243 (9.72) 0.229				
Fathoccu	0.037 (8.13) 0.152	0.114 (7.53) 0.146	0.088 (5.15) 0.093		0.010 (2.26) 0.048
Kurashi	0.559 (8.47) 0.150				

TABLE 7.2. Continued

	Education	Occupation I	Occupation II	Hierarchy	Earning
Age 1	0.102 (4.08)	0.079			
Experience			0.087 (6.21)	0.113	0.020 (10.00)	0.199	0.029 (5.14)	0.110
Aspiration				0.210 (3.96)	0.073	
Age					0.016 (2.73)	0.071
Marriage					0.772 (5.11)	0.119
Size					0.156 (5.00)	0.108
Const	4.203	21.54	6.647	−1.797	−0.171
R^2	0.349	0.244	0.360	0.388	0.342
S.E.	2.281	7.751	8.660	1.068	2.152

Notes. Fatheduc: father's education; Motheduc: mother's education; Fathoccu: father's occupation; Kurashi: Living standard at age 15; Age 1: age at first job; Experience: current Age minus age at first job; Size: size of firm.
The numbers written at the right of the estimated coefficients are the beta coefficients, and the numbers in parentheses are the t-ratios.

France. There must be factors other than education for explaining the achievement of occupation in Japan.

Hierarchical position is of great interest. Education is not so important in the presence of current occupation with which it is positively correlated strongly. Experience has a considerable influence on hierarchical position. Promotion is largely determined by the seniority of the workers. It must be remembered, however, that seniority is not a necessary condition. It was shown in Tachibanaki (1986) that education was a necessary condition for promotion. In other words, education sorts workers into two groups: workers with higher education are placed in the line of future promotion, while workers with lower education are largely excluded from the process of promotion.

Finally, earnings are discussed at length. The earnings function in Table 7.2 presents the results which exclude independent workers. The most surprising observation is the fact that hierarchy has the most important influence on the determination of earnings. The influence of hierarchy is by far the strongest on the basis of the beta coefficients. This is true even when the indirect effect of occupation, which becomes the second most important factor, via hierarchy, is added to the direct effect of occupation. A superior position in the hierarchical order of an organization contributes enormously to higher monetary reward in Japanese society. This study seems to confirm empirically recent theoretical works of the hierarchical earnings differentials, which have been discussed before. I had believed, before launching the work of this book, that Japanese society could be characterized as egalitarian except for the notorious male/female discrimination, at least with respect to pay, in view of the fact that neither education nor occupation was very important in differentiating earnings. The fact that age and experience, which could be achieved by all as their natural endowment, were the most crucial factors was additional evidence for egalitarianism in Japan. The evidence of this study may have to reverse the egalitarian characteristics of earnings distribution if the effect of hierarchy is explicitly brought in.

The other factors which are influential on earnings distribution are experience, marriage, and size of firm. They have almost equal importance, judging from the beta coefficients. Experience (i.e. job tenure) is fully understandable not only from the Japanese seniority wage system (see Tachibanaki, 1975; 1982), but also from the concept of post-school human investment in terms of Mincer (1962; 1974). It would be possible to include the square of experience in the earnings equation, as has been done often in US studies. There are two reasons why it was not included: first, the Japanese data do not necessarily reject the linear form of experience, at least until a certain age (see Tachibanaki, 1975); secondly, since experience was always linear in the previous occupation and hierarchy equations, the linear form was adopted to maintain consistency for the purpose of comparison. Nevertheless, the square of experience is a worthwhile attempt in future.

The importance of marriage is somewhat surprising. Father's occupation, which was included as representing the social-background variable, and age in the presence of experience show relatively weak effects.

A final comment is necessary on the earnings function: R^2, namely 0.342, is not very high; it is considerably lower than that for France, but it is slightly higher than the values in various studies for the USA. It is considerably lower than R^2 in the estimated wage equations in Chapters 4 and 5 for Japan, which used a much larger number of explanatory variables. There may remain several unrecognized elements which help to explain earnings distribution in Japan when the analysis is performed for individual data. Some of these unrecognized variables may be equivalent to the variables used in Chapters 4 and 5. Since the aggregate sample with the log-earnings tends to give a higher value of R^2 than the individual sample with the untransformed earnings, the low R^2 of this work is not as discouraging as it looks. The earnings variable in this study is not transformed into the log of earnings, as was described before. This is one of the reasons.

7.3.1.2. Case 2. Errors; dependent. Table 7.3 presents a partial result which was estimated by the two-stage least-squares method. See Malinvand (1976) on the estimation method. The estimated parameters differ slightly from the previous results. For the hierarchy equation, the coefficient of occupation is marginally lower, while the coefficient of education is considerably higher; for the earnings equation, the coefficient of hierarchy is marginally higher, while the coefficient of occupation is fairly higher. Nevertheless, it is possible to conclude that the overall result is similar, judging from the fact that the pattern of statistical significance has not been

TABLE 7.3. *A simple recursive: 2SLS*

	Hierarchy	Earning
Education	0.154	0.101
	(0.016)[a]	(0.027)
Occupation II	0.052	0.079
	(0.010)	(0.005)
Hierarchy		0.573
		(0.161)
Experience	0.038	0.021
	(0.003)	(0.009)
Aspiration	0.417	
	(0.077)	
Age		0.019
		(0.011)
Marriage		0.996
		(0.156)
Size		0.055
		(0.032)
Const.	−4.043	−2.082
SE	1.476	2.237

[a] The numbers in parentheses are the estimated standard errors.

altered. It may be safely assumed that the error terms of the equations are statistically independent.

7.3.2. Quantification Is Discrete

This section presents the case in which quantification is made discretely. We consider, however, only the pure recursive type.

Eq. (D), which describes the hierarchical achievement process in the model, and eq. (E), on earnings, are discussed here. Table 7.4 shows the estimated results, which are based on explanatory variables such as education, occupation, experience, aspiration, and a constant term. It should be remembered that, since occupation is included as an independent variable, 289 occupations are considered in this equation. Aspiration was included as representing the individual desire for promotion. The variable has nothing to do with the economic variables, but is intended to symbolize a kind of

TABLE 7.4. Estimated coefficients for hierarchical position[a,b]

	Education	Occupation	Experience	Aspiration	Const.
$\log_e\left[\frac{\text{Hierarchy 2}}{\text{Hierarchy 1}}\right]$	0.014 (0.048)	−0.196 (0.013)	−0.059 (0.010)	−0.824 (0.225)	13.761 (0.879)
$\log_e\left[\frac{\text{Hierarchy 3}}{\text{Hierarchy 1}}\right]$	−0.009 (0.065)	−0.217 (0.017)	0.032 (0.013)	0.355 (0.290)	11.844 (1.081)
$\log_e\left[\frac{\text{Hierarchy 4}}{\text{Hierarchy 1}}\right]$	0.184 (0.055)	−0.143 (0.014)	−0.030 (0.012)	−0.566 (0.258)	6.752 (0.945)
$\log_e\left[\frac{\text{Hierarchy 5}}{\text{Hierarchy 1}}\right]$	0.191 (0.049)	−0.056 (0.011)	0.013 (0.011)	−0.682 (0.234)	1.200 (0.897)
$\log_e\left[\frac{\text{Hierarchy 3}}{\text{Hierarchy 2}}\right]$	−0.023 (0.044)	−0.021 (0.011)	0.026 (0.008)	0.469 (0.183)	−1.917 (0.629)
$\log_e\left[\frac{\text{Hierarchy 4}}{\text{Hierarchy 2}}\right]$	0.171 (0.027)	0.053 (0.005)	0.029 (0.007)	0.258 (0.126)	−7.009 (0.347)
$\log_e\left[\frac{\text{Hierarchy 5}}{\text{Hierarchy 2}}\right]$	0.178 (0.010)	0.140 (0.007)	0.072 (0.005)	0.142 (0.064)	−12.560 (0.179)
$\log_e\left[\frac{\text{Hierarchy 4}}{\text{Hierarchy 3}}\right]$	0.193 (0.035)	0.075 (0.010)	0.002 (0.005)	−0.211 (0.132)	−5.092 (0.525)
$\log_e\left[\frac{\text{Hierarchy 5}}{\text{Hierarchy 3}}\right]$	0.200 (0.043)	0.162 (0.013)	0.045 (0.007)	−0.327 (0.171)	−10.644 (0.603)
$\log_e\left[\frac{\text{Hierarchy 5}}{\text{Hierarchy 4}}\right]$	0.007 (0.025)	0.087 (0.009)	0.043 (0.005)	−0.116 (0.109)	−5.552 (0.207)

[a] Hierarchy 1: ordinary; Hierarchy 2: foreman (*shokucho*); Hierarchy 3: section head (*kakaricho*); Hierarchy 4: division head (*kacho*) and director (*bucho*); Hierarchy 5: executive (*torishimariyaku*) and highest civil servant (*seifu kokan*).
[b] The numbers in parentheses are the asymptotic standard errors.

psychological characteristic. The particular question with respect to aspiration was the following: 'Have you always liked being a leader in groups?' Although the variable is imperfect in revealing one's aspiration, it was included since it was believed that no consideration of an aspiration variable is worse than the inclusion of even an imperfect variable.

Education is quite significant for promotion because many cases are statistically significant and give positive values. Statistical tests can be performed in view of a property that the ratios of the estimated coefficients to their estimated asymptotic standard errors are asymptotically normally distributed with mean zero and variance one. Two cases show negative values; as the standard errors are very large, these two cases can be ignored. In sum, more education makes it more likely that an individual will be promoted.

Occupation is somewhat disturbing, because half of the cases are negative and statistically significant. It was expected that the coefficients would be positive in the sense that the higher the occupational status, the more superior the hierarchical status. The partial reason for the somewhat puzzling outcome is likely to arise from the inclusion of education, which is highly correlated with occupation. Moreover, it may be possible to hypothesize that higher occupational achievement does not necessarily result in promotion of all workers to superior hierarchical status. Another reason may be that hierarchy and occupation are not completely independent, although they are measured separately. Experience shows, in general, positive influences on promotion, which confirms the implication of the preliminary result. Aspiration does not provide any definitive answers with respect to the effect on promotion.

As McFadden (1974; 1976) admits, it is difficult to interpret the estimated coefficients given in the form of Table 7.4. One way of avoiding such hard interpretation is to derive the elasticities with respect to their explanatory variables. I prefer, instead, to estimate the probability of occupying a given position with respect to the representative group of people. Table 7.5 presents the estimated probabilities for various combinations of education and of experience. Occupation is deliberately excluded from a list of independent variables in this exercise because the effect of occupation was somewhat ambiguous in the previous estimated coefficients. Table 7.5 (a) is the result for all observations, while 7.5 (b) is the one for observations of those who belong to organizations with more than 1,000 employees (called 'large organizations' for simplicity). Both tables, in general, show that the probability of promotion to a superior hierarchy is an increasing function of both education and experience.

We find, moreover, several notable corollaries on the basis of Table 7.5 (a). First, education seems to be a necessary condition for promotion. For example, junior high-school graduates with thirty years' experience have only 7 per cent chance of being promoted to Hierarchy 3 (section head) or Hierarchy 4 (director or division head). Moreover, about 60 per cent of junior high-school graduates with even thirty years' experience stay in the lowest hierarchy. A fairly high probability, 13 per cent, is observed for Hierarchy 5. This is probably due either to the contribution of smaller

TABLE 7.5. *Estimated probability of occupying each of five hierarchical positions*[a]

	Junior high			Senior high			Junior college			University		
	10	20	30	10	20	30	10	20	30	10	20	30
(a) All observations												
Hierarchy 1	0.817	0.734	0.615	0.714	0.582	0.420	0.596	0.437	0.278	0.447	0.289	0.163
Hierarchy 2	0.085	0.101	0.10	0.064	0.068	0.065	0.048	0.046	0.039	0.033	0.028	0.020
Hierarchy 3	0.048	0.061	0.073	0.096	0.111	0.114	0.138	0.144	0.130	0.179	0.165	0.132
Hierarchy 4	0.016	0.035	0.072	0.052	0.102	0.177	0.102	0.181	0.277	0.181	0.283	0.384
Hierarchy 5	0.033	0.068	0.130	0.074	0.137	0.224	0.115	0.191	0.276	0.160	0.235	0.301
(b) Large organizations												
Hierarchy 1	0.845	0.758	0.623	0.795	0.652	0.444	0.715	0.516	0.285	0.581	0.344	0.150
Hierarchy 2	0.105	0.138	0.168	0.079	0.096	0.096	0.062	0.066	0.054	0.043	0.038	0.024
Hierarchy 3	0.043	0.078	0.131	0.096	0.160	0.222	0.153	0.225	0.253	0.222	0.267	0.236
Hierarchy 4	0.007	0.025	0.077	0.029	0.091	0.235	0.069	0.189	0.396	0.148	0.333	0.546
Hierarchy 5	0.000	0.000	0.000	0.000	0.001	0.003	0.001	0.004	0.013	0.005	0.018	0.043

[a] The numbers beneath the educational level indicate years' experience. The meaning of each hierarchy is the same as the one in Table 7.3.

organizations which do not require education for promotion or to the contribution of the owners of extremely small firms who are junior high graduates. In other words, extremely small firms could be owned by anybody, regardless of his educational level. University graduates, contrary to junior and senior high school graduates, have a considerably higher chance of being promoted to Hierarchy 3 and 4 (0.132 and 0.384 respectively). Hierarchy 4, in particular, seems to require university-level education (0.238 with twenty years' experience and 0.384 with thirty years' experience). Junior college-level education with thirty years' experience, 0.277, is roughly equivalent to university-level education with twenty years' experience, 0.238. Calvo and Wellisz (1979) and Rosen (1982) proposed theoretically that a profit- (or output-) maximizing firm would select the better-quality workers for the higher ranks. Although it is somewhat premature to believe that educational attainment is a sole criterion, it is certainly one of the indicators of workers' quality.

Second, it must be pointed out that, even though education is a necessary condition for promotion, it is not a sufficient condition. About 45 per cent, 29 per cent, and 16 per cent of university graduates and about 60 per cent, 44 per cent, and 28 per cent of junior college graduates with ten, twenty, and thirty years' experience respectively are not promoted to a superior rank but stay at the lowest. These numbers are by no means negligible, and imply that education is not a sufficient condition. This contrasts with the US studies which propose that experience (i.e. job tenure) is not a very important factor in the determination of promotion (see Medoff and Abraham (1980) and Abraham and Medoff (1985)). Japan and the USA present different pictures regarding internal promotion at firms.

Third, suppose that we accept a proposition that education is a necessary condition for promotion, but not a sufficient one. What, then, are the additional factors determining the probability of promotion? One of the most important factors is experience (or tenure). It is observed that the probability with respect to hierarchy decreases, for all the educational levels, at an almost constant rate as experience increases from zero years to ten, twenty, and thirty years. In superior hierarchical positions, it is found that more experience (or tenure) raises the probability of being promoted further if the education level is held constant. This suggests the importance of internal promotion. See Williamson (1975) about the relation between internal promotion and incentives. Japanese organizations do not recruit outside workers to fill higher-rank positions, but select among their employees for higher positions. Tachibanaki (1982) showed the importance of tenure for promotion using the aggregate data. It is also important to notice that accumulation of specific skill in the particular organization will raise the productivity of workers, and thus that management will choose these qualified internal persons for promotion, as the theory of organization suggests.

Fourth, Hierarchy 2 is somewhat different, especially for junior college and university graduates, because they have extremely small probabilities of being in it. Hierarchy 2 (foreman) consists of mainly manual workers; therefore they are normally promoted from Hierarchy 1 to Hierarchy 3 (section head) without being in Hierarchy 2. One idea may be to combine Hierarchies 2 and 3; however, this was not attempted, because Hierarchy 3 is superior to Hierarchy 2 in job assignments and hierarchical orders. Some successful foremen in Japan are promoted to Hierarchy 3, despite the fact that they were originally manual workers; it is worthwhile considering them separately.

Fifth, our psychological variable, namely aspiration, turned out to contribute nothing significant. There may remain 'latent ability', 'responsibility', 'leadership', and possibly 'luck' which could contribute to an individual probability of promotion. Data which contain such information will disclose such unknown factors; see e.g., Wise (1975) for a study of a particular firm.

The distinction between Table 7.5 (a) and 7.5 (b) is of interest. Without discussing the results in detail, the following may be concluded. Education becomes much more important in deciding the level in the hierarchy in the case of larger organizations than in the case of all organizations. Having only junior or senior high-school education is extremely disadvantageous for promotion. The case for Hierarchy 5 (executives and highest civil servants) shows no possibility; Hierarchies 3 and 4 are almost similar stories, except for the case of those with extremely long experience. On the contrary, junior college and university graduates have a greater advantage in larger organizations than in all organizations. These are particularly true for Hierarchies 3 and 4. However, the story for the top hierarchy (5) is the opposite. The probability of being promoted to the highest level in the hierarchy is extremely small; competition seems to be very severe to obtain the highest rank.

Now consider the earnings equation. When hierarchy measured discretely enters as an independent variable in the earnings equation, it is in reality equivalent to a familiar form: they are included as the usual 0–1 dummy independent variables.

Table 7.6 shows the estimated result derived from the maximum-likelihood (ML) method. Due to the pure recursive nature of the model, the joint ML estimator with the hierarchy equation is equivalent to maximizing each likelihood function separately. Table 7.6 (a) provides the results for all organizations, while Table 7.6 (b) provides results for those who belong to organizations with

TABLE 7.6. *Estimated coefficients for earnings*

	Earning (a)[a]		Earning (b)[a]	
Education	0.141	0.142	0.069	0.090
	(6.46)		(2.07)	
Occupation	0.051	0.203	0.046	0.232
	(8.72)		(5.38)	
Experience	0.010	0.054	0.015	0.096
	(2.51)		(2.27)	
Marriage	1.104	0.156	1.154	0.214
	(8.00)		(5.60)	
Hierarchy 2	0.778	0.061	1.369	0.164
	(3.34)		(4.69)	
Hierarchy 3	0.644	0.060	0.869	0.148
	(3.20)		(4.10)	
Hierarchy 4	1.170	0.112	1.748	0.269
	(5.44)		(6.72)	
Hierarchy 5	2.583	0.225	2.240	0.091
	(10.7)		(2.61)	
Independent	0.379	0.061		
	(3.07)			
Const.	−0.110		1.094	
SE	2.340		1.655	
R^2	0.245		0.350	

[a] (a) = all observations. (b) = workers who belong to organizations with more than 1,000 employees. The numbers written at the right of the estimated coefficients are the beta coefficients, and the numbers in parentheses are the t-ratios.

more than 1,000 employees. Consequently, Tables 7.5 (a) and 7.6 (a) can be treated as one set for all organizations, while Tables 7.5 (b) and 7.6 (b) provide another set for larger organizations. The choice of explanatory variables was made on the basis of the results of earnings equations given in the previous section. Education, occupation, experience, and marriage, which were found to be important, are used in addition to hierarchy.

Hierarchical position seems to be the most important. Not surprisingly, membership of Hierarchy 5 (executives and senior civil servants) is extremely advantageous for receiving higher monetary remunerations, judging from the estimated coefficients. Hierarchy 4 (director and division head) in larger organizations is also quite advantageous. This confirms the proposition that the distribution of hierarchical earnings is more skewed than the distribution of effectiveness of the workers.

It is possible to conjecture that the differences in working hours is one reason for explaining the wider inter-hierarchical annual earnings differentials: workers in superior positions may work longer hours. Since the data contain no information on working hours, it is impossible to test this hypothesis. Another element is the payment of bonuses in Japanese firms; earnings figures in the data include bonus payments (see Tachibanaki, 1982; 1987a on the effect of bonuses).

One interesting outcome appears in Hierarchy 2 (foreman). This hierarchy receives higher earnings than Hierarchy 3 (section head) in view of higher estimated coefficients, despite the fact that it is inferior to Hierarchy 3 in status. Extremely skilled manual workers who are heads of a group of manual workers are paid better than section heads, who are essentially non-manual workers but who belong to the smallest segment of office workers. The reason for this interesting outcome is unclear, but two conjectures are possible. First, Hierarchy 2 (foreman) is normally occupied by experienced (i.e. longer-tenured) manual workers, while Hierarchy 3 (section head) is likely to be occupied by both experienced and inexperienced non-manual workers. Since experience is quite important in differentiating earnings, the effect of the low earnings of inexperienced workers lowers the average earnings of Hierarchy 3. Since experience was included as an explanatory variable, the influence of experience is already controlled to a certain extent; consequently, the above conjecture is not so convincing. Second, Japanese firms may value the productivity of extremely skilled manual workers who are responsible for the production line more highly than that of some lower-level office workers.

7.4. CONCLUSIONS AND COMMENTS

The overall results suggest a strong causal relationship between social background, education, occupation, hierarchy, and earnings. First occupation is largely determined by one's educational attainment; promotion process is determined not only by one's education and occupation but also by one's seniority in the organization. Job ranks have a very strong effect on the determination of earnings. Finally, it is noted that several unrecognized factors contribute considerably to explain earnings distribution in Japan, at least in comparison with France. Some of the unrecognized factors in this chapter appeared in many control variables for wage figures in Chapters 4 and 5.

The economic and sociological implication of the effect of education on promotion may be interpreted in the framework of the sorting role of education. The findings of this work suggest that neither junior nor senior high-school graduates had much chance of promotion even if they had longer experience, say twenty or thirty years, and that only junior college and university graduates had the opportunity of promotion. In other words, the entry-point or the initial stage of the career sorts workers into two categories: the first comprises workers whose future promotion possibility is extremely limited (except for Hierarchy 2), and the second comprises workers whose potential for promotion is open. The actual promotion probability for the second group is determined by several factors, including experience. Alternatively speaking, the continuous selections and sortings are held as they continue to work. The above story is particularly true in the case of larger firms. Competition is very severe because the number of superior hierarchical positions is limited. The monetary reward of promotion to superior positions, in return, is very large. This extraordinary benefit, which is paid to a limited number of 'successful' educated workers who have been promoted to superior positions, may cast new doubt on the egalitarianism of earnings distribution in Japan.

This sorting practice may be called 'educational credential', although the term 'credential' in Japan is used normally for the graduates of several prestigious universities who are assured bright and successful careers in their professional life. This chapter concludes that strong separation (or sorting) is observed between less educated people (mainly junior and senior high school graduates), and educated people (mainly junior college and university graduates) where promotion is concerned. The sorting role of education is judged as a screening role by Arrow (1973) and Spence (1973).

Although it has been widely accepted that education is relatively unimportant in deciding earnings distribution in Japan, the current work proposes that hierarchical position, which is determined by educational attainment of workers to a considerable extent, plays an important role in earnings distribution. This *may* lead to the conclusion that education is important for explaining earnings distribution in Japan. Is it an apparent contradiction of past knowledge? I do not believe so, as explained below. It is true that education is an important factor for promotion; but, it should not be overlooked that experience and unrecognized factors also contribute significantly to the promotion of workers to superior hierarchical positions. These two propositions imply that there are a considerable number of educated workers who are not promoted to superior hierarchical positions but stay at inferior levels; this was actually confirmed by this study. There are many educated workers who cannot receive higher earnings simply because they are unable to occupy superior positions. This is a primary reason why education is still less important for earning differentials, even when the effect of hierarchy is considered. I have stated that experience and unrecognized factors in addition to education were necessary for promotion. For experience, this is quite understandable, because experience by itself plays an important role in the earnings distribution, as shown by Tachibanaki (1975) and many other studies. For unrecognized factors such as ability, responsibility, leadership, luck, and 'pull', it is possible to regard these as the main reasons why an apparent contradiction should be rejected.

The theory of inter-hierarchical wage differentials cited in the Introduction suggested that large firms would observe wider differentials in wages by hierarchies. Our two samples, the small organizations (*a*) and the large organizations (*b*), support this conjecture. Moreover, the result shows that it is the employees in larger organizations who compete more keenly. See Tachibanaki (1995*a*; 1995*b*) on the recent story.

8

A Theoretical and Empirical Model of Wage Determination

8.1. INTRODUCTION

The purpose of this chapter is to estimate an empirically testable wage function. It presents a theoretical development of wage determination which aims to incorporate several stylized facts in Japan, and shows its empirical results. Empirical observations obtained in Chapters 3, 4, 5, and 7 provide several stylized facts; we use the *Employment Status Survey* as the data source. Section 8.2 discusses a recent controversy over the effect of job tenure on wages; section 8.3 develops a theory of wage determination in Japan; and section 8.4 presents its empirical results based on the theory.

8.2. WAGE DETERMINATION AND THE EFFECT OF TENURE

Several theoretical advances have explained how the wage level of an individual worker is determined, with particular emphasis on the effect of job tenure. Such theories include the human-capital model, the job-matching model, the wage deferral and effort–incentive theory, and the efficiency wage theory; these theories have already been discussed in Chapter 2. These theories are not totally exclusive, being related to each other to a certain extent.

Mincer (1974), and Mincer and Jovanovic (1981) are typical early examples of the human-capital approach, emphasizing the effect of human capital on wage growth. When a positive growth rate of the wage by job tenure is observed, it is found to be due mainly to the accumulation of firm-specific human capital (or training). They showed, in fact, that the tenure–earnings profile was upward-sloping.

There have been several challenges to the positive return to seniority (or job tenure) in recent years. First, several econometric studies have appeared which do not necessarily support the positive return to seniority (e.g. Altonji and Shakotko, 1987; Abraham and Farber, 1987). Altonji and Shakotko (1987) propose that, when positive bias in the least-squares estimates which arises from both individual heterogeneity and job match heterogeneity is removed, the return to tenure is greatly reduced. It is found by the instrumental-variable estimates that a more important factor in growth of wages is total labour market experience. Abraham and Farber (1987) also propose that the measured positive cross-sectional return to seniority is largely a statistical bias, which arises from the positive correlation of tenure with an omitted variable such as the quality of the worker, job- or worker–employer match. Marshall and Zarkin (1987) claim that the observed wage levels, which are used in the analysis of the effect of tenure on wages, are not wage offers made by firms but wages accepted by workers. According to Marshall and Zarkin, this discrepancy causes censoring bias and thus gives an overstated return to tenure in the wage determination. However, Topel (1991) and Topel and Ward (1992) provided counter-examples, proposing strong evidence that wages do rise with job seniority; in particular, Topel (1991) is critical of Abraham and Farber (1987) and Altonji and Shakotko (1987), and presents significant problems of measurement error and methodological bias. It is impossible to state that technical arguments have been settled.

All the studies mentioned above emphasize the importance of omitted variables—individual heterogeneity, job-matching heterogeneity, censoring bias, etc. These are largely statistical or econometric problems. One non-econometric issue must be mentioned: both the firm-specific human capital theory and the effort-incentive wage deferral theory, (see Lazear, 1979; 1981) propose that the return to tenure is positive, although their reasonings for obtaining the positive return, and economic interpretations differ. Since the empirical formulations, however, based on the human-capital theory and the agency theory (non-shirking deferral theory) are nearly the same, it is hard to identify which theory is supported by data unless some special devices are used to separate the two theories; therefore it is not easy to assert which theory is superior in the empirical context.

A Model of Wage Determination

Regarding empirical issues concerning wage growth rate by job tenure in Japan, panel data are required to test rigorously whether or not wages rise with job tenure, as shown by several US studies. Japan has no panel data like the US Panel Study of Income Dynamics (PSID); so it is nearly impossible to perform a rigorous statistical test. It is important, nevertheless, to point out that the observed growth rate of wages by job tenure in Japan is higher than in the USA, as shown by Hashimoto and Raisian (1985) and Mincer and Higuchi (1988). It should be reasonable to assume that wages grow with job tenure, at least in Japan, although a possible panel data study in Japan may give a somewhat lower rate of wage growth with job tenure than the currently observed growth rate. In other words, it is reasonable to assume that the positive wage growth rate with job tenure is a stylized fact, at least in Japan.

8.3. THEORETICAL DEVELOPMENT

This section develops a theory of the wage determination process in Japan. It aims to incorporate some of the stylized facts which were discussed in Chapters 3, 4, 5, and 7, and to show a different theoretical and empirical development from past studies.

The starting observations and postulates which are taken into account in developing this formulation are as follows:

(a) The wage level is equal to worker's marginal productivity. This is called simply 'productivity' in this chapter. We therefore adopt the marginal-productivity theory from the various wage-determination theories surveyed in Chapter 2.

(b) Workers' productivity is not basically observable, but firms evaluate it with observable information about their employees.

(c) Workers' productivity is normally higher when educational attainment, formal training, and on-the-job training are higher (see Chapter 3 and 7). Therefore, we do not reject the notion of human capital, but we shall borrow it in order to relate productivity to other observable variables. A crucial development in this chapter is that the growth rate of workers' productivity differs according to the stage of one's career. For example, Brown (1983), Parsons (1986), Tan (1987), and Mincer (1984) all show that the tenure profile of wages is decomposed into three segments: wages grow slowly before the training period,

A Model of Wage Determination

grow rapidly during and immediately after the training period, and level off after it. This phenomenon gives us an important clue: that productivity (or wages) grow slowly in the early career, rapidly in the middle stage, and again slowly in the later stage. The second and third stages are important in Japan, but the first is almost negligible.

(d) The curve which matches the above shape (i.e. the two stages of productivity growth) is the logistic curve, since this curve fits well with observation (c).

(e) There are two points of productivity levels in an individual's career, the initial starting level and the maximum attainable level of productivity. Denoted by $P(0)$ and $P(A)$, these levels are determined by a worker's latent ability and educational attainment, and by working conditions (firm size, etc.). Firm size, discussed in Chapter 4, is taken into account. These two levels are basically unobservable.

(f) The shape of a worker's productivity path differs both by worker's occupation and by firm size, (see Chapter 4 and 7).

(g) The shape of a worker's productivity path is determined both by his current level of productivity and by the difference between his maximum attainable level of productivity and his current level, formally speaking.

The basic model, which incorporates the above hypotheses and mechanisms, may be stated by equation (8.2):

$$dP/dt = kP(A - P) \tag{8.2}$$

where P denotes the worker's productivity, k is a parameter which shows the shape of individual productivity path, and A is the maximum attainable level of individual productivity. P is a function of time (t) and, in fact, is measured by job tenure in the firm. This formulation is a modified version of the model of life earnings by Rosen (1977), who specified a learning production function.

A brief description for solving (8.2) is given here. (8.2) is equivalent to (8.3):

$$P'(t) - kAP(t) = -k\left(P(t)\right)^2 \tag{8.3}$$

This is the Bernoulli differential equation. Dividing (8.3) by $(P(t))^2$, and replacing $(P(t))^{-1}$ by $q(t)$,

A Model of Wage Determination

$$q'(t) + kAq(t) = k \tag{8.4}$$

Multiplying exp (kAt) for both sides of (8.4),

$$q'(t)\exp(kAt) + kAq(t)\exp(kAt)$$
$$= \{q(t)\exp(kAt)\}' = k\exp(kAt) \tag{8.5}$$

Integrating both sides of (8.5) by t;

$$q(t)\exp(kAt) = A^{-1}\exp(kAt) + C$$

where C is the integration coefficient is, in fact, equal to $\{q(0) - A^{-1}\}$. Thus, we obtain $q(t)$ as follows,

$$q(t) = \frac{\{A - P(0)\}\exp(-kAt) + P(0)}{AP(0)} \tag{8.6}$$

Finally, $P(t)$ is given by (8.7),

$$P(t) = \frac{AP(0)}{P(0) + \{A - P(0)\}\exp(-kAt)}$$
$$= \frac{A}{1 + \{A/P(0) - 1\}\exp(-kAt)} \tag{8.7}$$

where $P(0)$ is the initial condition of the function $P(t)$, and is equivalent to the starting level of individual productivity.

Equation (8.7) is the fundamental equation, which should be tested by empirical data. There are, needless to say, several deficiencies in this formulation. First, (8.7) is not a formulation which has not been derived from any solid behaviours of workers or firms (say, maximization of lifetime utilities or of profits), but rather a formulation which seeks the best empirical wage equation. The sole theory, if any, is a learning production function as presented by Rosen (1977). Since several recent attempts (e.g. Abraham and Farber, 1987; Altonji and Shakotko, 1987; Topel, 1991) are concerned with finding better empirical functions which do not necessarily depend on solid behaviours, our approach also may be approved. Secondly, the basic model considered here is, in principle, applied to a worker who stays in the same firm during his entire career. It is not easy to apply the model to female workers who often interrupt their careers, or to male workers who change employers. Although some remedies are attempted below for the latter, female workers are eliminated from consideration. Thirdly, there are several unobservable variables in equation (8.7); it is necessary to give observable information which indicates the contribution of those unobservable variables.

8.4. EMPIRICAL RESULTS

8.4.1. Estimation Procedure

Equation (8.7) is estimated by non-linear least-squares method. Since several variables, namely A (the maximum attainable level of individual productivity) and k (the parameter indicating the shape of productivity path), are unobservable in this analysis, it is necessary to transform them into manageable forms. We assume that both A and k are dependent upon a worker's educational attainment and working conditions (i.e. the size of firm to which he belongs); if he had reached a higher educational level, both his maximum attainable productivity and the shape of the productivity path would probably be higher. It was shown in Chapter 4 that wage differentials by firm size were substantial in Japan; we hypothesize that the productivities of workers in larger firms are higher than those in smaller firms for the following reasons (as was argued in Chapter 4). First, able and productive workers prefer to work in larger firms, at least in Japan. Second, higher capital intensities, better equipment, economies of scale, higher R&D, etc. make workers in larger firms more productive than those in smaller ones. Third, oligopolistic competition may provide larger firms with extra profits which are likely to raise their employees' wages (see Chapter 9). Consequently, we consider the functional forms as follows.

$$A = a_1 + a_2 \text{ school} + a_3 \text{ size} \qquad (8.8)$$

$$k = k_1 + k_2 \text{ school} + k_3 \text{ school}^2 + k_4 \text{ size} + k_5 \text{ size}^2 \qquad (8.9)$$

where 'school' specifies the years of schooling and 'size' specifies the size of firm to which a worker belongs; a_i and k_i are the parameters. A squared form was introduced in the equation of k in order to consider a marginally increasing (or decreasing) effect of each variable.

Substituting A and k in (8.7), we obtain the final formulation, which is explained basically by school, size, and tenure in a highly non-linear fashion. Note that these three variables were concluded to be the main determinants of wage differentials in Chapter 5. The parameters are estimated by non-linear least squares method. A rough initial value, $P(0)$, which is equal to the starting wage, must be given. The following simple linear form was estimated preliminarily:

$$\ln W = C_1 + C_2 \text{ school} + C_3 \text{ size} + C_4 \text{ tenure} \qquad (8.10)$$

The exponential of the estimated value of C_1 may be regarded as one of the initial values, and it is in fact used in the final calculation of (8.7).

We shall explain briefly the treatment of a job-changer. We suppose that a job-changer, regardless of a voluntary or involuntary turnover, departs from the productivity (wage) path given by equation (8.7). Concretely speaking, the maximum attainable level of productivity is strongly affected. The reason is that his forecasted attainable productivity is no longer achieved, since he is not in the same company. We thought that if one person was in the same company for his entire career, it would be possible to forecast the maximum attainable productivity; once that individual changed company, however, it would be necessary to modify the maximum attainable productivity, partly because of the change in the environment and partly because of a loss of the learning capacity accumulated at the previous company. This distinction between changers and no-changers adopts the notion of specific human capital, which differentiates the growth path of their productivities. The US evidence supports the hypothesis that more productive or able persons change jobs less often, (e.g. Topel, 1991).

We believe, moreover, that the degree of change in an individual's attainable maximum level of productivity depends upon whether he moves from a smaller to a larger firm or vice versa. Since the firm-size effect is crucial in Japan, it should be reasonable to argue that the direction of the change in employers (to a larger firm or to a smaller firm) is also crucial: we take the view that if an individual moves to a larger firm, his maximum attainable productivity will be increased. This is due to the fact that larger firms in Japan provide workers with higher productivity for various reasons, as explained previously. On the other hand, if an employee moves to a smaller firm, his productivity will decrease. When we perform a regression analysis, the above mechanism (the change in an individual's maximum attainable productivity) is incorporated in the coefficient of the firm size (namely a_3) in equation (8.8) of the maximum attainable productivity equation. Specifically, a dummy variable, indicating unity if a worker moves to a larger firm and minus unity if a worker moves to a smaller firm, is multiplied to the coefficient a_3.

It would have been possible to consider another similar dummy variable in the coefficient of 'school' (education), technically speaking. This was not done, however, partly because we believe that the component of productivity attributable to education would be much less affected by labour turnover than would that attributable to the effect of size of firm, and partly because education-specific knowledge would be common and useful to all the firms. This is the implication of general human capital. It would be reasonable to assume that equation (8.9), the parameter which indicates the shape of the productivity path, might also be affected by labour turnover. Since the contribution of (8.8) is larger than the contribution of (8.9) in determining the overall productivity path given by (8.7), the consideration of a dummy variable was made only for (8.8).

This section has discussed extensively the implication of both general human capital and specific human capital; and this chapter is a strict application of human-capital theory. It should be noted, nevertheless, that the model developed here draws on many other factors and theories as well as human capital.

8.4.2. Data

Before the empirical results are discussed, we shall explain the data. The main data source is the *Employment Status Survey* published by the Statistical Office. This survey was conducted every three years before 1982, but it is now conducted every five. We use the years 1979 and 1982 for this study. This data source is different from the *Wage Structure Survey* on which several other chapters of this book have drawn.

The number of original observations is about 800,000, and the Survey contains a large number of useful information on workers' employment status and wages. Since it is extremely costly to use all observations for the extensive non-linear calculation adopted in this investigation, we reduced the number of samples, using only one-tenth of the total observations, which were selected purely randomly. Note that even if the sample number is reduced, the number (male observations) is about 40,000, which is still large. The reason for selecting only males is that the model developed here is suitable only for males who do not interrupt their careers.

8.4.3. Empirical Results

We present the estimated results based on equation (8.7) for three occupational groups: white-collar workers, blue-collar workers, and sales workers. Each occupation has two samples: workers who have never changed employer ('no-changers'), and workers who change employer at least once ('changers'). We consider only the latest change for changers, and the effect of previous changes in employer is ignored in this econometric estimation. See Table 8.1 for the proportion of changers and no-changers. The number of changers is smaller for each occupation in this data set because we use all observations regardless of the age of employees. It is noted,

TABLE 8.1. *Share of 'changers' and 'no-changers' in Employment Status Survey*

Occupation	Changers	No-changers
White-collar	1,469	3,165
	(31.7%)	(68.3%)
Blue-collar	3,949	4,913
	(44.6%)	(55.4%)
Sales	1,222	1,766
	(40.9%)	(59.1%)

Note. The number of observations in this table comes from the sample used in this chapter.

Source: *Employment Status Survey* (1982).

158   A Model of Wage Determination

however, that the difference by occupation between no-changers and changers is considerable in the samples (see Tachibanaki, 1984a). Table 8.2 presents some descriptive statistics of the sample used in this study; only the result for no-changers is presented, to save space. The following regression analysis adopts only three explanatory variables: school, size, and tenure.

Tables 8.3(a) and 8.3(b) show the estimated regression coefficients for no-changers and changers in 1982 and 1979. Several empirical observations may be based on Table 8.3(a). First, the

TABLE 8.2(a). *% Share of blue-collar workers (no-changers) distinguished by education (years of schooling) and size of firm (number of employees)*

Size of firm	Years of schooling				
	9	12	14	16	Total
1–9 (1)	10.48	6.98	0.33	0.61	18.40
10–29 (2)	7.39	6.64	0.41	0.47	14.90
30–49 (3)	3.22	2.97	0.22	0.26	6.68
50–99 (4)	3.22	3.99	0.16	0.61	7.98
100–299 (5)	3.44	6.05	0.47	0.94	10.89
300–499 (6)	1.08	3.11	0.24	0.45	4.88
500–999 (7)	1.57	3.44	0.26	0.55	5.82
1,000– (8)	6.51	20.68	1.02	2.24	30.45
TOTAL	36.90	53.86	3.11	6.13	100.00

Note. Averages—schooling: 11.20 years; size; 4.68; tenure: 13.99 years; wage: 1,666 yen. Average size is calculated by the numbers written in parentheses under the numbers of employees. In other words, the numbers in parentheses show the quantification method for the size of firm.

Source: Employment Status Survey (1982).

estimated R^2s are much higher for no-changers than those for changers. Our formulation of the wage determination for no-changers is fairly successful, in view of the lower estimated R^2s based on the human-capital model performed in the past (see e.g. Mincer and Higuchi (1988), who obtained low R^2s by using the same survey data as here). The present model is capable of predicting the wage path by job tenure for workers who have never changed employer. This is also supported by the fact that nearly all the estimated coefficients are statistically significant, and have the

TABLE 8.2(b). % share of white-collar workers (no-changers) Distinguished by education (years of schooling) and size of firm (number of employees)

Size of firm	Years of schooling				
	9	12	14	16	Total
1–9 (1)	0.98	3.48	0.98	2.26	8.06
10–29 (2)	1.14	5.12	1.23	3.25	10.74
30–49 (3)	0.41	2.18	0.38	1.74	4.71
50–99 (4)	0.51	4.20	0.60	3.32	8.63
100–299 (5)	0.63	5.72	1.14	5.72	13.21
300–499 (6)	0.13	2.78	0.47	3.06	6.45
500–999 (7)	0.13	2.43	0.51	3.67	6.73
1,000– (8)	1.48	19.24	1.61	19.15	41.48
TOTAL	5.40	45.15	6.92	42.53	100.00

Note. Averages—schooling: 13.68 years; size; 5.62; tenure: 15.28 years; wage: 2,507 yen. Average size is calculated by the numbers written in parentheses under the numbers of employees. In other words, the numbers in parentheses show the quantification method for the size of firm.

Source: Employment Status Survey (1982).

TABLE 8.2(c). *% share of sales workers (no-changers) distinguished by education (years of schooling) and size of firm (number of employees)*

Size of firm	Years of schooling				
	9	12	14	16	Total
1–9 (1)	4.87	9.12	0.62	2.77	17.38
10–29 (2)	3.06	7.30	0.51	3.06	13.93
30–49 (3)	1.30	3.79	0.23	1.30	6.63
50–99 (4)	1.02	4.87	0.34	2.89	9.12
100–299 (5)	1.36	6.96	0.91	5.04	14.27
300–499 (6)	0.51	3.51	0.23	3.17	7.42
500–999 (7)	0.40	3.57	0.06	4.25	8.27
1,000– (8)	0.51	10.82	1.08	10.59	22.99
TOTAL	13.02	49.49	3.96	33.07	100.00

Note. Averages—schooling: 13.01 years; size: 4.35; tenure: 11.33 years; wage: 1,718 yen. Average size is calculated by the numbers written in parentheses under the numbers of employees. In other words, the numbers in parentheses show the quantification method for the size of firm.

Source: *Employment Status Survey* (1982).

right signs in the case of no-changers. Incidentally, the results for changers are also marginally better than in the human-capital model.

Secondly, our basic equations, (8.7), (8.8), and (8.9), consist of only three variables, school, size, and tenure, although the way in which these three variables are introduced is fairly complicated. The estimated R^2s in the *ad hoc* statistical models for wage differentials explained in Chapter 2 are normally higher than those estimated here. However, it should be noted that the current model,

TABLE 8.3(a). *Estimated non-linear regression coefficients for wage equations in 1982*

	No-changers			Changers		
	W	B	S	W	B	S
k_1	396.0	257.0	131.0	908.0	337.0	699.0
	(2.70)	(6.05)	(1.73)	(1.86)	(2.32)	(1.49)
k_2	−49.1	−9.53	7.02	−115.0	−58.4	−67.0
	(−2.33)	(−1.49)	(0.64)	(−1.63)	(−2.10)	(0.99)
k_3	1.99	0.624	0.0466	4.03	3.20	2.14
	(2.65)	(2.30)	(0.11)	(1.61)	(2.44)	(0.89)
k_4	−12.1	−46.9	−37.2	−6.77	1.67	−20.7
	(−2.67)	(−7.08)	(−3.93)	(−0.63)	(0.29)	(1.56)
k_5	1.06	3.48	2.47	1.99	1.22	2.12
	(2.68)	(6.58)	(3.23)	(1.42)	(1.68)	(1.45)
a_1	1058.5	569.9	601.3	565.1	1418.2	246.4
	(3.66)	(5.68)	(2.79)	(1.89)	(9.30)	(0.83)
a_2	131.2	65.4	74.3	180.2	47.8	148.0
	(6.41)	(6.87)	(4.40)	(7.62)	(3.54)	(5.84)
a_3	99.9	192.9	207.5	15.7	42.0	35.0
	(5.05)	(27.38)	(12.66)	(1.47)	(8.64)	(3.73)
R^2	0.214	0.381	0.337	0.137	0.204	0.134
Sample	3,165	4,913	1,766	1,469	3,949	1,222

Notes
1. The meanings of the parameters are given by equations (8.7), (8.8), and (8.9).
2. W stands for white-collar workers, B for blue-collar workers, and S for sales workers.
3. The numbers in parentheses are the t-ratios.
4. The real coefficients for $k_1, k_2, k_3, k_4,$ and k_5 must be multiplied by 10^{-6}.

which consists of only three variables, is not inferior to the *ad hoc* statistical model, which normally uses a much larger number of explanatory variables.

Thirdly, the results for changers are not so satisfactory in comparison with those for no-changers, in view of lower R^2s and of the presence of several statistically insignificant variables. Two possible reasons may be suggested. First, the productivity (wage) growth path formulated in this study may be inadequate for workers who changed employer; in other words, we may need a different theoretical development of wage determination for changers. Second, the statistical (econometric) treatment of a job-changer may not be sufficient. In any case, further work is necessary.

TABLE 8.3(b). *Estimated non-linear regression coefficients for wage equations in 1979*

Parameters	No-changers		
	W	B	S
k_1	33.4	420.0	646.0
	(0.74)	(6.40)	(2.98)
k_2	4.01	−17.7	−36.7
	(0.57)	(−1.92)	(1.17)
k_3	0.0277	0.0976	1.52
	(0.96)	(2.67)	(1.35)
k_4	−11.7	−68.9	−95.1
	(−2.08)	(−6.59)	(5.87)
k_5	0.0717	4.91	7.21
	(1.51)	(5.91)	(5.57)
a_1	1404.2	472.3	29.6
	(5.72)	(6.25)	(0.20)
a_2	50.7	44.9	87.3
	(3.11)	(6.67)	(7.15)
a_3	88.5	144.5	149.2
	(6.40)	(27.4)	(12.31)
R^2	0.269	0.374	0.302
Sample	2,794	4,472	1,703

Notes
1. The meanings of the parameters are given by equations (8.7), (8.8), and (8.9).
2. W stands for white-collar workers, B for blue-collar workers, and S for sales workers.
3. The numbers in parentheses are the t-ratios.
4. The real coefficients for k_1, k_2, k_3, k_4, and k_5 must be multiplied by 10^{-6}.
5. It is impossible to estimate the case of 'changers' in 1979 because of data limitation.

Fourth, with respect to the difference by occupation it is possible to conclude that the model is best suited to blue-collar workers, and that the order of superiority is roughly (1) blue-collar, (2) sales, and (3) white-collar. This is justified by both the estimated R^2s and the statistical significance of the coefficients. One reason for the inferior performance by white-collar workers is that several omitted variables, in particular the effect of position (i.e. the hierarchical position associated with supervising jobs), might have a significant effect. This was shown in Chapter 7, which suggested a strong influence of the hierarchical positions in organizations on earnings differentials. Since white-collar workers are diversified by hierarchical positions in comparison with blue-collar worker, an omission of this variable necessarily reduces the explanatory power of the empirical result.

Fifth, the effect of both school (education) and size (size of firm) on the wage path is examined. Since it is somewhat cumbersome to examine the estimated coefficients in Table 8.3(a), Table 8.4 gives the estimated values of both the maximum attainable productivity (A) and the shape parameter (k) is presented. Table 8.4 is cross-tabulated by education and size of firm.

Table 8.4(a) presents the following observations. The value of A is an increasing function of both the educational attainment and of

TABLE 8.4(a). *Estimated values of the maximum attainable productivity (A) and the shape parameter (k) by education and size of firm (no-changers)*

	Size of firm[a]					
	10–29		100–299		1,000–	
	k[b]	A	k	A	k	A
White-collar						
Junior high	9.58	2,439	8.17	2,738	8.68	3,038
Senior high	7.39	2,832	5,98	3,131	6.49	3,352
University	10.00	3,357	8.63	3,657	9.13	3,956
Blue-collar						
Junior high	10.4	1,545	7.47	2,123	6.97	2,702
Senior high	15.3	1,740	8.54	2,319	8.05	2,899
University	18.4	2,002	11.70	2,584	11.20	3,160
Sales						
Junior High	13.3	1,685	7.37	2,308	5.84	2,930
Senior High	15.7	1,908	9.77	2,530	8.24	3,153
University	19.1	2,205	13.10	2,828	11.50	3,450

[a] We considered only 3 representative groups of firms regarding their size. This is true also for Table 8.4(b).
[b] The real values in k should be multiplied by 10^{-5}.

164 A Model of Wage Determination

TABLE 8.4(b). *Estimated values of the maximum attainable productivity (A) and the shape parameter (k) by education and size of firm (changers)*

	Size of firm								
	10–29			100–299			1,000–		
	k[a]	A^+[b]	A^-[b]	k	A^+	A^-	k	A^+	A^-
White-collar									
Junior high	19.3	2,218	2,155	21.5	2,265	2,108	27.2	2,312	2,061
Senior high	10.2	2,758	2,696	12.4	2,806	2,648	18.1	2,853	2,601
University	9.37	3,479	3,416	13.1	3,526	3,369	17.2	3,573	3,321
Blue-collar									
Junior high	7.91	1,932	1,764	11.0	2,058	1,638	16.2	2,184	1,512
Senior high	10.5	2,075	1,908	13.6	2,201	1,782	18.9	2,327	1,656
University	23.0	2,266	2,099	26.1	2,392	1,973	31.4	2,518	1,847
Sales									
Junior high	29.4	1,649	1,508	27.6	1,753	1,403	29.7	1,859	1,298
Senior high	24.6	2,093	1,952	22.9	2,163	1,882	22.9	2,198	1,847
University	24.3	2,685	2,544	22.6	2,790	2,439	24.6	2,895	2,334

[a] The real values in k should be multiplied by 10^{-5}.
[b] A^+ signifies that a worker moved to a larger firm than the current size, and A^- signifies that a worker moved to a smaller firm.

the size of firm. Simply speaking, the higher the educational attainment, the higher the maximum attainable productivity. This is also true for the size of firm. The value of k, however, shows a somewhat different result, due mainly to the squared form of the equations. For example, while the value of k is a decreasing function of the size of firm for blue-collar and sales workers, it is not a simple decreasing function for white-collar workers. The value of k is an increasing function of the educational attainment for blue-collar and sales workers, while it is not a simple increasing function for white-collar workers.

Most surprisingly, the value of k turned out to be a non-increasing function of the size of firm, contradicting the assumption that the larger the size of firm, the higher would be the shape parameter of productivity (k). The value of A satisfies the prior expectation: it is always an increasing function of the size of firm, as noted previously. We need to evaluate the effect of education and firm size on wages in the form of the product of k and A, because the denominator of equation (8.7) contains the multiple form of k and A. In sum, it is risky to evaluate the effect of education or firm size on wages on the sole basis of the numbers in Table 8.4: these numbers show the effects of education and firm size on the values of k and A only, whereas the product of k and A has a more significant meaning, if we are concerned with the effect of k. The effect of A, however, may be interpreted straightforwardly.

The results in Table 8.4(b), which are estimated for changers, differ considerably from those in Table 8.4(a). Most importantly, the value of k is an increasing function of size of firm, and a decreasing function of educational attainment for white-collar workers. These values are quite different from no-changers among white-collar workers. Also, the value of k is an increasing function of size of firm for blue-collar workers, while the opposite is true for no-changers among blue-collar workers. The parameter A in changers, however, has the same property as no-changers with respect to the influence of educational attainment and size of firm. It would be premature to emphasize the effect of educational attainment and firm size on k and A separately; the combined effect of k and A on the wage path is more reliable and appealing. This does not imply, however, that the separate effect on k and A is entirely useless.

No serious interpretation is applied to Table 8.3(b) because almost the same interpretations as those in Table 8.3(a) (in 1982) can be applied to Table 8.3(b) (in 1979) for no-changers. The data limitation did not allow us to perform a regression analysis for changers in 1979.

Finally, it is necessary to evaluate the effect of job tenure on the wage path. Since equation (8.7), which is our basic formulation, is a function of job tenure, it is in principle possible to specify the contribution of job tenure to wage determination. Equation (8.7), however, is also influenced by both educational attainment and firm size, and its form is highly non-linear. We therefore adopted a simple way of expressing the influence of job tenure on wage path; the estimated wage figures through (8.7) on the basis of various tenure levels are presented. These estimations were made for various combinations of educational level and firm size. Some of the results are shown in Fig. 8.1 for no-changers and Fig. 8.2 for changers. Table 8.5 shows the exact numbers of wage figures only

TABLE 8.5. *Estimated wage figures (yen) according to tenure levels by educational attainment (firm size: 100–299 employees)*

Tenure	School: white-collar			School: blue-collar		
	Junior high	Senior high	University	Junior high	Senior high	University
0	632.70	788.40	1,057.86	651.97	735.10	862.64
1	748.07	903.94	1,309.74	752.75	838.02	1,044.15
2	875.72	1,028.98	1,585.01	803.32	946.74	1,236.38
3	1,014.06	1,162.29	1,871.99	883.95	1,059.48	1,431.05
4	1,160.63	1,302.19	2,156.84	966.73	1,174.16	1,619.47
5	1,312.27	1,446.55	2,426.10	1,050.70	1,288.57	1,794.02
6	1,465.32	1,592.98	2,669.15	1,134.80	1.400.50	1,949.25
7	1,615.99	1,738.94	2,879.58	1,218.00	1,507.93	2,082.40
8	1,760.73	1,881.93	3,055.26	1,299.27	1,609.17	2,193.10
9	1,896.53	2,019.62	3,197.56	1,377.72	1,702.96	2,282.76
10	2,021.15	2,150.06	3,310.00	1,452.56	1,788.45	2,353.87
11	2,133.21	2271.72	3,397.14	1,523.16	1,865.26	2,409.33
12	2,232.15	2,383.55	3,463.64	1,589.06	1,933.36	2,452.02
13	2,318.10	2,484.98	3,513.82	1,649.98	1,993.04	2,484.55
14	2,391.73	2,575.87	3,551.35	1,705.77	2,044.82	2,509.15
15	2,454.04	2,656.44	3,579.23	1,756.46	2,089.34	2,527.64
16	2,506.24	2,727.17	3,599.84	1,802.15	2,127.33	2,541.48
17	2,549.59	2,788.73	3,615.03	1,843.06	2,159.53	2,551.80
18	2,585.34	2,841.93	3,626.19	1,879.47	2,186.68	2,559.48
19	2,614.66	2,887.60	3,634.37	1,911.69	2,209.47	2,565.19
20	2,638.57	2,926.60	3,640.36	1,940.07	2,228.52	2,569.42
21	2,658.01	2,959.75	3,644.74	1,964.97	2,244.39	2,572.56
22	2,673.76	2,987.81	3,647.95	1,986.72	2,257.57	2,574.88
23	2,686.48	3,011.48	3,650.29	2,005.66	2,268.50	2,576.60
24	2,696.74	3,031.40	3,652.00	2,022.12	2,277.55	2,577.87
25	2,704.99	3,048.11	3,653.24	2,036.37	2,285.02	2,578.81
26	2,711.63	3,062.11	3,654.15	2,048.70	2,291.19	2,579.51
27	2,716.96	3,073.81	3,654.82	2,059.33	2,296.27	2,580.02
28	2,721.24	3,083.59	3,655.30	2,068.49	2,300.46	2,580.40
29	2,724.67	3,091.74	3,655.66	2,076.38	2,303.90	2,580.68
30	2,727.41	3,098.53	3,655.91	2,083.15	2,306.74	2,580.89

in the case of no-changers to save space. The maximum tenure is limited to twenty-five years in those figures because tenure lasting longer than that does not raise the wage figures significantly.

Fig. 8.1 shows the cases of white-collar and blue-collar workers who are both working in firms with between 100 and 299 workers. Both figures clearly show that the growth rate of wages by job

A Model of Wage Determination

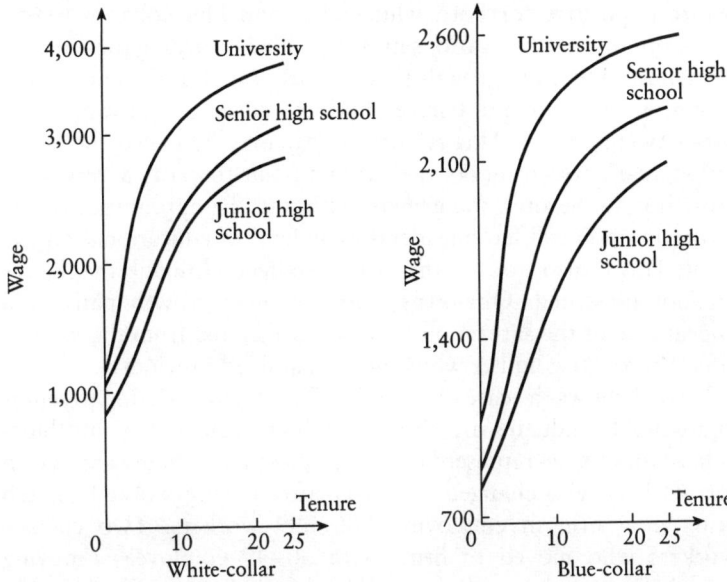

FIG. 8.1. a The effect of job tenure on wage growth in 1982 (no-changers)

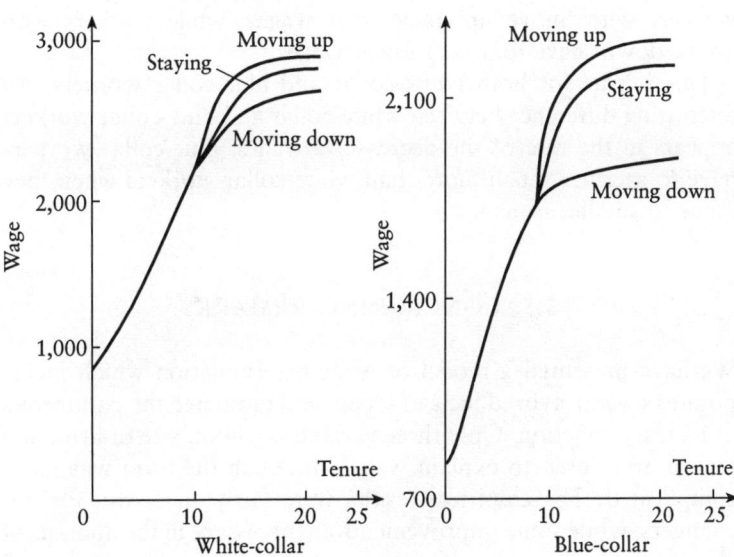

FIG. 8.2. a The effect of job tenure on wage growth of junior high-school graduates in 1982 (changers who moved after ten years)

tenure is positive for both white-collar and blue-collar workers. Three important observations must be added regarding the effect of job tenure. First, the growth path is fairly rapid in the early years (say up to fifteen years' tenure), and it declines considerably after about twenty years. This twentieth year may be called the 'saturation year', which marks the turning-point towards a very slow growth path. Second, the growth path and the appearance of the saturation point differ considerably by level of educational attainment. This is also true for the firm size effect, although the figures are not presented. Obviously, those various growth paths and appearance of the saturation years are originated from the various effects through k and A which were examined previously.

Fig. 8.2 shows the case of changers. Two figures relating to senior high-school graduates are shown for both white-collar and blue-collar workers, as representative examples. These figures are given for workers who changed employer after having worked for ten years in a firm in employing 100–299 workers. Two cases—workers who moved to firms with 30–49 employees ('moving down') and workers who moved to larger firms, with 500–999 employees ('moving up')—are shown in Fig. 8.2, in addition to workers who stayed in the same firms. This figure suggests that workers who 'move up' raise their wages, while workers who 'move down' have to accept lower wages.

This is true for both white-collar and blue-collar workers. An interesting difference between white-collar and blue-collar workers appears in the rate of the decrease in wages. Blue-collar workers have to sacrifice much more than white-collar workers when they move to smaller firms.

8.5. CONCLUDING REMARKS

We have presented a model of wage determination which incorporates several stylized facts in Japan, and estimated the parameters of its wage function. Only three variables, school, size of firm, and tenure, were used to explain wages, although the form was fairly complicated. The empirical results were fairly successful for no-changers, while some improvements are necessary in the analysis of changers. The Japanese wage growth path is explained fairly well by the above three variables, if a relevant theoretical model is applied. The arguments for omitted variables and heterogeneity bias in the American case are not major issues in Japan, at least for workers who never change employer. The effect of job tenure on wage growth was estimated: the case of no-changers was fairly successful, but the 'changers' case needs further refinement. The next task is a theoretical and empirical development of this approach for females.

9

The Effect of Discrimination and of Industry Segmentation on Wage Differentials

9.1. INTRODUCTION

The purpose of this chapter is to investigate wage differentials by both sex and industry. We investigate these issues by applying the labour market segmentation concept and noting its effect on wage determination. At the same time, the interaction between human capital and labour segmentation is taken into account.

Our view of labour market segmentation differs from the traditional view of a dualistic economic structure and labour market in Japan which has focused on firm-size differentials.[1] Our view is related to industrial division (or sectoral division). While most segmentation theories in the USA are based on occupational division, there has been a development of studies in industrial division, based on the view that the existence of labour market segmentation is the consequence of the more fundamental process of segmentation in the economic order. Baran and Sweezy (1966), Averitt (1968), Edwards *et al.* (1975), Bluestone *et al.* (1973), and Gordon *et al.* (1982) define distinct economic sectors—oligopolistic and

---

[1] As for the labour market in the traditional view, large firms have a highly structured internal labour market in the sense of Doeringer and Piore (1971). Such firms hire new graduates to fill entry-level jobs; higher positions are filled through internal promotion. The *nenko-joretsu* wage system is characterized by a low starting wage and a subsequent steep increase with age and seniority. Lifelong commitment to the same firm is common, and changing firms is severely penalized. Small firms, in contrast, have many entry points and a high turnover rate. Labour mobility between large firms and small firms is restricted, however. Wages are directly influenced by the operation of the competitive labour market. There is an important difference in the power of unions within large firms and small firms. See Tachibanaki (1993*a*) for unions in Japan and Shinohara (1970) for Japanese economic duality.

competitive sectors, or centre/core and periphery—in terms of market power concentration. Beck *et al.* (1978), following Shepherd's (1970; 1979) multifactor approach, present a definition of core and periphery industrial segments. They use indicators of industrial oligopoly which are categorized as (1) measures of the capacity for oligopoly in an industry, (2) measures of oligopolistic behaviour in the industrial product market, and (3) measures of oligopolistic behaviour in the industrial labour market. In Carnoy and Rumberger (1976), the industrial segments are defined by the percentage of total business receipts accounted for by the sales of firms in the top two asset categories in each industry. The idea of labour market segmentation was proposed by Doeringer and Piore (1971) and Piore (1975), and more recently by Dickens and Lang (1992*a*; 1992*b*). In Japan, Ishikawa (1989; 1991) is a main advocate.

The analysis of industrial division in relation to wage differential has been little explored in Japan, except for the group of studies mentioned in Chapter 5, which paid attention to average wages in industries. It may be argued that the industrial differences in average wage are merely a reflection of the different proportion of firms of different size, and different sex and age composition of workers in various industries. A simple comparison of average wages, however, by industry and by firm size shows that, although there are considerable wage differentials by firm size within each industry, the differences by industry are even greater. There is quite a high correspondence between the wage level of the industry and the proportion of large firms in that industry; the wage level of a small firm in an industry with a high proportion of large firms is close to that of large firms in an industry mainly composed of small firms. (This finding was partly supported by Chapter 5.)

The discussion above suggests that the analysis of wage differentials between industries might offer us a useful insight into the nature of wage differentials in Japan, beyond the theory of dualism based on firm size across all industries. For this reason, we use the notion of concentration of market power within an industry as the operational criterion by which to define the labour market segments in the private economic sector. This chapter differs from Chapter 5 because industrial power given by market share is its main concern; more importantly, the relationship with male/female difference is also investigated here.

9.2. THE HYPOTHESIS, METHODOLOGY, AND DATA

We will test the following hypotheses:

1. The labour market in the concentrated sector and the labour market in the competitive sector are different in terms of worker characteristics, employment practices, career patterns, and wage determination.
2. Within each sector, women and men face different treatments in wage determinations.
3. Differences in worker characteristics such as education are not important sources of wage differentials by sex.

We define the two economic sectors on the basis of the degree of concentration of market power. Following Shepherd (1970: 33), market power is defined as the ability of a market participant to influence price, quality, and nature of the product in the market. This is departure from the traditional view of a dualistic economic structure and labour market in Japan, which focuses on firm size differences. The underlying assumption of the inter-scale dualism is that large size alone produces various benefits which small firms cannot capture, such as economies of scale, higher productivity, and an internal labour market. These differences due to firm size are considered to be the primary causes of the dualism. (See Chapter 4).

In contrast, this study assumes that large size alone does not necessarily confer important advantages over small firms; but large size accompanied by market power ensures long-term profitability (see, e.g. Edwards, 1979: 82), and possibly raises wages further. Some of the reasons for the advantages by oligopolistic firms may be: (1) some oligopolistic firms have capacity to increase their product prices; (2) monopoly (or oligopoly) rent theory may be applied; (3) some oligopolistic firms in Japan have some extra advantages in productivity—e.g. easy access to the financial market within the ex-*zaibatsu* groups (i.e. familial conglomerates) market, better information, and R&D aided sometimes by the government. The traditional marxian school in Japan was concerned with these observations. See Kawashima (1983) for details.

It is true that market segmentation due to market power and inter-scale dualism are interrelated, and that it may be difficult to distinguish them empirically, because the proportion of large firms in non-competitive sectors is higher than that in competitive sectors. The following analysis, however, tries to control the firm size variables within each sector, thus removing a large part of intercorrelations and ambiguities.

There are many measures of market power.[2] Commonly used measures include concentration of production, sales, shipment, assets, value added, employment, expenditure on advertisement, amount of political contribution, and numbers of government contracts. (see Oster, 1979). Although each measure reveals some aspect of concentrated market power, none is sufficient on its own to represent the complex structure and behaviour of oligopolistic firms.

This study uses product concentration because this is the most consistent and reliable information among those available. The concentration ratio is calculated in terms of the production share of the largest three, five, and ten firms within each two-digit industry. If the concentration ratio is 25 per cent or more for the three largest firms, or 35 per cent or more for the five largest firms, or 45 per cent or more for the ten largest firms, then the industry is defined as non-competitive/concentrated. If the concentration ratios are less than these values, then the industry is defined as competitive. This procedure, however, covers only manufacturing industries. Information about the concentration of production or sales is not available for non-manufacturing industries. It is sometimes difficult to measure output in non-manufacturing industries. Concentration of workers is used as a measure of concentration of market power for these industries, because this is the most reliable of the limited range of information available for non-manufacturing industries. If the proportion of workers employed in large firms hiring 1,000 or more workers in 30 per cent or more, the industry is defined as non-competitive, and otherwise as competitive.

Table 9.1 summarizes the results. Fifteen industries are defined as concentrated and fourteen industries as competitive. There is a close parallel between production concentration and worker

---

[2] Nakao (1980) finds that a firm's market power (measured by the top three-firm concentration ratio for 1966) has a significant impact upon the average wage rate (the total expenditure by a firm on its workers divided by the total number of workers); and that the wage rates are positively related to the firm's advertising expenditure (the stock of goodwill), which lends support to the hypothesis that advertising constitutes a barrier to entry.

TABLE 9.1. *Definition of sectors and unionization rates*

Industry[a]	Worker concentration[b]	Production concentration by			Sector[c]	Unionization[d]
		Top 3 firms	Top 5 firms	Top 10 firms		
80 Electricity, gas, water	77.2				N	0.923
50 Finance, insurance	76.0				N	0.735
36 Transportation equipment	63.8	31.5	41.2	57.2	N	0.714
31 Iron, steel	63.8	31.0	38.8	49.5	N	0.654
70 Transport, communication	58.3				N	0.740
26 Chemical products	55.0	27.5	37.3	53.9	N	0.718
32 Non-ferrous metal	47.4	42.0	55.4	69.9	N	0.634
35 Electrical machinery	47.4	30.6	40.2	51.8	N	0.530
27 Petroleum, coal	46.1	36.1	50.4	69.3	N	0.594
10 Mining	45.1				N	0.526
28 Rubber products	43.9	42.0	48.9	57.6	N	0.574
37 Precision machinery	33.9	32.1	41.7	53.6	N	0.498
34 Machinery	31.6	26.1	35.0	44.9	N	0.455
40 Retail trade	25.4				C	
24 Pulp, paper	25.0	22.8	29.9	40.8	C	0.354
18 Food, tobacco	24.0	29.7	36.3	44.2	C	0.309
30 Ceramics, stone, clay	21.1	26.0	32.4	41.2	N	0.327
20 Textile mills	20.1	23.2	29.4	38.1	C	0.387
25 Publishing, printing	19.7	20.5	24.7	30.4	C	0.285

Effects of Discrimination and Industry Segmentation

Code & Industry	Worker concentration[b]	Unionization rate[d]			N/C[c]	Production concentration
41 Wholesale trade	18.2				C	0.287
15 Construction	17.5				C	0.105
60 Real estate	16.7				C	0.250
33 Fabricated metal	14.1	17.5	22.2	28.5	C	0.469
90 Service	13.7				C	0.182
38 Other manufacturing	13.1	18.2	23.0	30.5	C	0.133
23 Furniture	5.1	7.9	10.8	15.8	C	0.193
21 Apparel	5.1	11.5	15.0	20.8	C	0.130
22 Lumber, wood	4.4	5.9	7.4	10.8	C	0.120
29 Leather	2.7	10.3	14.1	20.0	C	

[a] Industries are ordered according to the degree of worker concentration. The figure preceding the industry name is the code number.
[b] Worker concentration is the % of workers in firms with 1,000 or more workers. Firms of under than 10 workers are excluded from the survey.
[c] N = non-competitive; C = competitive.
[d] Each of the unionization rates is computed by dividing the number of union members by the total number of workers in the industry, including those who work in firms with under than 10 workers. The unionization rate for retail and wholesale trade together is 0.143. The separate rates are not obtainable. The average unionization rate in the competitive sector is 0.217, while that in the non-competitive sector is 0.546.

Sources: For worker concentration, Ministry of Labour, *Wage Structure Survey*, 1978. For production concentration, Ministry of International Trade and Industry, *Kogyo Tokei-hyo (Survey on Manufacturing Industries)*, 1978. For unionization rate, Ministry of Labour, *Rodokumiai Kihon Chosa (Survey of Labour Unions)*, 1978.

concentration. The only contradictory results in the two sets of criteria are seen in industries located around the dividing line between the two sectors. This means that worker concentration is a good proxy for the concentration of market power for non-manufacturing industries.

Use of the product concentration ratios in some top firms has drawbacks: they do not reveal whether the oligopolies are asymmetrical or equal-sized, imports and exports and ignored, and product diversification is not taken into account. However, the weakness of the single-measure approach is partly reduced, since product concentration ratios are positively correlated with the other measures of market power, as shown in Table 9.2. Tables 9.1 and 9.2 in fact show that unionization rate, capital intensity (measured by capital : labour ratio), and productivity (measured by value added per worker) are all positively correlated to product and worker concentrations.

Our methodologies to test the hypotheses are (1) to examine how worker characteristics are different by sector and sex, (2) to perform regression analysis on the wage first of the whole population and then of each of the populations grouped by sector and sex, and then to examine whether worker characteristics are treated differently in wage determination, and (3) to estimate the total size of wage differentials by sector and sex, and the relative importance of each of the components (or causes).

We use two main data sources: *Basic Survey on Manufacturing Industries*, 1978 (Ministry of International Trade and Industry) for the product concentration, and *Wage Structure Survey*, 1978 (Ministry of Labour) (the latter was also used in Chapters 3, 4, 5, and 10). The former uses the four digit classification of industries, while the latter uses the two-digit classification. We aggregated the concentration ratios to the two-digit classification of industry in order to match both data. Since the sample sizes of both surveys are enormous, the results based on them are robust.

9.3. ANALYSIS OF WORKER CHARACTERISTICS BY SECTOR AND SEX

Tables 9.3, 9.4, and 9.5 demonstrate how the labour force is distributed between the competitive sector and the concentrated sector.

TABLE 9.2. *Capital intensity differentials, productivity, and wage differentials in manufacturing industries (1,000 yen, 1978)*

Industry[a]	Capital:labour ratio[b]	Value added per worker[c]	Wage payment per worker
36 Transportation equipment	4,000 (100)	6,241 (100)	2,792 (100)
31 Iron, steel	15,587 (390)	8,192 (131)	3,189 (114)
26 Chemical products	10,113 (253)	12,048 (193)	3,146 (113)
32 Non-ferrous metal	8,099 (202)	6,867 (110)	2,818 (101)
35 Electrical machinery	1,907 (48)	5,255 (84)	2,209 (79)
27 Petroleum, coal	40,072 (1,002)	15,029 (241)	3,421 (123)
28 Rubber products	2,871 (72)	5,008 (80)	2,265 (81)
37 Precision machinery	1,795 (45)	4,390 (70)	2,138 (77)
34 Machinery	2,862 (72)	5,420 (87)	2,561 (92)
24 Pulp, paper	6,737 (168)	5,387 (86)	2,225 (80)
18 Food, tobacco	3,395 (85)	5,009 (80)	1,695 (61)
30 Ceramics, stone, clay	4,342 (109)	5,597 (90)	2,066 (74)
20 Textile mills	2,113 (53)	3,123 (50)	1,419 (51)
25 Publishing, printing	2,517 (63)	5,992 (96)	2,616 (94)
33 Fabricated metal	2,813 (70)	4,622 (74)	2,000 (72)
38 Other manufacturing	2,694 (67)	4,354 (70)	1,795 (64)
23 Furniture	1,928 (48)	3,466 (56)	1,589 (57)
21 Apparel	766 (19)	2,329 (37)	1,162 (42)
22 Lumber, wood	2,580 (65)	3,425 (55)	1,593 (57)
29 Leather	752 (19)	3,398 (54)	1,522 (55)

[a] Industries are ordered according to the degree of worker concentration.
[b] Capital : labour ratio is computed by dividing the total assets at the end of year by the total no. of workers. 'Asset' refers to corporate fixed assets including (i) land, (ii) buildings, (iii) machine and equipment, (iv) transportation equipment.
[c] Value added = value product − (consumption tax + cost of materials + depreciation).

Source: Ministry of International Trade and Industry, *Kogyo Tokei-hyo* (*Survey on Manufacturing Industries*), 1978. Figures in parentheses are indices.

TABLE 9.3. *Distribution of workers by sector and sex (000)*

Sex	Sector total	Competitive sector	Concentrated sector
Female	6,100 (100)	3,881 *35.4* (63.6)	2,219 *24.0* (36.4)
Male	14,106 (100)	7,070 *64.6* (50.1)	7,036 *76.0* (49.9)
Total	20,206 (100)	10,951 *100* (54.2)	9,255 *100* (45.8)

Source: Ministry of Labour, *Wage Structure Survey*, 1978. The figures in parentheses show the % sectoral distribution by sex, and those in italics show the % sex composition by sector.

TABLE 9.4. *Distribution of workers by firm size (%)*

	Large firms	Medium firms	Small firms
FC	13.3	35.3	51.4
FN	47.9	29.3	22.4
MC	17.6	36.5	45.9
MN	54.4	26.4	19.2

Source: Ministry of Labour, *Wage Structure Survey*, 1978. F = female; M = male; C = competitive sector; N = non-competitive (concentrated) sector; B = blue-collar worker; W = white-collar worker. These abbreviations will be used in the following tables and figures.

Location of women and men. Table 9.3 shows the sex composition of the labour force in the two sectors. Males are equally distributed between the two sectors, whereas 64 per cent of females are in the competitive sector against 36 per cent in the concentrated sector. Table 9.4 presents the distribution of workers by firm size, which indicates that women are more likely to work in small firms than men. In brief, women are most likely to work in small firms in the competitive sector.

Educational composition. Table 9.5 shows the educational composition by sector, sex, and occupation (blue-collar versus white-collar). Since we find that the comparisons between eight sector/

TABLE 9.5. *Educational composition of workers and average length of service by sector and sex*

		Education (%)				Length of service (years)
		Junior high school	Senior high school	Junior college	University	
Blue-collar workers	FC	76.7	23.3	—	—	6.3
	FN	71.4	28.6	—	—	6.5
	MC	66.2	33.8	—	—	8.7
	MN	58.1	41.9	—	—	11.1
White-collar workers	FC	43.0	41.3	12.3	3.4	5.4
	FN	15.4	76.6	6.7	1.3	6.8
	MC	19.2	48.9	4.7	27.2	9.2
	MN	28.9	47.2	2.8	21.1	13.2

Source: Ministry of Labour, *Wage Structure Survey*, 1978.

sex/occupation groups are more useful than the comparisons between four sector/sex groups, we use the eight-group comparisons in the subsequent analysis. As for blue-collar workers, those in the concentrated sector have a higher average educational level than those in the competitive sector, and males overall have a higher educational level than females. The shortage of blue-collar workers after 1960 and the general increasing trend of the educational level shifted the main source of blue-collar workers from junior high-school graduates to senior high-school graduates. The concentrated sector has been able to react to this shift more quickly than the competitive sector.

White-collar workers have very different educational backgrounds from those of blue-collar workers. Males in the competitive sector have, on average, a higher educational level than males in the concentrated sector. The picture for females is not clear. The share of higher education graduates is more important in the competitive sector than in the concentrated sector for both sexes; one possible explanation is that the proportion of workers in managerial positions relative to the proportion of subordinate workers is generally lower in the concentrated industries than in the competitive industries. Another interesting fact is that the distribution of female educated graduates is 81 per cent in the competitive sector and 19 per cent in the concentrated sector, because it is likely that female higher-education graduates can find job opportunities more easily in the competitive sector. Large firms which have hierarchically structured internal job ladders tend not to hire women for the jobs linked to the higher positions. The job opportunities are more open to them in the competitive sector composed of smaller firms with less developed job ladders.

Length of service (job tenure). Table 9.5 lists the workers' average length of service by sector and sex. Workers in the concentrated sector have a longer length of service, on average, than workers in the competitive sector. In the concentrated sector, the internal labour market is more developed and workers have more stable employment patterns than in the competitive sector. The difference between sectors is particularly large for men; for women it is fairly minor. Men's length of service is considerably longer on average than women's. See Tachibanaki (1984*a*) for further findings on length of service and lifetime employment.

9.4. DIFFERENTIAL TREATMENT OF WORKER CHARACTERISTICS IN THE LABOUR MARKET

To test how worker characteristics are treated differently between different groups in the labour market, we estimate the wage functions expressed as follows:

$$\ln(\text{WAGE}) = f(\text{ED, LS, SECTOR, SEX, OCCUP, AGE, SIZE}),$$

where the dependent variable is the natural logarithm of hourly wages. The explanatory variables are given in Table 9.6; few of these are new, since we use the *Wage Structure Survey* throughout the chapter.

Workers are classified by means of two-digit industrial classification, sex, occupation (blue-collar or white-collar), education (junior high school, senior high school, junior college, or university), and firm size (small, medium, or large). Length of service and wages are the sample mean values for the group of workers; see Tachibanaki (1975; 1982) for more details. While length of service and wages are continuous variables, the others are all dichotomous variables. Each group of workers is treated as a unit of observation;

TABLE 9.6. *List of variables*

Variable		Explanation
Education	JHS	JHS = 1 if a worker has a junior high-school degree, JHS = 0 otherwise
	SHS	Variable (reference group: workers with senior high-school education)
	COL	COL = 1 if a worker has a Junior college degree, COL = 0 otherwise
	UNIV	UNIV = 1 if a worker has a university degree, UNIV = 0 otherwise
Length of service	LS	Length of service in years
	(LS)²	The square of LS is included to take into account the fact that the wage growth path is quadratic
Sector	SEC	SEC = 1 if a worker works in the non-competitive sector
		SEC = 0 if a worker works in the competitive sector
Sex	SEX	SEX = 1 for male, SEX = 0 for female
Occupation	BW	BW = 1 for white-collar, BW = 0 for blue-collar
Age	AGE 17	A17 = 1 if a worker is 17 or under; A17 = 0 otherwise
	18	A18 = 1 if a worker is 18.9; A18 = 0 otherwise
	20	A20 = 1 if a worker is 20/24; A20 = 0 otherwise
	25	A25 = 1 if a worker is 25–9; A25 = 0 otherwise
	30	Variable (reference group: workers aged 30–4)
	35	A35 = 1 if a worker is 35–9; A35 = 0 otherwise
	40	A40 = 1 if a worker is 40–4; A40 = 0 otherwise
	45	A45 = 1 if a worker is 45–9; A45 = 0 otherwise
	50	A50 = 1 if a worker is 50–4; A50 = 0 otherwise
	55	A55 = 1 if a worker is 55–9; A55 = 0 otherwise
	60	A60 = 1 if a worker is 60–4; A60 = 0 otherwise
	65	A65 = 1 if a worker is 65 or over; A65 = 0 otherwise
Firm size	SIZEL	SIZEL = 1 for large firm; SIZEL = 0 otherwise
	SIZEM	SIZEM = 1 for medium-size firm; SIZEM = 0 otherwise
	SIZES	Variable (reference group: small firm)

then each group of observations classified by the variables is weighted by the number of workers within each group to take account of the variation in the size of the group. This implies that we apply weighted least squares rather than simple least squares as in Chapter 3.

The explanatory variables fall into two groups. The first group consists of human capital variables, namely education and length of service (i.e. job tenure), which indicate general and specific human capital (or training). The second group comprises structural variables or segmentation variables which, we believe, operate to differentiate workers in the labour market; they include sector, sex, occupation, age, and firm size. Three regression analyses are performed on the whole population, which are based on human capital variables, structural variables, and the composite of the two. The results are shown in Table 9.7. All the models have high values of R^2.

Of the human-capital variables, length of service alone accounts for 56.8 per cent of the variance of the dependent variable (wage), while education alone explains 13.3 per cent. This suggests that length of service is an important explainer of wage differentials. Among the structural variables which are used for grouping workers, sex has the largest coefficient, whereas sector has a rather small value. Similar results were obtained by Shimada (1981) and Tachibanaki (1975; 1982).

The above result, however, does not tell us how the labour market treats worker characteristics differently between different groups. In order to deal with this problem, regression analysis is performed separately on each of the eight sector/sex/occupation groups, using the composite regression model of ln (WAGE) = f (ED, LS, AGE, SIZE). The results are shown in Table 9.8. Each coefficient can be interpreted as the weight given to that variable in explaining the wages of each group.

Since the logarithm of wages is used as the dependent variable, direct interpretations of coefficients in terms of yen are impossible. To make the comparison easier, the coefficients are converted to be *multiplicative with regard to the reference group (left-out variable)*.[3]

---

[3] The exponentiation of the coefficients is performed by using the following formula:

TABLE 9.7. Comparison of human capital model, structural model, and composite model [a]

Variable	Human capital model ln(wage) = f(LS, ED)	Structural model ln(wage) = f(SEC, SEX, OCCUP, AGE, SIZE)	Composite model ln(wage) = f(LS, ED, SEC, SEX, OCCUP, AGE, SIZE)
(R^2)	(0.777)	(0.754)	(0.879)
Intercept	6.264	6.323	5.975
LS	0.0990		0.0957
$(LS)^2$	−0.00167		−0.0018
JHS	−0.238		−0.109
COL	0.183		0.204
UNIV	0.382		0.289
SECTOR		0.018	0.018
SEX		0.406	0.213
OCCUP		0.249	0.130
AGE 17		−0.655	−0.096
18		−0.574	−0.023
20		−0.317	0.035
25		−0.154	0.014
35		0.101	−0.017
40		0.132	−0.047
45		0.146	−0.074
50		0.143	−0.088
55		0.028	−0.133
60		−0.123	−0.205
65		−0.200	−0.343
SIZEL		0.429	0.175
SIZEM		0.191	0.077

[a] The coefficients are all significant at 1% level.

$$\ln\left(\text{hourly wage}\right) = \exp\left(\alpha + \Sigma \beta_i\, x_i\right)$$

where α is the intercept and β_i are the coefficients for the variable x_i. For the dichotomous variable x_i,

$$\text{if } x_k = 0, \text{ then } \exp(\ ) = 1$$
$$\text{if } x_k = 1, \text{ then } \exp(\ ) = \exp(\beta k)$$

TABLE 9.8. Regression coefficients of log of hourly wage by sector, sex, and occupation[a]

Variables	Blue-collar				White-collar			
	Female		Male		Female		Male	
	C[b]	N[b]	C	N	C	N	C	N
Intercept	5.913	5.885	6.691	6.593	5.781	6.317	6.413	6.448
ED JHS	-0.083	-0.080	-0.074	-0.078	0.039	-0.170	-0.183	-0.126
COL					0.255	0.180	0.152	0.188
UNIV					0.408	0.167	0.297	0.315
LS	0.06715	0.08719	0.02786	0.04274	0.15376	0.03902	0.08561	0.08048
(LS)²	-0.00065	-0.00177	0.0000*	-0.00051	-0.00357	-0.00082	-0.00154	-0.00147
AGE 17	-0.008*	0.083	-0.594	-0.475	0.059	-0.152	-0.312	-0.204
18	0.048	0.115	-0.464	-0.357	0.236	-0.329	-0.270	-0.153
20	0.089	0.153	-0.236	-0.159	0.215	-0.082	-0.164	-0.064
25	0.041	0.066	-0.072	-0.067	0.116	0.007	-0.061	-0.016
35	-0.024	-0.021	0.020	0.028	-0.070	0.042	0.008	0.216
40	-0.058	-0.054	-0.013	0.022	-0.153	0.100	0.007	0.017
45	-0.090	-0.107	-0.062	-0.001*	-0.207	0.180	0.003	0.012
50	-0.159	-0.172	-0.114	-0.045	-0.329	0.189	0.009	0.057
55	-0.240	-0.256	-0.184	-0.119	-0.422	0.179	-0.001	0.028
60	-0.318	-0.344	-0.289	-0.250	-0.520	0.147	-0.093	-0.057
65	-0.420	-0.495	-0.387	-0.365	-0.741	0.002	-0.250	-0.221
SIZEL	0.172	0.337	0.224	0.263	0.181	0.463	0.146	0.085
SIZEM	0.094	0.152	0.086	0.120	0.106	0.254	0.062	0.018
R²	0.588	0.880	0.874	0.941	0.736	0.849	0.922	0.856
Mean of log of hourly wage (yen)	6.235	6.407	6.837	7.047	6.604	6.843	7.092	7.250
	(510)	(606)	(932)	(1,149)	(738)	(937)	(1,129)	(1,408)

[a] All coefficients are significant at 1% level. The exceptions are marked *.
[b] C = competitive; N = non-competitive (concentrated).

Take firm size as an example. The reference group is workers in small firms. The coefficient for female blue-collar workers working in a medium-size firm in the competitive sector is 0.094. This means that their hourly wage is 1.099 ($e^{0.094}$) times the female wage in small firms, when all other characteristics are held constant. Therefore, if the hourly wage in small firms is indexed as 1.0, then the wage in medium-size firms is 1.099.

The results of the conversion of all the variable coefficients are shown in Fig. 9.1. The slope of the line does not show the final level of wage, but it shows the differences *vis-à-vis* the reference group in the multiplicative term.[4]

We shall now discuss how the relative return for each variable differs by sector/sex/occupation group in terms of wage determination.

9.4.1. Education

Senior high-school graduates are the reference group (indexed as 1.0) for this variable. The higher the education, the higher the wages for all groups, except for white-collar women with junior high-school education in the competitive sector.

Among blue-collar workers, junior high-school graduates earn about 8 per cent less than senior high-school graduates of the same group. The shortage of blue-collar workers, particularly at the junior high-school level, due to the high enrolment in senior high school explains the slight disadvantage of the junior high school relative to the senior school degree among blue-collar workers.

For white-collar workers, the disadvantage of the junior high-school diploma and the advantage of the university diploma

---

[4] To make this point clear, let us take a concrete example. Female blue-collar workers in the competitive sector whose wage is equal to the value of intercept as described above earn 370 yen ($e^{5.913}$) on average. Female blue-collar workers with the same characteristics, but working in medium-size instead of small firms, earn 406 yen (370 × 1.099). On the other hand, male blue-collar workers with the same characteristics and working in small firms in that sector earn 805 yen ($e^{6.691}$). Since the coefficient for the medium-size firm is 0.086 ($e^{0.086}$ = 1.090), males in the medium-size firm earn 877 yen (805 × 1.090). What the slopes in the graph compare is the value of converted coefficients, which are 1.099 for the female blue-collar workers and 1.090 for the male blue-collar workers in this case. The actual levels of wages are not considered. *Relative return or advantage* of working in a medium-size firm compared to a small firms is large for the females than for the males, although the wage is higher for the males than for the females.

vis-à-vis the senior high-school diploma vary considerably between groups. Disadvantages of having only a junior high-school diploma are greater for white-collar than for blue-collar workers; the only exception is the case of white-collar females in the competitive sector; but their gain relative to senior high-school graduates is very small. A possible explanation for this is the following: as we saw in the previous section, the most important source of female labour in this sector is junior high-school graduates. They may be in high demand in this sector, which would have raised their wages close to the level for senior high school graduates.

The advantage of a higher education degree over a senior high-school degree is greatest for women in the competitive sector and smallest for women in the concentrated sector. We saw also earlier that 81 per cent of females with higher education are employed in the competitive sector, as against 19 per cent in the concentrated sector. These results imply that the concentrated sector offers women with higher education very limited job opportunities, and relatively small returns on their education. The competitive sector, in contrast, offers the major job opportunities and also a greater return on their education. A greater demand for female employees in this sector might be the main reason for the favourable payoff for higher education.

The sectoral difference is smaller for men than for women. The competitive sector employs a larger percentage of male higher-education graduates than the concentrated sector (60 per cent against 40 per cent), but the advantage of higher education is greater in the concentrated sector than in the competitive sector. This is not the case for women.

9.4.2 Length of Service (or Job Tenure)

Length of service is highly rewarded for all groups, but the degree of reward varies by sector, sex, and occupation.

Among blue-collar groups, the two female groups have greater relative return on seniority than the two male groups. Sectoral differences within the same sex groups are minor. White-collar groups show very different patterns from blue-collar groups. Relative return on seniority is greatest for women in the competitive sector and smallest for women in the concentrated sector. Between the two extremes of the female groups, the male groups show little sectoral difference. This observation is similar to the case of education.

The finding that relative return on seniority is greater for women than for men (except for white-collar women in the concentrated sector) is a surprise. The average lengths of service are 5.4 and 6.8 years for women and 8.7 and 13.2 years for men (see Table 9.5). The proportion of workers who have remained in the same firm is much smaller for women than for men, as pointed out by Tachibanaki (1984a). This means that many women quit their jobs before they accumulate length of service and benefit from it. But since an increase in age counteracts the effect of length of service (see below), it is necessary to consider the effect of length of service and age together.

9.4.3. Age

The 30–34 age category is taken as the reference group, indexed as 1.0. For female blue-collar workers in both sectors, youth is highly rewarded and older ages are disadvantaged. On the other hand, for male blue-collar workers in both sectors, youth is at the great disadvantage, and wage decline with age is smaller than for women. Sectoral differences between the two same-sex groups are minor. Among white-collar workers, as in the cases of education and length of service, the two female groups show extreme cases, and between these two the male groups show small sectoral differences. For white-collar women in the competitive sector, being young is a great advantage and disadvantage increases with age. For the other three groups, youth is a disadvantage and old age does not imply disadvantage. In particular, women in the concentrated sector enjoy advantages with increased age.

One of the characteristics of the Japanese wage system is said to be a steep rise in wage with worker's age. There is a controversy about the nature of such a system: paternalism based on the Japanese sociocultural tradition as against economic rationality in accommodating the economic situation of the time (see Chapter 3).[5] Our regression estimates reveal that increased age contributes

---

[5] Abegglen (1958: 54) writes: 'The pay system rests on the base-pay formula which is not seen by the kind of work done, the performed efficiency, or the worker's capacity. Base pay is a function of age and education . . . and further increments to the base pay are primarily a function of length of service.' The importance of age in

to wage increases for male workers, but is a negative factor for most female workers. Since an important proportion of workers stay a long time in the same firm, length of service is accumulated with age; consequently, Japanese wages still seem to be highly age-related. However, when age and length of service are analysed separately, holding other variables constant, length of service turns out to be a far more important contribution to wage increase than age. If it can be correctly assumed that skill acquired by working in a firm is specific to that firm and largely non-transferable to other firms, then length of service is a good measure of skill. Therefore, the finding that length of service is more important than age in wage increase seems to be judged as economic rationality.[6]

9.4.4. Firm Size

The larger the firm size, the higher the wage for all groups. The degree of advantage, however, differs largely among groups. Women from both types of occupation in the concentrated sector gain an important advantage by working in larger firms; white-collar women, who receive the smallest advantages from higher education and accumulation of length of service, gain the greatest advantage by working in larger firms.

It is interesting to see that inter-scale differences are relatively small for the other three white-collar groups, particularly for males in the concentrated sector, since inter-scale wage differentials have

---

wage determination is often described as the paternalistic aspect of the Japanese wage system. Taira (1970: 184) contends that the the apparently age-related wage was brought about by trade unionsocioeconomic insistence during hardship of the immediate post-war period: the concept of a 'living wage' was derived from the need for survival. In particular, the *Densan-gata* wage system proposed by the electrical industry workers' union in 1946 initiated a wage formulation in which the 'living wage' component was an important portion. A recent study (Tachibanaki, 1992*a*) nevertheless suggests that the kind of work done, the efficiency of performance, and the contribution of an employee are taken into account more significantly than the past in the determination of wages.

[6] Tachibanaki (1975) gave the findings which differ from this finding that length of service, i.e. job tenure, is a major contributor to the wage increase, but age is not. This difference may be due partly to the difference in statistical methods. Tachibanaki uses the analysis of variance, and a unit of analysis is a group of workers who have the same characteristics in terms of sex, occupation (blue-collar or white-collar), educational level, age, and firm size. A variation in the size of groups is ignored. This study uses regression analysis, and although a unit of analysis is the same, each unit is weighted by the number of workers within a group.

been regarded as one of the most important sources of wage differentials in the traditional dualistic view of the Japanese labour market. When the sector is used as a grouping variable and separate regressions are performed on different groups, these results show a great reduction in the inter-scale difference within the group (compare the coefficients for firm size in the structural model and the composite model, Table 9.7).

The above results imply, for example, that small firms in the concentrated sector and in the competitive sector treat worker characteristics differently, while small and large firms in the concentrated sector treat them rather similarly. There is another segmentation of the labour market due to industries which are classified by market power, and this segmentation sometimes reduces the power of inter-scale differentials to a certain extent.

9.4.5. SUMMARY

It is concluded that worker characteristics are treated differently by sector, sex, and occupation. The detailed explanations are as follows. Among blue-collar groups, whereas return on education is almost the same for all groups, treatment of length of service (i.e. job tenure) and age in the labour market are significantly different for women and men. Sex plays a major role in differentiation; in contrast, the role of the sector is small. Among white-collar groups, sex is again an important differentiating parameter. Sector has very different meanings for women and men. Whereas sectoral location produces little difference among men, it does divide women between the two extremes.

The finding that returns on higher education and length of service, i.e. two human-capital variables, are greatest for women in the competitive sector is a surprise. However, this does not necessarily mean that their wage level is the highest. The above discussion is not concerned with the *absolute* level of wages. We saw earlier that the average wage (converted from the mean of the logarithm hourly wage) is lower for women than for men, and lower in the competitive sector than in the concentrated sector. How can we explain these seemingly contradictory findings? Is it that, despite favourable treatment of their human capital in the labour market, the average wage of women in the competitive sector is the lowest because they have the smallest amount of human capital? We need to know the wage levels of different groups in absolute terms, estimate the magnitude of the differences, and search for the causes of the differences. The next section deals with this problem.

9.5. THE MEAN COST–BENEFIT OF SEX AND SECTOR

The question to be addressed here is how much of the difference in mean wage is due to differences in worker characteristics and how much to factors which are related, not to worker characteristics, but to the working of the labour market. To deal with this problem, we ask a question: how much would workers earn on average if they were working in a different sector or were of the opposite sex (adjusted mean wage)? The difference between the adjusted mean wage and the actual or observed mean wage can be regarded as the cost–benefit of sector/sex; using regression coefficients, we can simulate adjusted mean wage and compute the cost–benefit of sector/sex. Similar methods were used in Blinder (1973), Carnoy and Rumberger (1976), and Tolbert et al. (1980).

There is a problem of unexplained wage differentials. The following analysis is based on an assumption that an inclusion of additional variables would not bring about important changes. Among the variables in the regression equation, education, length of service, and age are the worker characteristics, while firm size is a sector characteristic. For this reason, worker characteristics and firm size need to be treated differently.

Take, as an example, a case in which female blue-collar workers in the competitive sector (FBC) would move into the concentrated sector. Two changes would occur: a change in treatment of worker characteristics in the labour market and a change in firm size composition. It is necessary to estimate the effects of these two separately; and this requires a two-step operation. If each mean of the regression variables for FBC is multiplied by the corresponding regression coefficient for FBC and the intercept and all the products are added up, the total indicates the mean of the logarithm of hourly wage that FBC actually earn; this is equivalent to 510 yen. If the same kind of operation is performed using the regression coefficients of worker characteristics for the female blue-collar workers in the concentrated sector (FBN), the result yields 541 yen. This is the hourly wage FBC would earn if their worker characteristics were treated in the same way as FBN. The difference of 31 yen (541–510) is the part of wage differential due to the difference in treatment of worker characteristics between the two sectors. To express it differently, this is the cost of discrimination by sector that FBC bear on average.

For the next step, both the means and the regression coefficients of firm-size variables for FBC are replaced by the values for FBN, and the same kind of operation is repeated. This result gives the wage FBC would earn if they worked in the concentrated sector under the actual distribution of firm sizes in the concentrated sector. As already seen, the concentrated sector has a higher proportion of large firms, and since the large firms offer higher wages, the average wage is increased. The result is 590 yen. The difference of 49 yen (590–541) is due to the difference in firm-size composition between the two sectors. The FBN actually earn 606 yen; therefore, the remaining difference of 16 yen (606–590) is due to the differences in worker characteristics between FBC and FBN.

To sum up, the total difference of 96 yen can be explained by three components: 16 yen due to the difference in worker characteristics, 31 yen due to the difference in treatment of worker characteristics, and 49 yen due to the difference in firm-size composition. The second component can be regarded as the average hourly cost of sectoral discrimination of FBC. The differential firm-size composition and treatment of characteristics in the labour market are fundamentally different in nature from the first component; they are not related to workers, but stem from the working of the labour market. The total of these two is the cost for FBC of working in the competitive sector instead of the concentrated sector.

Table 9.9 lists the results. For each group of workers, the total wage differential by sector and its breakdown into three components are shown on the left-hand side of the table, and the total wage differential by sex and its breakdown into three components on the right-hand side. The three components are (1) amount due to the difference in worker characteristics, (2) amount due to the differential treatment of worker characteristics (cost–benefit of

Effects of Discrimination and Industry Segmentation

TABLE 9.9(a). *Total wage differential by sector and sex, and cost–benefit of discrimination: blue-collar workers—yen, (%)*[a]

Group of workers	Wage differential by sector			Wage differential by sex		
	Total	Component		Total	Component	
FBC	−96	(1) −16 (17) (2) −31 (32) (3) −49 (51)	−80 (83)	−422	(1) −91 (22) (2) −329 (78) (3) 2 (0)	−331 (78)
FBN	96	(1) 14 (15) (2) 18 (19) (3) 64 (67)	82 (85)	−543	(1) −172 (32) (2) −350 (64) (3) −20 (4)	−372 (68)
MBC	−217	(1) −94 (43) (2) −19 (9) (3) −104 (48)	−123 (57)	422	(1) 75 (18) (2) 344 (81) (3) 3 (1)	347 (82)
MBN	217	(1) 81 (37) (2) 25 (12) (3) 110 (51)	136 (63)	543	(1) 167 (31) (2) 360 (66) (3) 16 (3)	376 (69)

[a] Total wage differential is divided into three components: (1) amount due to the difference in worker characteristics; (2) amount due to the differential treatment of worker characteristics (cost–benefit of discrimination); and (3) amount due to the difference in firm size composition. The percentages of each of the three components are written in parentheses. The sum (2) + (3) indicates the amount due to the market structure, that is, the total cost–benefit of sector/sex. A positive value indicates an advantage (benefit) to the group, and a negative value indicates a disadvantage (cost) to the group. Figures in parentheses are percentages.

TABLE 9.9(b). *Total wage differential by sector and sex, and cost–benefit of discrimination: white-collar workers—yen, (%)*[a]

Group of workers	Wage differential by sector			Wage differential by sex		
	Total	Component		Total	Component	
FWC	−199	(1) −45 (23) (2) 50 (−25) (3) −204 (103)	−154 (77)	−463	(1) −365 (79) (2) −108 (23) (3) 10 (−2)	−98 (21)
FWN	199	(1) 59 (30) (2) −134 (−69) (3) 274 (138)	140 (70)	−471	(1) −417 (89) (2) −406 (86) (3) 352 (−75)	−54 (11)
MWC	−207	(1) −145 (70) (2) −59 (29) (3) −3 (1)	−62 (30)	463	(1) 305 (66) (2) 170 (37) (3) −12 (−3)	158 (34)
MWN	207	(1) 161 (78) (2) 43 (21) (3) 3 (1)	46 (22)	471	(1) 208 (44) (2) 563 (120) (3) −300 (−64)	263 (56)

[a] See note to Table 9.9(a).

discrimination), and (3) amount due to the difference in firm-size composition. Let us start with the blue-collar workers.

1. Wage differential by sex is far more important than wage differential by sector.

2. The major part of wage differential, whether by sector or sex, is due to the working of the labour market; only a small proportion of *wage differential* is due to differences in worker characteristics.

3. There are, however, clear differences in the components between wage differentials by sex and by sector. Wage differentials by sex are due mostly to the differential treatment of worker characteristics, in other words, discrimination. Firm-size component is not an important cause. Both female groups bear 330–50 yen hourly as the cost of sex discrimination. When their mean hourly wages are 510 and 539 yen respectively, the cost of discrimination is all too clear. Both male groups receive almost the same amount of extra gain as the benefit of sex discrimination.

4. The different composition of firm size is the most important determinant of wage differential by sector, and the differential treatment of worker characteristics is not important (this was one of the conclusions in Chapter 5). Thus, although we applied different methods, we obtained the same result.

For white-collar workers:

1. As for white-collar workers, wage differential by sex is much more important than the sectoral differential. The causes, however, of wage differentials are different compared with the case of blue-collar workers.

2. The major part of wage differentials by sex is explained by the differences in worker characteristics. We saw earlier that there are substantial differences in length of service between women and men (see Table 9.5), and length of service is the most important element for wage increase. This explains the importance of the worker characteristics in explaining wage differentials.

The only exception to this is the extra gain male white-collar workers in the concentrated sector (MWN) receive with regard to FWN. This is because of the extremely low return on length of service for FWN, which raises the weight of the component related to the treatment of worker characteristics.

Yet neither cost of discrimination for females nor the benefit of discrimination for males is small. The effects of discrimination and that of firm size are inverse, offsetting each other; as a result, the final effect of the working of the labour market is reduced. In particular, FNW bear 406 yen as the average cost of discrimination, whereas MWN benefit 563 yen from discrimination. But the firm size component works in favour of FWN, offsetting a large portion of the cost of discrimination, owing to the greatest return for FWN on working in larger firms (see Fig. 9.1). Consequently, the importance of labour market structure in explaining wage differentials is reduced.

3. The sectoral wage difference between the female groups is mostly due to the labour market structure. As far as the treatment of worker characteristics is concerned, women are better off in the competitive than in the concentrated sector. Nevertheless, FWN have a higher average wage than FWC because of the firm-size component, which works in favour of FWN.

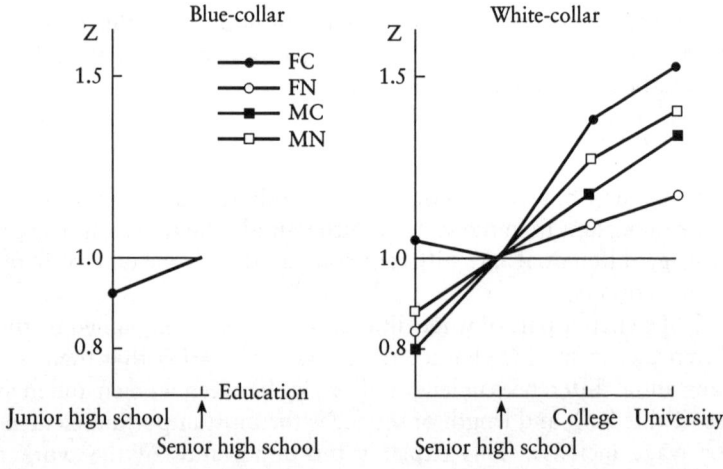

FIG. 9.1. Exponentiated regression coefficients indexed to the reference group: (a) education (reference group: senior high-school graduates); (b) length of service (years) (reference group: workers with zero length of service); (c) age (reference group: age 30–4); (d) firm size (reference group: small firm). (Z = exponentiated regression coefficients indexed to the reference group: F = female; M = male; C = competitive industry; N = non-competitive industry.)

Effects of Discrimination and Industry Segmentation

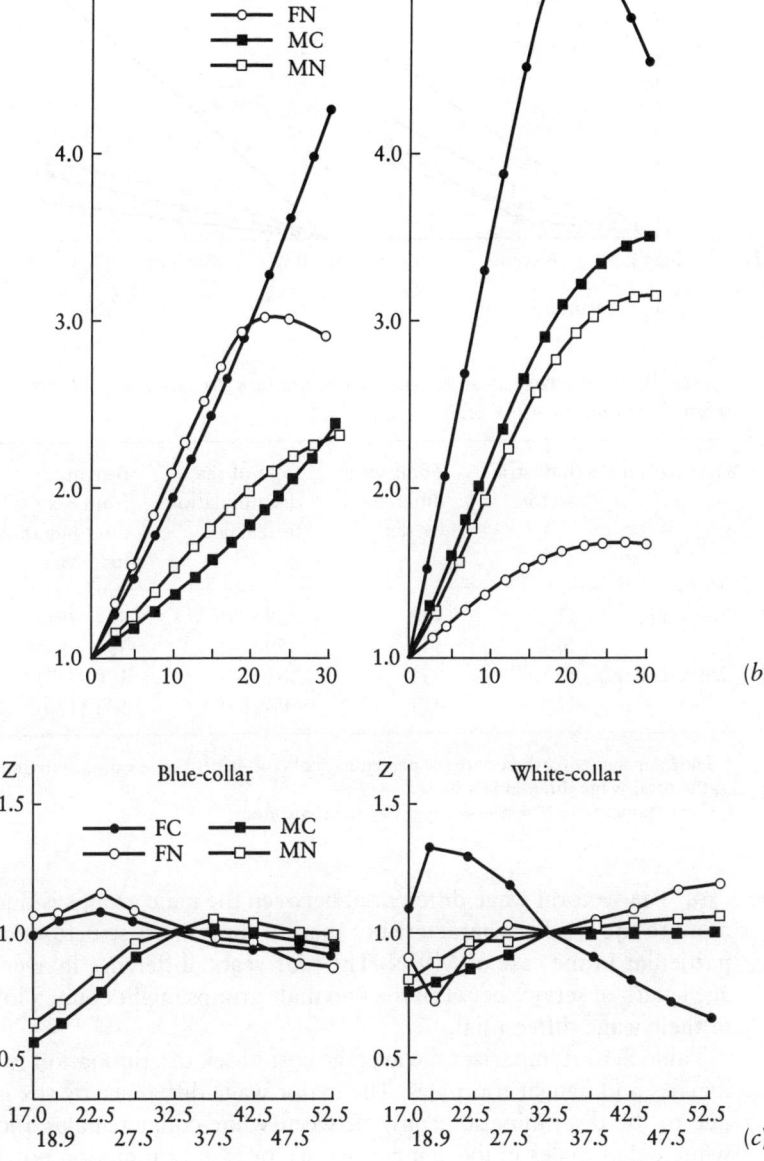

FIG. 9.1. Continued

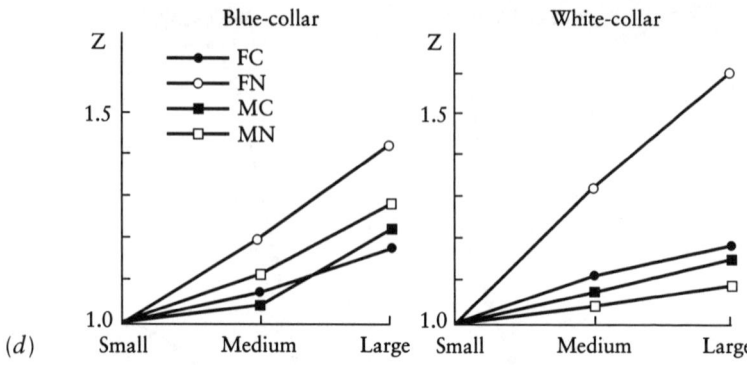

(d)

FIG. 9.1. Continued

TABLE 9.10. *Average cost of sex discrimination to females and benefit from discrimination for males—yen, (%)*[a]

Occupation	Industrial sector	Total wage differential by sex	Cost of sex discrimination to females	Benefit from sex discrimination for males
Blue-collar	C[b]	422	329 (78)[a]	344 (81)
	N	543	350 (64)	360 (66)
White-collar	C	391	108 (23)	170 (37)
	N	471	406 (86)	563 (120)

[a] The figures in parentheses are the percentages of cost–benefit of sex discrimination in the total wage differentials by sex.
[b] C = Competitive; N = non-competitive (concentrated).

4. The sectoral wage differential between the male groups is due more to the worker characteristics than to the market structure, in particular in the case of MWN. The four years' difference in average length of service between the two male groups might count a lot in their wage differential.

Table 9.10 summarizes the average cost of sex discrimination for females and benefit for males. The major wage difference by sex is due to the discrimination; only between white-collar females and white-collar males in the competitive sector is discrimination not a major cause of wage differential.

9.6. POLICY IMPLICATIONS

We examine to what extent changing workers' human capital, in particular workers' educational level, can reduce the existing wage differential. If the wage differentials are due mainly to the market structure, changing worker characteristics would not help to reduce the wage differentials. On the contrary, if the wage differentials are due mainly to the differences in worker characteristics, then changing worker characteristics can be expected to produce an equalizing effect.

Using the regression coefficients, we calculate the wage increase female workers would gain if they had the same amount of education or length of service as their male counterparts in the same sector, assuming that workers' other characteristics and the market conditions remained the same. Although such an assumption may be too simplistic in a sense, this method allows us roughly to evaluate equalization policies.

Table 9.11 shows the total wage differential by sex within each sector, and the amount of wage increase which might be brought about by equalizing female workers' educational level or length of service to that of male workers. It must be noted, however, that

TABLE 9.11. *Expected amount of reduction in wage differentials by sex, by equalizing education or length of service—yen, (%)*[a]

Differential by sex			Expected amount of reduction in wage	
Occupation	Industrial sector	Total wage differential by sex	By equalization of educational level	By equalization of length of service
Blue-collar	C[b]	422	5 (1)	71 (17)
	N	543	6 (1)	145 (27)
White-collar	C	463	52 (11)	297 (64)
	N	471	6 (1)	116 (25)

[a] Equalization of educational level or length of service means equalization of female workers' educational level or length of service to that of the male level in the same sector. The figures in parentheses show the percentage reduction in total wage differentials by sex.
[b] C = competitive; N = non-competitive (concentrated).

equalization of length of service is not a practical tool; in reality, only equalization of educational level would be conceivable and practicable. For blue-collar females in both sectors and white-collar females in the concentrated sector, we find that educational equalization to the male level would have only a negligible effect in reducing the wage differentials. Equalization of length of service to the male level would be more effective; yet even this would not reduce wage differentials by more than 30 per cent. For white-collar females in the competitive sector, equalization of their educational level to that of male counterparts would have a slightly more important effect, reducing 11 per cent of the total wage differential. Equalization of their length of service would further reduce a great part of their wage differentials. Equalization of both their education and length of service would eliminate 75 per cent of the actual wage differential by sex in the competitive sector.

In brief, since wage differentials by sex are mostly rooted in the market structure (differential treatment of worker characteristics and firm-size component), changing workers' human capital would not greatly reduce the wage differentials. Only in the case of female white-collar workers in the competitive sector would changing their human capital result in an important equalization of wages. A policy of educational equalization based on the assumption that human capital is equally rewarded among individuals, would be ineffective for wage equalization, as the differential reward to human capital itself is a more important cause of wage differentials in most cases. One of the reasons for this failure is that the increase in the potential female labour force resulted in the marginalization of female workers such as part-timers and temporary workers, rather than the improvement of their wages, despite increased human capital stock of females. Equal employment opportunity, equal promotion, equal wage (the equal treatment of worker characteristics) are more important than equal education and training for equalization.

It may be useful to provide a brief survey of the USA regarding the effect of discrimination against women. Blinder (1973) attributed 66 per cent to discrimination, and Corcoran and Duncan (1979) 56 per cent, in explaining wage differentials by sex. There is some evidence suggesting that this proportion has declined slightly in recent years in the USA, as shown by Gunderson (1989). In sum,

Japan has a stronger effect of sex discrimination than the USA, and needs affirmative action to reduce this gap.

9.7. CONCLUSION

This chapter has investigated Japanese wage differentials based on the industrial division; the labour market was examined for two sectors: the competitive sector and the concentrated sector. The effects of female/male difference, of human capital, and of occupation (blue-collar versus white-collar) also were examined. By applying several quantitative methods, it was found that worker characteristics such as education, length of service, and age were treated differently by sector, sex, and occupation. Also, wage differentials by sex were mostly rooted in differential treatment (discrimination) of worker characteristics, while wage differentials by sector were explained largely by the firm-size component. A somewhat similar result to the latter was obtained in Chapter 5. The above general results, however, are greatly modified by workers' occupations and industrial divisions. As a result, the current work suggests the importance of industrial division by market power in the analysis of wage determinations and the labour market, and confirms the prevailing discrimination against women in Japan. Finally, this chapter considered some policy implications for reducing wage differentials by sex.

10

Earnings Distribution and Inequality Over Time: Education versus Relative Position and Cohort

10.1. INTRODUCTION

Economists are usually dissatisfied with income distribution data collected at one point in time for individuals who have obviously different ages and experiences; the study of income and earnings distribution in a lifetime perspective is more desirable. If individual data of the entire history of income streams from birth to death (or at least from the beginning to the end of an individual's work history) were available, economists would be able to enquire fully into the lifetime earnings distribution; but it is nearly impossible to find such data, as Rosen (1977) notes.

This study explores the *male* earnings distribution over time for Japan, where data limitation is as usual in the sense that there are no panel data. We had to impose several assumptions to make the study feasible. However, as will be shown later, the assumptions are not so unrealistic in view of the Japanese social and economic system; the results obtained in this study describe realistic stories fairly well.

The data in this study can be briefly described. The *Wage Structure Survey* published by the Ministry of Labour provides average earnings figures for age intervals of five years based on three education levels each year. This data source has been frequently used in this book. Very fortunately, the data published in 1961 and 1976 give fairly comprehensive earnings distributions for each age class. In sum, the data source is a very reliable basis for a study of earnings over time. We use those two years' distributions and the each year's average earnings.

Two methodologies and tools can be applied to the study of

income and earnings over time. The first one is the estimated lifetime earnings along various 'age profiles' of percentiles of the annual distribution; the second is the process of mobility and/or lifetime inequality. We provide results based on both in this study. The two adopt different behavioural assumptions. First, the study of lifetime earnings assumes normally that income mobility does not exist; note, however, that we actually allow for small degree of inter-class mobility in this study. Second, the study of lifetime inequality explicitly assumes the existence of mobility. The first question will be discussed mainly in section 10.3(*b*), and the second will be discussed mainly in 10.3(*c*).

The study is organized as follows. Section 10.2 will present the motivation of this research, and the theoretical framework as well as the estimation procedures. The theoretical framework will explain the methodology in relation to Gibrat's and the Galtonian assumptions, and serial correlation are incorporated under the log-logistic distribution. Section 10.3 will present and discuss the empirical results estimated.

10.2. THEORETICAL FRAMEWORK AND ESTIMATION PROCEDURE

Analysis of lifetime earnings and/or income dynamics over time can be classified largely in terms of two approaches, on the basis of the estimation procedures: the first may be called the British approach (e.g. Creedy, 1974; 1977; Hart, 1976*a*; 1976*b*; Creedy and Hart, 1979), while the second may be called the American approach (e.g. Hause, 1974; Lillard 1977; Parsons, 1978; Lillard and Weiss, 1978; 1979; Weiss and Lillard, 1978; Eden and Pakes, 1981). Although the two approaches overlap in some aspects, the distinction originates from the difference in available data: while the UK lacks panel data, the USA provides fruitful individual panel data. The present study stays basically within the British approach methodologically, because no individual panel data exist in Japan. A loss of interest in lifetime income studies has been observed recently among economists, for the following reasons. First, data problems are severe, even in the USA. Second, economists are currently interested in the decomposition of inequality. This does not necessarily deny the importance of studies of lifetime income.

The principal theoretical model developments and estimation procedures are explained in the main text.

Under the assumption of Gibrat's so-called 'law of proportionate effect', the variance σ_t^2 of x_{it} (log-earnings) is written as a linear function of time, t:

$$\sigma_t^2 = \sigma_0^2 + \sigma_\varepsilon^2 \cdot t \qquad (10.1)$$

where σ_0^2 is the variance of x_{it} at initial time and σ_ε^2 is the constant variance of stochastic component u_{it} for all t.

Considering the assumption of Galtonian 'regression towards the mean', equation (10.1) is modified as follows:

$$\sigma_t^2 = \beta^{2t}\sigma_0^2 + \left(\left(1-\beta^{2t}\right)/\left(1-\beta^2\right)\right)\sigma_\varepsilon^2 \qquad (10.2)$$

where β is the regression coefficient. See Hart and Prais (1956) and Creedy (1974; 1977) for equations (10.1) and (10.2).

So far the possibility of serial correlation in the stochastic component has been excluded. Creedy (1974; 1977) and Hart (1976a, 1976b) introduced first-order serial correlation (10.3) into equation (10.2) in the analysis of earnings dynamics, and Creedy (1974) derived the variance, equation (10.4) below, which is analogous to equation (10.2).

$$u_{it} = \rho\mu_{it+1} + \varepsilon_{it} \qquad (10.3)$$

where ρ is assumed to be the same for all individuals, and ε_{it} is distributed independently of previous values with constant variance σ_ε^2.

$$\sigma_t^2 = \beta^{2t}\sigma_0^2 + \sigma_\varepsilon^2 \sum_{j=1}^{t}\sum_{i=0}^{j}\beta^{2(t-i)}\rho^{2t} + \sigma_\varepsilon^2 \sum_{j=1}^{t-1}\sum_{i=j+1}^{t}\sum_{r=0}^{i}\beta^{2t-(i+j)}\rho^{2r-(i-j)}. \qquad (10.4)$$

Since equation (10.4), which is equal to equation (10.10) in Creedy (1974), is clearly intractable, Creedy considered a special case where $\beta = 1$ (i.e. Gibrat's case). As will be shown later, however, we try explicitly to use equation (10.4) to estimate each year's variances and σ_ε^2 under the given estimated values of β and ρ.

The estimation procedure of the variances σ_ε^2 in (10.2) and (10.4) adopted in this study, which represent (i) the Galtonian case and (ii) the Galtonian and serial correlation case respectively, is briefly explained. Two years' observations (1961 and 1976) of the variances σ_t^2 for each cohort satisfy (10.2) and (10.4). Thus the two unknowns, σ_0^2 and σ_ε^2, can be estimated by solving the simultaneous equations. The system of two equations and two unknowns produces a unique solution of σ_0^2 and σ_ε^2 for each (10.2) and (10.4).

So far no assumptions have been imposed on the distribution function of earnings variables. Assuming that earnings for each age group are log-normally distributed, Creedy (1974; 1977) derived the formula for the coefficient of variation over time, and provided us with impressive empirical results. As is shown in Atoda *et al.* (1988), Japanese data do not necessarily support the log-normality assumption, but rather indicate that the earnings distribution by earning class shows a better result given by a log-logistic distribution.[1] See Johnson and Kotz (1970) for the log-logistic distribution. This is a crucial observation, and it forced us to depart from the British methodology in which the log-normal distribution in earnings was assumed. The log-normal and log-logistic distributions are, in a way, similar to each other, because their log-transformed observations are distributed symmetrically. However, their shapes and, in particular, their mathematical density functions differ. In sum, the theoretical model developments in this study try to explore the inequality of earnings over time under the log-logistic condition; we investigate it also under the log-normal condition.[2]

The coefficient of variation of lifetime income (Y) over time (T) is defined by

---

[1] The purpose of this study is not to enquire into the generating process of earnings distribution and the difference in functional forms by educational level, but to estimate the lifetime earnings inequality under a more plausible assumption of earnings distribution. Takahashi *et al.* (1959) uses the log-normal distribution for the Japanese income distribution. Since they do not attempt other distributions, one cannot conclude that the log-normal is the most appropriate distribution in Japan.

[2] To save space, the result based on the log-normal distribution is only briefly described here. See Aitchison and Brown (1958) for the log-normal distribution. Lifetime earnings at both the first and third quartiles of the log-normal function are considerably lower than those of the log-logistic function, while lifetime earnings at the second quartile are the same values. The difference in estimated coefficients of variation over time also reflects them quite firmly. In sum, although it is true that we do not find very different results, we do obtain significantly different results when the density functions in earnings are specified differently. Thus, it is crucial to adopt an appropriate density function when performing this kind of analysis. The estimated results of the log-normal function can be obtained from the author.

$$\eta(Y) = \sqrt{V(Y)} / \sum_{r=t}^{T} c_r E(y_r). \qquad (10.5)$$

where $V(Y)$ is the variance of earnings over time T, y_r is individual earnings at time r, and c_r is the discounting factor. The variance $V(Y)$ is written as follows:

$$V(Y) = \sum_{r=t}^{T} c_r^2 V(y_r) + 2 \sum_{r=t}^{T-1} \sum_{s=r+1}^{T} c_r c_s \operatorname{cov}(y_r, y_s) \quad \text{for } s > r \quad (10.6)$$

where $V(y_r)$ is the variance in the rth year, and $\operatorname{cov}(y_r, y_s)$ is the covariance between earnings in the rth year and sth year. $V(y_r)$ is given by

$$V(y_r) = \left[E(y_r)\right]^2 \left[(\tan k_r \pi)/k_r - 1\right] \qquad (10.7)$$

under the assumption of a log-logistic distribution. In addition, the mean $E(y_r)$ is given by

$$E(Y_r) = e^{\mu_r} \frac{k_r \pi}{\sin k_r \pi} = e^{\mu_r} \frac{\sqrt{3\sigma_r^2}}{\sin \sqrt{3\sigma_r^2}} \qquad (10.8)$$

Where y_r is distributed as log-logistic with mean $E(\ln y_r) = \mu_r$, variance $V(\ln y_r) = \sigma_r^2$ and $k_r \pi = \sqrt{3\sigma_r^2}$. Alternatively, the following relation can be used: $V(\ln y_r) = k_r^2 \pi^2 / 3$. By definition, $\operatorname{cov}(y_r, y_s)$ is given by

$$\operatorname{cov}(y_r, y_s) = E(y_r y_s) - E(y_r)E(y_s) \qquad (10.9)$$

It is necessary to calculate $E(y_r y_s)$ in order to evaluate (10.9). $E(y_r y_s)$ is obtained by finding out the arithmetic mean of the log-logistic distribution with parameters $E(x_r + x_s)$ and $V(x_r + x_s)$ which are given as follows:

$$E(x_r + x_s) = \mu_r + \mu_s \qquad (10.10)$$

$$V(x_r + x_s) = \sigma_{rs}^2 \qquad (10.11)$$

where

$$k_{rs} = \sqrt{3\sigma_{rs}^2}/\pi \qquad (10.12)$$

It is important to note that equation (10.11) is different in two alternative cases: (i) Galton and (ii) Galton and serial correlation. Using (10.7), we can derive $E(y_r y_s)$ as follows:

$$E(y_r, y_s) = e^{\mu r + \mu s} \frac{\sqrt{3\sigma_{rs}^2}}{\sin\sqrt{3\sigma_{rs}^2}} \qquad (10.13)$$

Equation (10.4) shows the formula of $\text{cov}(y_r, y_s)$ (equation (10.9)), which is derived by using equations (10.8) and (10.13).

$$\text{cov}(y_r, y_s) = e^{\mu r + \mu s} \left[\frac{\sqrt{3\sigma_{rs}^2}}{\sin\sqrt{3\sigma_{rs}^2}} - \frac{\sqrt{3\sigma_r^2} \cdot \sqrt{3\sigma_s^2}}{\sin\sqrt{3\sigma_r^2} \sin\sqrt{3\sigma_s^2}} \right] \qquad (10.14)$$

Replacing σ_{rs}^2 in (10.14) by equations (10.15) and (10.16) and putting the estimated $\text{cov}(y_r, y_s)$ into equation (10.6), we obtain the estimated variances $V(Y)$.

(i) Galtonian case:

$$\sigma_{rs}^2 = \left[1 + 2\beta^{(s-r)}\right]\sigma_r^2 + \sigma_s^2 \quad \text{for } s > r \qquad (10.15)$$

(ii) Galtonian case and serial correlation:

$$\sigma_{rs}^2 = \left[1 + 2\beta^{(s-r)}\right]\sigma_r^2 + \sigma_s^2 + 2\sigma_\varepsilon^2 \sum_{i=1}^{r} \sum_{j=k+1}^{s} \sum_{k=0}^{j} \beta^{(r-i)+(s-j)} \rho^{2k+j-1} \quad \text{for } s > r$$

$$(10.16)$$

Finally, it is easy to estimate the coefficients of variation over time given by equation (10.5) under the two alternative hypotheses because $V(Y)$ and $E(y_r)$ are now available. The empirical result is presented by Table 10.5.

A primary purpose of this work is to take account of the *estimated* serial correlation coefficients, instead of using hypothetical values for serial correlation, as was done by Creedy (1977), into the analysis of inequality over time. The estimation procedure can be briefly explained. A first-order serial correlation coefficient is given by equation (10.3). Combining (10.3) and the Galtonian equation, we obtain the following equation:

$$z_t = (\beta + \rho)z_{t-1} - \beta\rho z_{t-2} + \varepsilon_t \qquad (10.17)$$

where z_t is log-earnings at time t and ε_t is serially independent.

There may be a criticism against an $AR(1)$ process in u, Ideally, several alternative AR processes should be examined in order to obtain the least biased result. Since the Galton and serial model developed in this study is already complicated enough, it requires another piece of work which takes account of alternative AR processes rather than an AR (1) process. This is certainly a task for the future.

If cross-sectional individual data for three consecutive years were available, the OLS estimator would give asymptotically unbiased and meaningful results; however, it was necessary for us to substitute the time-series approach for the cross-sectional one simply because cross-sectional three-year data are unavailable. We used actually time-series data on average (Z_t), and adopted the Cochran and Orcutt method to minimize the bias of the estimated parameters which arises form using the long-run time-series data on average rather than consecutive cross-sectional data. One advantage of using long-run time-series data is the fact that they meet more suitably the assumption of the constancy of the regression coefficient during the period. This does not necessarily cancel the deficiency of the time-series data fully, because we have to believe that the coefficient on average would describe the whole story. If we were interested in investigating the influence of income mobility among individual persons, the use of average data would not be justified. In this study, the influence of income mobility is not our principal concern.

We have based our discussions on the earnings inequality over time, under the empirically supported condition that the density function of the earnings distribution remained log-logistic for a particular cohort over time. Under this presumption, it is possible to estimate the gross earnings of a person who stays in a particular position (say, the median or lower quartile) during the period. This is the task of the estimation of lifetime earnings.

For the log-logistic distribution, equation (10.18) shows the earning figure under the percentage (decile or quartile) point:

$$y = \exp\left\{\mu - k\ln\left[(1-\alpha)/\alpha\right]\right\} \qquad (10.18)$$

Equation (10.18) is easily obtained from the cumulative function of the log-logistic curve.

$$\alpha = \frac{1}{1+\exp\left[-(\ln y - \mu)/k\right]} \qquad (10.19)$$

Empirical estimations of earning figures under the given α are obtained by replacing k in (10.18) by the estimated value of k under the two alternative hypotheses: (i) Galtonian case and (ii) Galtonian and serial correlations. Specifically, the estimated value of k is derived from the relation $k\pi = \sqrt{3\sigma^2}$ under the log-logistic distribution and from the estimated variances given by (10.2) and (10.4) respectively under the two alternative hypotheses. Since the mathematical forms of the lifetime earnings are fairly messy but straightforward, we need not write them here. The empirical result is presented by Table 10.3.

10.3. EMPIRICAL RESULTS

10.3.1. Data and Preliminary Discussions

The data source was explained in the introduction to this chapter. Before undertaking the actual estimation, it was necessary to create consecutive annual average male earnings figures for each cohort so as to meet with our data requirement. We made an extensive job of preliminary interpolations to create earning figures for each age. We have chosen three educational levels to analyse income dynamics over time; junior high-school graduates (approximately 8–9 years of schooling); senior high-school graduates (11–12 years); and college and university graduates (14–16).[3] The chosen four cohorts for this analysis are given by birth years: 1924, 1929, 1934, and 1939. Finally, the figures are given in real terms. The nominal earnings were adjusted by the consumer price index.

10.3.2. Discussions of the Estimated Results

10.3.2.1. *Variances, Galtonian Coefficients, and Serial Correlations.* We begin our discussions with Table 10.1, which shows the actual variances of log-earnings by three educational levels of

---

[3] Although schooling years are slightly different within a graduation level, due in part to educational reform after the Second World War, this does not significantly affect the result for the following reasons: in Japan graduation level is considered much more important than schooling years; since we perform in principle a cohort analysis, the difference in schooling years in fact disappears.

TABLE 10.1. *Estimated variances of log-earnings by three educational levels and by four cohorts*

Birth cohort	Variances	Sample	Variances	Sample
1924	*Age 35–9*		*Age 50–4*	
Junior high school	0.7268	262,199	0.2443	281,140
Senior high school	0.6559	36,469	0.3293	76,880
College and university	0.4973	22,470	0.2648	23,620
1929	*Age 30–4*		*Age 45–9*	
Junior high school	0.6863	320,672	0.1887	356,600
Senior high school	0.6315	73,550	0.2437	135,050
College and university	0.4520	40,568	0.2106	44,860
1934	*Age 25–9*		*Age 40–4*	
Junior high school	0.6457	379,549	0.1541	401,960
Senior high school	0.5663	134,711	0.2437	223,640
College and university	0.4153	82,289	0.1714	86,730
1939	*Age 20–4*		*Age 35–40*	
Junior high school	0.6420	431,340	0.1330	391,320
Senior high school	0.5295	232,478	0.1312	341,610
College and university	0.2963	33,017	0.1269	123,620

the male labour force in 1961 and 1976. The most important finding in Table 10.1 is that the actual variances in male log-earnings decrease as age increases.[4] Since the decreases are observed for all cohorts and for all age ranges, the decreasing trend in the variances is a universal phenomenon in Japan, and one which is contrary to empirical observations in the UK. We can conceive of several reasons.

First, there has been a strong tendency towards equalization in earnings over time, promoted not only by modernization and democratization but also by rapid economic growth after the Second World War. Secondly, a tradition of age-related payment has been fostered by the paternalistic nature of society. An important

[4] We do not aim at considering the relationship between the variances in log-earnings and ages in the cross-sectional data, but in each cohort data. It may be necessary to build up another model which takes account of age, time, and cohort effects to analyse the difference of tendency in the variances between the cross-section data and cohort data.

part of wages is determined by a worker's age because firms feel that the family expenditure increases as a person becomes older (see Chapter 3). Finally, it is possible that an exogenous shift occurred not only in the distribution of earnings but also in the shape of the functions. Further serious analysis is required, however, to verify this point statistically. In sum, we accept the decreasing tendency in the variances as a general rule, which is not surprising at all.

The empirical result in Table 10.1, namely the decreasing tendency in variance, is apparently incompatible with equation (10.1) because the estimated σ_ε^2 are negative. The variance of u_{it} (or ε_{it}) should be positive. We conclude, therefore, that our data do not support the simple form of Gibrat's case. This suggests that we should pay attention to (10.2) and (10.4) rather than to (10.1).

The Galtonian case in Table 10.2 presents the estimated values of σ_ε^2 and β based on (10.2), and the Galton-serial case in the same table shows the estimated values of σ_ε^2, β and ρ based on (10.4) in combination with equation (10.3). Under the Galtonian hypothesis all the signs of the estimated σ_ε^2 are positive, as required a priori. Thus, we should accept equation (10.2) as a meaningful hypothesis.

The introduction of a serial correlation coefficient into the Galtonian hypothesis makes the estimated results somewhat vague in the two cases, namely junior high-school graduates of the 1934 and 1939 cohorts, because the negative values of σ_ε^2 have been obtained. There may be several interpretations of these negative values. First, since both 1934 and 1939 cohorts are younger, there may be an estimation bias. Both senior high and university graduates of 1934 and 1939 cohorts, however, produced positive values; thus this interpretation is not so persuasive. Secondly, it is possible to reject equation (10.4) as a meaningful hypothesis because of the negative estimated variances, provided that there is no estimation bias. In other words, the introduction of a serial correlation is redundant. We choose the second interpretation: that junior high-school graduates of the 1934 and 1939 cohorts do not follow the Galton-serial case, but do follow the Galton-only case; thus we do not report the Galton-serial case in Table 10.2.

Table 10.2 suggests that we should follow other observations. First, the estimated Galtonian coefficients are statistically significant. Also, they are not so different, not only across the two alternative hypotheses—Galton and Galton-serial—but also across

TABLE 10.2. *Estimated values of variances of the stochastic term, the Galtonian coefficient, and the serial correlation coefficient under the two alternative hypotheses*

Education parameters		Junior high			Senior high			university		
Cohort	Models	σ_ε^2	β	ρ	σ_ε^2	β	ρ	σ_ε^2	β	ρ
1924	Galton	0.0572	0.8707 (0.0141)		0.0721	0.8809 (0.0148)		0.0524	0.8922 (0.0144)	
	Galton-serial	0.0102	0.9192 (0.0236)	0.4565 (0.1681)	0.0258	0.9131 (0.0099)	0.3086 (0.1794)	0.0120	0.9336 (0.0200)	0.3815 (0.175)
1929	Galton	0.0347	0.8930 (0.0125)		0.0468	0.8927 (0.0139)		0.0174	0.9436 (0.0156)	
	Galton-serial	0.0043	0.9345 (0.0198)	0.4728 (0.1671)	0.0095	0.9330 (0.0198)	0.3953 (0.1734)	0.0048	0.9572 (0.0233)	0.3226 (0.1920)
1934	Galton	0.0118	0.9312 (0.0112)		0.0082	0.9516 (0.0120)		0.0139	0.9418 (0.0202)	
	Galton-serial				0.0033	0.9550 (0.0181)	0.2810 (0.2007)	0.0042	0.9433 (0.0388)	0.4543 (0.2046)
1939	Galton	0.0043	0.9404 (0.0112)		0.0085	0.9357 (0.0170)		0.0187	0.9145 (0.0312)	
	Galton-serial				0.0002	0.9529 (0.0325)	0.4857 (0.2067)	0.0031	0.9447 (0.0590)	0.4627 (0.2373)

Note. σ_ε^2: variances of stochastic term (Galtonian-serial case shows serially independent stochastic term); β: Galtonian coefficient; ρ: serial correlation coefficient. Numbers in parentheses are estimated standard errors.

the three educational levels. Slightly different Galtonian coefficients were obtained across the four cohorts. On average the values are about 0.9, which suggests that Galtonian regression towards he mean takes place gradually. When individual error components had been introduced into the model, as was done by Lillard and Weiss (1979), the result would have been somewhat different from the current one with respect to the implication of β; we await panel data to verify this. Secondly, the serial correlation coefficients differ marginally, not only across education levels but also across cohorts. The highest coefficient, 0.5911, is observed for the 1939 senior high-school cohort, while the lowest, 0.2810, is observed for the 1934 senior high-school cohort. It is important, however, to note that almost all the coefficients are statistically significant, and that they are positive. This signifies that the mechanism 'success breeds success' is a general phenomenon in Japan, which is again in contrast to the British case (see Hart, 1976a; 1976b; Creedy and Hart, 1979).

10.3.2.2. Lifetime Earnings Figures. The next task is to estimate the male lifetime earnings figures under our model framework. Table 10.3 shows the estimated lifetime earnings for various combinations of educational level, cohort, discount rate, and quartile level. The following remarks may help the reader understand Table 10.3.

First, labour market experiences obviously differ not only from cohort to cohort but also from educational level to educational level, because of various starting ages of work. The numbers in Table 10.4 show the lengths of work history for various combinations of educational level and of cohort. The comparable cohort is 1924, since it has 30 years' work history for all educational levels. Although 30 years' work history for junior and senior high graduates is common for cohorts 1924 and 1929, their observation ages are somewhat different because of data availability. In other words, earnings for cohort 1924 are adopted during the relatively older ages, while earnings for cohort 1929 are adopted during the relatively younger ages. This difference in the observation ages is likely to produce the finding that the 30 years' income for the 1929 cohort is lower than that for the 1924 cohort, even if the growth rate of productivity is positive. Thus it is impossible to compare the lifetime earnings across cohorts, despite the fact that junior and

TABLE 10.3. *Estimated lifetime earnings by various educational levels, discount rates, cohort and quartiles under the Galton–serial model, discounted to 15 years old at 1967 price level (million yen)*

Discount (%)	Cohort	First quartile			Second quartile			Third quartile		
		JH	SH	Univ.	JH	SH	Univ.	JH	SH	Univ.
4	1924	18.35	20.30	28.36	30.21	33.00	42.59	53.16	55.93	64.85
	1929	16.04	17.10	22.13	24.92	26.40	31.64	40.40	41.94	45.50
	1934	14.30*	14.74	17.35	21.16*	21.42	23.71	32.43*	31.43	32.54
	1939	13.44*	13.61	14.66	18.97*	18.62	18.78	27.20*	25.66	24.08
16	1924	3.36	3.70	5.13	6.85	7.14	8.57	15.45	14.80	14.66
	1929	2.68	2.85	3.35	5.00	5.12	5.11	9.94	9.63	7.84
	1934	2.56*	2.52	2.49	4.45*	3.97	3.55	8.19*	6.34	5.08
	1939	3.36*	3.10	2.80	5.19*	4.47	3.65	8.21*	6.51	4.75

* Figures calculated using the Galton-only model.

TABLE 10.4. *Working years for various educational levels and birth cohorts*

Cohort	Education		
	JH	SH	Univ.
1924	30	30	30
1929	30	30	30
1934	28	25	21
1939	23	20	16

senior high graduates of the 1924 and 1929 cohorts have a common work history. We stress that we need a further study to compare between cohorts. The figures on cohorts 1934 and 1939 should be called earnings *over time* rather than lifetime earnings, because of the insufficient work history; for simplicity, however, both are called lifetime. In sum, attention should not be given to the comparison of lifetime earnings across cohorts.

Secondly, we adopted two different discount rates, 4 and 16 per cent, to estimate the earnings discounted to age 15 (at which junior high-school graduates start to work), since it is not easy to define the appropriate rate of discount which would be accepted universally in one society. A rate somewhere between 4 and 16 per cent would be a likely choice, in view of the rate of return on securities and the rate of interest in Japan.

Finally, three different lifetime earnings—the first quartile, the median (1/2), and the third quartile—are estimated on the basis of both the Galton model and the Galton-serial model. The calculation, based on the three different positions in the earnings distribution, assumes that a person who was at a particular position in distribution at his starting time always stays in the same position during the observation period. Although it is true that no person satisfies such a condition in his stream of lifetime earnings, the reality is not so different from this assumption in view of the Japanese social and economic system, where seniority and age are very important in determining wages and promotions. Tachibanaki and Takata (1994) investigated the case in which mobility of income from one time to another was allowed.

Table 10.3 gives estimated lifetime earnings under the

Galton-serial correlation hypothesis. Since this is more general than the Galton-only hypothesis, more attention is paid to the former. One difference, which is not reported here, to save space, between the Galton-only hypothesis, and the Galton-serial hypothesis is that the estimated lifetime earnings under the latter at the third-quartile level are smaller, while the opposite outcome appears at the first-quartile level. The following observations are obtained from Table 10.3.

First, lifetime earnings differ considerably between senior high-school and university graduates, in contrast to the difference between junior high and senior high graduates. Similar results were also obtained by Tachibanaki (1975; 1982), who analysed earnings distribution at one point in time. At the median level, university graduates earned 25.6 per cent and 14.1 per cent higher, at an 8 per cent discount rate, for the 1924 and 1929 cohorts respectively, although the figures are not shown in the table. At the third-quartile level, however, lifetime earnings are almost equal between the two educational levels, namely 20 million yen for the 1929 cohort. Successful senior high graduates earn almost the same as university graduates ('successful' means in this study that a person is at a higher position in the distribution). Higher discount rates such as 12 per cent show an inverse ranking; younger cohorts, like 1934 and 1939, also show an inverse order. It is somewhat risky, however, to generalize this inverse ranking at younger cohorts, because the length of labour market experiences differs between senior high-school and university graduates in those cohorts.

Secondly, the effect of relative position in the earnings distribution, represented by quartile level in this analysis, is much more important than the effect of educational level as a reason for lifetime earning differentials. For example, the third-quartile lifetime earnings of junior high-school graduates is higher than the median lifetime earnings of both senior high-school and university graduates at any discount rate for both the 1924 and the 1929 cohorts. An analogous result is obtained between the median earnings and the first quartile earnings. Comparison between senior high-school and university graduates supports a similar story.

This second point is interesting, and suggests a caveat concerning the conventional understanding of lifetime earnings; it is quite inadequate to discuss the effect of education on lifetime earnings without referring to different positions in the distribution. It is true that, at a common position in the distribution, higher educational attainment normally provides higher lifetime earnings, as suggested by this work. When different relative positions in earnings distribution are taken into account, the above story is not usually supported. Our result suggests that relative position in distribution affects the difference in lifetime earnings much more significantly than does the level of education. Accordingly, it may be suggested that policies which can reduce the inequality (or the variance) of earnings distribution at a given level of education would be more effective than policies which pursue equalization of educational attainment, if the equality of lifetime earnings is regarded as an important policy goal. We do not discuss in depth how such reductions can be achieved because we have not discussed the exact significance of unobserved ability, risk, luck, or other factors in explaining the inequality of earnings at a given level of education. Alternatively speaking, the result showed that education did not work as a factor which increased the degree of income inequality; education did not contribute to inequality, at least in the field of earning differentials. This does not necessarily imply, however, that education has no influence (see Chapter 7, which examined the influence of education in relation to occupation and hierarchy).

Thirdly, Table 10.3 suggests that the choice of discount rates is crucial for evaluating the figures of lifetime earnings because they differ significantly by adopted discount rates. Although we regarded an approximate 8 per cent rate of discount as the most relevant for Japan, discount rates are not free from subjective judgement; thus, use in the tables of two different levels of discount rate is intended to show merely that the estimated lifetime earnings differ considerably from discount rate to discount rate.[5]

10.3.2.3. Coefficient of Variations over Time. Finally, the empirical results of Table 10.5 are examined. The observation periods for the coefficients of variation over time were limited to

---

[5] Related to the argument of discount rates, it is possible to calculate the (internal) rate of return on education for different positions of the distribution. The rate of return certainly enables us to show the profitability more compactly. It might be somewhat misleading, however, to estimate the rate of return based only on the foregone earnings and lifetime earnings, without taking into account the cost of education. It would require another study to estimate the educational and training cost for various combinations of cohort and education.

TABLE 10.5. *Estimated coefficients of variation over time and cross-age, under the Galton and serial correlation model*

Discount (%)	Education Cohort	Coefficient of variations over time		
		JH	SH	Univ.
8	1924	1.1162	1.0773	0.9113
	1929	1.0110	1.0057	0.8418
	1934	0.8387*	0.9153	0.7322
	1939	0.8417*	0.7854	0.5790
12	1924	1.2599	1.1981	1.0036
	1929	1.1386	1.1228	0.9297
	1934	0.9481*	1.0210	0.8138
	1939	0.9547*	0.8829	0.6460

Notes.
1. Age covered 1924 cohort: 37–52; 1929: 32–47: 1934: 27–42: 1939: 22–37.
2. *signifies that the figures were calculated based on the Galton-only model.

fifteen years (1961–1976).[6] The following results are obtained on the basis of Table 10.5. First, it appears that the estimated coefficients of variation over time under the Galton-serial correlation hypothesis are somewhat larger than those under the Galton-only hypothesis. The above result is observed in all cohorts and at all educational levels; this is quite reasonable if we compare the two formulations. Secondly, the impact of the discount rate is quite strong, as was true for lifetime earnings. The higher the discount rate, the higher the estimated coefficient of variation. Thirdly, the estimated coefficient of variation over time for university graduates is smaller than that for junior and senior high-school graduates: for example, at an 8 per cent discount rate it is

[6] The following three reasons have led us to limit the observation periods. First, extrapolation has produced extraordinarily large variances in several cases, unlike log-transformed earnings, because the variances are measured in terms of untransformed earnings figures. It is very risky to include such large estimated variances at an early stage of an individual's career in the calculation of coefficients of variation over time, since an excessively heavy weight is given to that early stage. Secondly, shortening the period covered does not necessarily produce significantly different measures in comparison with a longer period. Thirdly, the calculations of the coefficients of variation for a longer period were, practically speaking, quite expensive computationally.

0.7067 for university graduates and 0.8195 and 0.8557 for junior and senior high-school graduates respectively, for the 1924 cohort, although the result is not given in the table. Similar results are obtained for the other cohorts, although the ranking between junior high and senior high is occasionally reversed. Consequently, it may be concluded that the dispersion in earnings is larger among junior and senior high-school graduates than among university graduates. This conclusion is consistent with Weiss (1972), who found for the USA that the variance in the earnings distribution for college graduates is smaller than that for non-college graduates. It should be noted, however, that Parsons (1978) found the opposite result for the USA. At all events, investment in higher education in Japan carries little risk as far as monetary reward is concerned. Finally, it is noted that the estimated coefficient of variation in Japan is higher than that in the USA as given by Lillard (1977). The main cause of the high values in Japan lies in the difference in model specifications. Our model is likely to increase the coefficient of variation, when the values of β and/or ρ (the regression coefficient and the serial correlation coefficient) are high because of the larger values of the covariance at earlier careers. We obtained significantly high positive values of β and/or ρ.

10.4. SUMMARY

This chapter constructed a theoretical model for analysing earnings distribution over time, and provided an estimation procedure for the inequality of earnings over time. The theoretical model framework attempted to incorporate Gibrat's 'law of proportionate effect', Galton's 'regression towards the mean', and serial correlation of the error terms, under the condition that the density function of earnings for each age cohort is distributed as log-logistic, which had been empirically observed in Japan. Three alternative model specifications, by combining the above three properties, were constructed and tested empirically. The estimated lifetime earnings and other related parameters were presented for several cohorts and for three educational levels. Emphasis was placed upon comparing the influence of the relative position in the distribution with the influence of education on earnings. Our result suggests that the relative position in the distribution is a much more significant factor in differentiating lifetime earnings than is the level of education. Finally, the coefficients of variation over time under the above behavioural assumptions were derived, and the estimated results were presented. It was found that the dispersion in earnings was larger among less educated than among highly educated people. These results imply that it is important to take account of dispersion in earnings distribution, and of the location of one's earnings in income rankings. A story based only on average earnings disguises many important facts about earnings distribution.

11
Labour Market Flexibility and Wage Determination

11.1. INTRODUCTION

There is a common belief outside Japan that the Japanese labour market is more flexible than those of the other industrialized nations, and that this flexibility has allowed a lower rate of unemployment with little fluctuation, and has in general facilitated a better macroeconomic performance. This chapter examines, on the basis of Japanese and non-Japanese studies, whether flexibility is the real story; it seeks the reasons for this flexibility, if any, with particular emphasis on a comparison between the Japanese economy and the economies of other industrialized nations, and the reasons for the very minor change in the rate of employment.

There are many dimensions to labour market flexibility. This chapter concentrates on a few, largely related to wage determination: labour adjustment, wages and labour demand, and labour cost. Some other dimensions, such as labour supply and labour mobility, are discussed in Tachibanaki (1987).

It might be useful to summarize the reasons for the relatively good performance in the Japanese labour market (especially the low rate of unemployment) during the 1970s and the 1980s. First, there was no strong pressure of labour supply by young people and female workers. The proportion of the working population which is young has been declining somewhat, due largely to a decrease in the youth population and an increase in the enrolment rate for higher education. The female labour force participation rate had been in a decreasing trend for a long time, although quite recently it has begun to increase somewhat. Secondly, the pressure of foreign workers was almost negligible, unlike the USA and Europe, where internationally immigrant workers became one of the main causes of unemployment, especially in Europe. Thirdly, the growth rate of employment in the tertiary sector was quite high; this sector absorbed a large proportion of the workforce, in contrast to a minor decrease in employment in manufacturing industries. During the most recent period of rapid economic growth, the manufacturing sector absorbed an incredibly large number of workers from the rural areas, where people were predominantly engaged in agriculture. The regional and industrial mobility of workers was extremely high, at least during the period of rapid economic growth. Fourth, the proportion of temporary employees such as part-time workers, employees on fixed-term contracts, and others (a very rough estimate is about 30 per cent of the total non-agricultural labour force), and of self-employed workers, including family workers (about 30 per cent), was high. As a result, the proportion of permanent employees was about 40 per cent. The high proportion of temporary employees suggests that employment may fluctuate rather easily, while the high proportion of self-employed workers implies that those people are rarely unemployed unless they change their labour force status (see Taki and Tachibanaki, 1994, on the effect of self-employed workers). Fifth, the effect of discouraged workers contributed significantly (see Tachibanaki and Sakurai, 1991; Sakurai and Tachibanaki, 1992). Sixth, the movement of labour productivity, working hours, and wages was quite flexible. This point was emphasized by Gordon (1982), Hamada and Kurosaka (1986), and others. Seventh, union power and 'search intensity', in terms both of the generosity of unemployment compensation and of the strictness of the unemployment protection laws, were weak. See Gordon (1982) on conflict avoidance as a social norm and the *Shunto* (annual spring offensive) in union power; Morishima (1991), Tachibanaki (1993a; 1993c), and Tachibanaki and Noda (1994) on the co-operative behaviour of unions; and Tachibanaki (1984b; 1984c), who found a minor disincentive effect of unemployment compensation. See also Layard and Nickell (1985) on its quantitative assessment. Eighth, several forms of labour adjustment to minimize the number of discharges (or layoffs) are adopted by Japanese firms and encouraged by the government. Ninth, the share of non-wage labour costs within the total labour cost has been relatively small. This is related to the relatively poor social-security system in Japan, at least in comparison with Europe. Several of the above arguments are examined carefully in this chapter.

11.2. LABOUR ADJUSTMENT

This section investigates how firms adjust employment. A considerable effort has been made in Japan to estimate the labour demand functions, in particular the labour adjustment functions. The main purpose of these studies is to estimate the degree of responsiveness or the speed of adjustment to labour demand. Some of the results are reviewed in comparison with the other countries.

A relatively simple labour demand function is a starting-point, which was originated by Brechling (1965), Ball and Cyr (1966), Nadiri (1968), and others.

$$\ln N_t - \ln N_{t-1} = \lambda \left(\ln N_t^* - \ln N_{t-1} \right)$$

where N_t is the employment at time t, N_t^* is the desired level of employment, and λ is the adjustment coefficient. This is a partial-adjustment model. When we take account of adjustment costs such as those of hiring, training, and firing (see e.g. Rosen, 1968; Ehrenberg, 1971; Nadiri and Rosen, 1974), the adjustment model with fixed costs is obtained.

Let us summarize the estimated speed of adjustment in employment. In the USA, those coefficients are calculated as 0.5–0.6 by Soligo (1966), 0.59 by Brechling and O'Brien (1967), 0.643 by Nadiri (1968), and 0.4 by Shinozuka and Ishihara (1977*a*). In the UK the coefficients are calculated as 0.307 by Brechling (1965), 0.185 by Ball and Cyr (1966), and 0.22 by Brechling and O'Brien (1967). The Japanese coefficients are calculated as 0.1 by Muramatsu (1983) and 0.04–0.08 by Shinozuka and Ishihara (1977*a*; 1977*b*; 1980). Abraham and Houseman (1989) confirmed these early results. Hashimoto and Raisian (1988), and Seike (1992) provided useful comparisons of Japan and the USA regarding labour demand adjustments. In sum, it is found that the Japanese speed of adjustment is considerably slower than those of the UK or the USA, thus, it may be concluded that the Japanese response to labour demand is very slow by the international standard.

Why has the Japanese speed of adjustment been slower? Labour input has been regarded as a quasi-fixed factor of production. This may be interpreted by the notion of specific human capital and of hiring and training fixed costs. A firm invests in a worker's human capital in order to achieve a higher expected marginal value product over his expected future working lifetime in the firm. The higher such an investment, the less adjustment there is in labour.

When the labour inputs are separated between employment and man-hours (employment times working hours), the speed of adjustment differs considerably. As Hamermesh (1976) concludes, in general the adjustment of employment is slower than that of working hours, although there are minor exceptions such as Hart and McGregor (1982) for West Germany and Briscoe and Peel (1975) for the UK. Incidentally, Hamermesh (1993) is a useful and comprehensive treatment of labour demand. Japan is no exception to this general rule, as Muramatsu (1983) and Shinozuka and Ishihara (1980) have shown. The latter, for example, found that the speed of adjustment of employment was 0.10 for firms with more than 30 employees and 0.30 for firms with 5–29 employees, while the speed of adjustment of hours was 0.37 for firms with more than 30 employees and 0.49 for firms with 5–29 employees. Shinozuka (1989) confirmed those findings. They attribute this to the following factors: first, higher fixed costs of hiring, training, and discharge than those of overtime premiums associated with a change in working hours are normal. In fact, it is no exaggeration to say that most of the labour adjustments in Japan were made through change in working hours, and to a lesser extent by reducing new hirings, as will be shown later. Secondly, Japanese firms prefer internal rather than external work-forces when they adjust labour input; for example, reallocation or transfer of workers to other establishments within a firm, or to other sections within an establishment, is frequently used, and labour-hoarding is also quite common. In other words, the internal labour market dominates the external labour market.

Several supplementary notes follow on labour adjustment in Japan. First, there is a considerable gap between men and women with respect to the speed of adjustment. Nakamura (1983; 1984) found that the coefficient for women is much higher than that for men when the speed of adjustment in employment is investigated. Shinozuka and Ishihara (1980) obtained a similar result to Nakamura's, but described another valuable finding: when the speed of adjustment in employment is estimated for large firms and small firms separately, the female coefficient is higher than the male coefficient in large firms, while the opposite result is observed in small firms. When we combine the two sexes, the speed is greater at small firms. They suggest the following order of priority when labour adjustment takes place in large firms: first, adjustment by working hours; second, use (or discharge) of temporary or part-time female workers; third, firing of female regular employees; and last, firing of male regular workers. Results for small firms are less clear, since almost the same values of the adjustment coefficients were obtained when man-hours were used instead of employment.

Secondly, a non-negligible difference is observed by industry in Japan, unlike the USA (see Hamermesh, 1976, for the USA). Seike (1985), Muramatsu (1986), and others conclude that the speed of adjustment in light industries is greater than in heavy industries. One of the reasons is that technology in heavy industries is more capital-intensive, and thus the fixity of labour input is higher.

Thirdly, labour adjustment in employment is made through a cut (or an increase) in new hiring rather than through a change in current stock (discharge or layoff) of workers. Fig. 11.1 shows a considerable rate of fluctuation in new hirings, particularly in manufacturing industries. This does not necessarily imply, of course, that there are no discharges or layoffs; for example, Muramatsu (1986) finds that when a firm has to cut more than 10 per cent of its man-hours in response to a fall in demand or output, the probability of adopting discharge is positive. A dismissal of workers by designation is the final step, probably because no rule (e.g. seniority) has been established for determining who is dismissed. The first step is to send workers (normally older workers) to subsidiary companies or to firms in the same group (say in the ex-*zaibatsu* group, for example). The second step is to call for voluntary quits by offering premiums. Finally, dismissals come.

Fourth, many studies suggest that the speed of labour adjustment by employment has been increasing, especially after the two oil crises. One reason is that Japanese firms do not have high expectations of a recurrence of the rapid growth rate of the past. In other words, they are somewhat pessimistic about the future, and thus tend to restrict the number of employees.

Finally, labour-hoarding, still a prevailing phenomenon, is a big issue currently because it is costly for firms. Some estimates show that the rate of unemployment may be about 5–6 per cent if labour-hoarding is included. Drastic method of adjusting the level of employment, such as discharges, may be unavoidable if

224 *Labour Market Flexibility and Wage Determination*

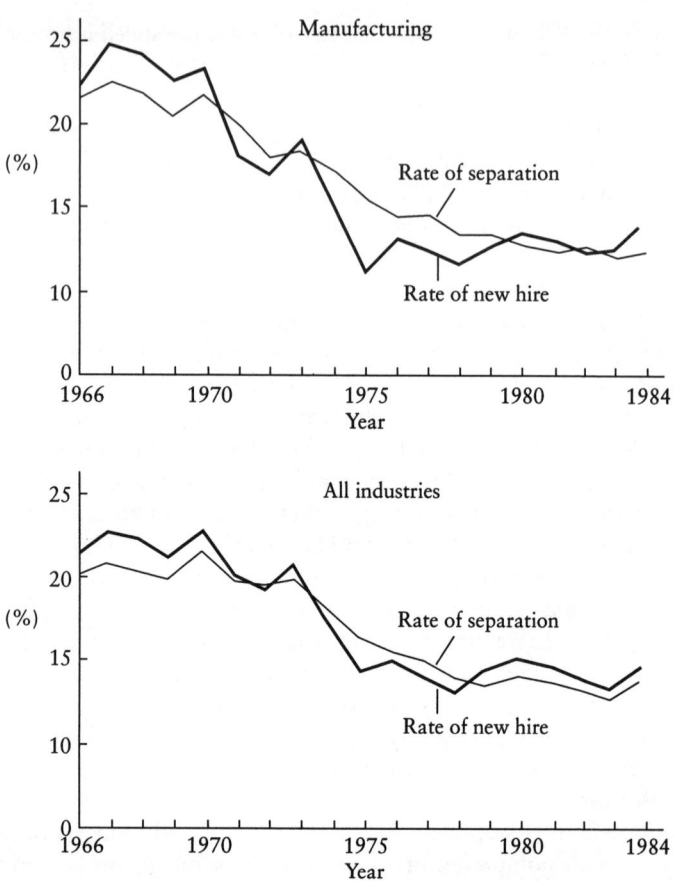

FIG. 11.1. Time-series change in the rate of new hires and separations. (*Source*: Ministry of Labour, *Employment Trends*.)

labour-hoarding becomes too costly. This possible change, however, would alter the entire process of the Japanese labour market.

Tables 11.1 and 11.2 confirm some of the above propositions from a different angle. The estimated standard deviations in Table 11.1 suggest that Japan shows the highest deviation in working hours and the lowest in employment among the major industrialized nations. Working hours are much more flexible than employment.

TABLE 11.1. *Estimated standard deviations of output, employment, working hours, and real wage per hour*[a]

	Production Corontput	Labour input			Real wage per hour
		Employment	Hours	Man-hours	
(A)[a]					
Japan	6.509	2.089	1.903		
USA	6.963	4.376	1.447		
UK	4.635	2.409	1.508		
W. Germany	4.014	2.325	1.509		
France	5.368	–	0.728		
(B)[a]					
Japan	0.147			0.048 (0.048)	0.111 (0.343)
USA	0.062			0.052 (0.050)	0.038 (0.045)
UK	0.045			0.056 (0.159)	0.052 (0.121)
W. Germany	0.070			0.062 (0.089)	0.057 (0.192)
France	0.069			0.037 (0.083)	0.036 (0.231)

[a] (A) signifies that the standard deviations are calculated for the rate of change in each index of the variable for 1970–83, while (B) signifies that standard deviations are calculated for log-transformed variables which are de-trended for 1964–83. The numbers in parentheses are the values for non-trended variables. Thus, (A) and (B) are not comparable.

Source: Higuchi *et al.* (1986); Ohtake (1986). (Original sources: Bank of Japan, *International Statistics*; OECD, *Main Economic Indicators*.

TABLE 11.2. *Decomposition of the change in total working hours into the change in regular hours and the change in overtime hours (% per year)*

	Total hours	Regular hours	Overtime hours
1955–60	0.9	0.3	0.5
1960–5	–1.1	–0.5	–0.5
1965–70	–0.5	–0.7	0.1
1970–3	–0.8	–0.6	–0.2
1973–6	–1.3	–0.6	–0.7
1976–80	0.2	–0.1	0.3
1980–5	–0.1	–0.2	0.1

Source: Ministry of Labour, *Monthly Labour Statistics*.

Moreover, it should be emphasized that the change in total working hours is strongly affected by the change in overtime hours. Table 11.2 shows a decomposition of the change in total working hours into the change in regular hours and the change in overtime hours. The table clearly indicates that the contribution of overtime hours is as strong as the contribution of regular hours. The overtime premium is 25 per cent in Japan, the UK, and West Germany, while it is 50 per cent in the USA. Thus Japan does not provide firms with an extra incentive to utilize overtime hours by the international standard. The mutual interest of both employers (coping with a fluctuation in demand and output smoothly) and employees (the desire to obtain higher wages by overtime hours and to avoid dismissals, and corporate loyalty to firms) may be another reason.

It is important to add the cost factor. The Ministry of Labour (1986) conducted a valuable study which compared the cost between a new hire and overtime hours by a currently employed person. It concluded that the cost to a firm of a new hire would be the same as the cost of overtime hours by a currently employed person if the overtime premium rate were 62.9 per cent. In view of the current premium, 25 per cent, no firms would hire new employees rather than utilizing overtime hours. Interestingly, the break-even premium rate is 74.4 per cent for larger firms (more than 500 employees), 61.0 per cent for medium-size firms (100–499 employees), and 47.4 per cent for smaller firms, (30–99 employees), respectively. This is due largely to the fact that the fixed cost is higher in larger than in smaller firms. This is one of the primary reasons why larger firms are inclined to use flexible overtime hours rather than changing the numbers employed, in comparison with smaller firms, which tend to use flexible employment.

Let us conduct a brief international comparison with respect to the level of working hours. The total annual working hours and overtime hours in 1983 were 2, 152 and 202 (the rate of overtime hours to total hours was 9.39 per cent) in Japan, 1,898 and 156 (8.22 per cent) in the USA, 1,938 and 140 (7.22 per cent) in the UK, 1,622 and 45 (2.77 per cent) in Italy, 1,613 and 78 (4.84 per cent) in West Germany, and 1,657 and 78 (4.71 per cent) in France. The reason for showing the figures in 1983 is that we are interested in the story immediately after the two oil crises. These years enable us to understand the difference in labour market conditions more clearly than do recent figures. Both total working hours and overtime hours (including the rate of overtime hours) are the longest in Japan among the six countries. The importance of overtime hours in Japan can be seen from this international comparison.

A higher fluctuation in working hours is confirmed internationally by Table 11.1. As noted before, Japan shows the highest standard deviation in working hours and the lowest in employment among the major industrial nations, despite very high fluctuations in output. When we use total man-hours, the story is considerably different: Japan shows the lowest fluctuation. In sum, a very high adjustment by working hours and a low adjustment by employment are the Japanese instruments of labour adjustment. The USA is the other extreme: a high adjustment by employment and a low adjustment by working hours. Europe stays between the two.

Which is more desirable as an adjustment policy? If there is a national consensus that to keep the rate of unemployment as low as possible should be the first goal of economic policy the Japanese way of labour adjustment is certainly desirable. However, achieving this goal involves far from negligible costs, such as inflation, redundancy wage costs, inefficient management of firms due to excess employment, profit squeeze, or foreign trade conflict. I do not believe, therefore, that the Japanese method of labour adjustment can easily be recommended to other industrialized nations. I evaluate the US temporary layoffs positively, provided that there is a real possibility of recall, and provided also that employees' income is protected during temporary layoffs. Each country has its own preference.

11.3. FLEXIBLE WAGE RATES AND LABOUR DEMAND

There is a common understanding internationally that Japanese wages (both nominal and real) are flexible, and that this flexibility has helped the Japanese economy to perform relatively well. This section intends to re-examine this issue on the basis of a large number of studies.

Japanese economists have not taken account of this aspect, namely flexibility of wages; it is ironic that foreign observers have opened Japanese economists' eyes to this issue (e.g. Sacks, 1979; 1983; Branson and Rotemberg, 1980; Gordon, 1982; Grubb *et al.*,

(1983). Most studies, except perhaps for Sacks, support the observation that flexibility of real wages in Japan is fairly high, and has thus helped towards a better performance. It is important to consider two issues separately. The first is to investigate whether the real wage is flexible, statistically speaking. Secondly, provided that this flexibility is supported empirically, is it possible to state that it has raised labour demand, and thus lowered unemployment?

11.3.1. Statistical Wage Flexibility

Since the seminal articles by Sacks (1979) and Gordon (1982) appeared, many investigations have been performed to re-examine whether real wages in Japan are flexible. Many studies (e.g. Yoshitomi, 1981; Shinkai, 1982; Komiya and Yasui, 1984; Mizuno, 1985; Brunello and Wadhwani, 1989; Hashimoto and Raisian, 1992; Koshiro 1992; except perhaps for Ohtake, 1986), support Gordon's view that Japanese real wages are more flexible than those of the other industrialized nations, although various reasons are provided by different authors to support it.

Gordon (1982) basically attributed the flexibility to 'bonus' payments twice a year. Mizuno (1985), however, emphasizes that not only bonus payments but also basic wages (total wage earnings minus bonus payments) are flexible. His point is that the proportion of bonus payments to total wage earnings is at most 25 per cent, and is declining constantly. Thus, if flexibility of total wage payments is observed statistically, its main cause is not flexibility of the bonuses but of the monthly wages. He actually estimated that the relative contribution of flexibility of bonus payments to the flexibility of total wage payments was about 10 per cent during the period 1960–83. The main source for the large contribution of the fluctuation of monthly wages is wage payments by overtime hours, due partly to overtime premiums. As emphasized previously in this chapter, overtime hours fluctuate considerably in Japan in response to business cycles.

Bonuses may be explained very briefly. In 1983, 97.9 per cent of firms paid bonuses and 99.3 per cent of all employees received some amount of bonuses; they are well-established and systematic payments. About 32 per cent of all firms say that they determine the total amount of bonus payments on the basis of firms' performances such as sales, value added, and profits. Smaller firms stress the consideration of performances and profits more than larger firms. The majority of Japanese firms, especially larger ones, regard bonuses as quasi-regular wage payments rather than as profit-sharing; Koshiro (1992) supports this view in his econometric work. Thus, although the bonus payments in Japan have a profit-sharing aspect (see Weitzman, 1984), it is not a pure profit-sharing scheme. This does not necessarily imply that the amount of bonuses is fixed; it is fairly varied in response to the firms' business conditions, as many authors have suggested (see e.g. Hashimoto, 1979; Tachibanaki, 1982; Freeman and Weitzman, 1987; Ohashi, 1989*a*; 1989*b*).

An interesting aspect of bonuses is the way in which the total amount of bonus payments is divided among individual employees. About 70 per cent of firms say that they take account of the individual employee's performance; only about 30 per cent pay the same amount (say, two or three months' regular wages) to all employees regardless of each employee's performance. The criteria for determining each person's performance include rate of absence, contribution to a firm, skill, responsibility, and leadership as a supervisor, and tenure at a firm. Thus, bonuses are used by firms as an incentive payment to a certain extent (see Okuno, 1984, on the theoretical aspects and Ohashi, 1989*b*, who supported it empirically). This, however, depends upon industries, and the incentive aspect should not be overemphasized, since the amount determined by it is fairly small.

Another method for estimating the degree of flexibility of wage payment is to rely upon the Phillips curve approach, which Grubb *et al.* (1983) have adopted. If a change in the wage rate were sensitive to the labour market condition (say, the rate of unemployment), it would be concluded that flexibility of wage determination is high. This method is likely to overestimate the degree of flexibility if an economy does not have a sizeable movement in the rate of unemployment. It is possible that Japanese flexibility has been somewhat overestimated because of the almost constant rate of unemployment. Thus, the study by Klau and Mittelstadt (1985), which showed that Japanese real wage rigidity was the lowest among the OECD countries, is somewhat dubious. The method utilized a change in the unemployment rate as well as a change in the consumer prices. Related to this, it is noted that the work by Hamada and Kurosaka (1984), who estimated the Okun coefficient as 10 times higher in Japan than in the USA, was accepted unfavourably not only by a non-Japanese (Mairesse, 1984) but also by several Japanese economists. An unbiased estimation of the Okun's coefficient requires a certain degree of fluctuation in the rate of unemployment. Tachibanaki and Sakurai (1991) modified the estimation of the Okun coefficient in the presence of disguised unemployment of female workers, and obtained a lower coefficient. In sum, a method for estimating the flexibility of wages which utilizes a change in the rate of unemployment in estimating wage or price equations (say, the Phillips curve approach) needs careful interpretation when the rate of unemployment does not fluctuate sufficiently, as in Japan's case.

It is possible to conclude from a large number of studies, in particular pure statistical studies which do not use the Phillips curve approach, that wages (both nominal and real) in Japan are fairly flexible. One important exception is Ohtake (1986), who found less flexibility when he considered the de-trended wage figures. He also examined real wages, which are standardized by a change in output. He suggests that a shock in output (say, the two oil crises), which gives an excessive impact on a change in wages, must be eliminated. Since his argument has a point, it is necessary to examine it further; however, he does not deny that real wages in Japan are variable, at least judging by the purely statistical evidence.

It is necessary to examine why real wages are flexible. Several economic and institutional factors, in addition to the bonus payments and flexible working hours examined before, are suggested here, but a serious discussion is avoided. (i) Wage contracts are determined largely on a yearly basis in the framework of the *Shunto*, unlike the three-year contract in USA. The past performance of productivity movement, inflation rate, macroeconomic conditions, and others is taken fully into account by both employers and trade unions at the *Shunto*. (ii) Several studies (e.g. Yoshitomi, 1981; Shinkai, 1982; Komiya and Yasui, 1984) propose that a change in wages is strongly affected by a change in terms of trade and productivity. (iii) Trade unions are concerned with the assurance of the employment of their members. When the utility function of trade unions was estimated by Hayami (1986), a preference for employment rather than for wage increase was found. Thus it is likely that trade unions are willing to sacrifice wages in exchange for the assurance of employment. This contrasts sharply with the European experience, especially the UK where the impact of union powers on wages is fairly strong, as shown by, for example, Minford (1983), Nickell and Andrews (1983; 1984), and Layard et al. (1991).

Furthermore, the rate of unionization in Japan is fairly low (below 30 per cent) by the international standard; more importantly, the rate is constantly declining (see e.g. Hamada and Kurosaka, 1986; Tachibanaki, 1993a). Weak union preference for wage increases and the low rate of unionization have both contributed to flexibility of wages. It is ironic but interesting that both Japan and the USA, where macroeconomic performances relatively better than the European countries, have lower unionization rates. It is crucial to point out that co-operative behaviour by trade unions raises average productivity in industries (Morishima, 1991; Tachibanaki and Noda, 1994).

I argue that the labour side should be able to demand higher wage payments in view of the fact that the properly measured labour share within the national income in Japan has declined constantly, and that some increase in wages in boom industries will encourage a higher domestic consumption, which has a positive effect on reducing the current huge trade surplus. Labour market flexibility, in terms of co-operative behaviour by trade unions vis-à-vis managements, may be regarded as one of the causes of the current foreign trade surplus, thus offering one example of the fact that labour market flexibility cannot always be evaluated positively.

11.3.2. Wages and Labour Demand

A second important issue is the relationship between wages and the demand for labour. Specifically, is it possible to propose that a flexible wage system increases employment? The US result was surveyed by Hamermesh (1976; 1993), and a consensus, namely stable and robust wage effects on the demand for labour, was obtained at least up to 1976. However, other papers by Hall (1975; 1980) have shown unresponsive wages, and Bell and Freeman (1985) find that flexible wages by industry in the USA have not contributed to employment growth. Thus, even in the USA, the recent story may differ from the past. In Europe the result was inconclusive (see Nickell, 1982; 1993). Recent studies, however, tend to confirm that there are some clear real-wage effects on the demand for labour when relative material/fuel prices are accounted for. See Nickell (1982), Symons (1985), and Layard *et al.* (1991); see also Symons and Layard (1984) for a rigorous international comparison, and Hamermesh (1993) for a comprehensive study of the relationship between wages and labour demand in the UK and USA.

What is the situation in Japan? Muramatsu (1985) gave a useful survey on the estimation of real-wage elasticities with respect to labour demand. His main conclusion, on the basis of about ten studies in Japan, suggests that real wage elasticities are considerably lower than the US elasticities surveyed by Hamermesh (1976). Under the constant assumption of capital cost and output, the average elasticities are at most −0.03 for total industries and −0.15 for manufacturing industries. The effect is smaller in Japan than in the USA. Incidentally, the output elasticities in Japan are on average 0.24 for total industries and 0.44 for manufacturing industries, even after two years' lag. Those values are smaller than the US values, which are about 0.75–1.00. Hashimoto and Raisian (1988) provided a useful comparison between Japan and the USA. In sum, it is possible to state that the real-wage effects on the demand for labour in Japan are weak.

Let us summarize this section. Although it is true that real-wage flexibility is high in Japan, it has not helped to increase the numbers employed; the role of wages as an adjusting factor has been quite limited. The growth of employment, if any, must be explained by reasons other than the real-wage effect. It should, however, be pointed out that flexibility has prevented current employment from falling to a certain extent, because the firm can save its cost considerably.

It is useful to discuss one recent topic in the relationship between wages and labour demand or, more concretely, between wages and unemployment—the '*International Wage Curve*' developed by Blanchflower and Oswald (1994). This curve intends to demonstrate a negative correlation between the level of pay and the level of unemployment. The original idea was addressed to the relationship between the rate of regional (or industrial) unemployment and its level of pay. Blachflower and Oswald estimated the unemployment elasticity of pay at approximately −0.1 for eight countries; Japan is not included in their study. They interpret this result as one reason to support efficiency wage theory, in which unemployment acts as a disciplining device that dissuades employees from shirking. They suggest a model which proposes that a high employment rate allows the firm to pay less in equilibrium.

Montgomery (1993) performed a similar work to Blanchflower and Oswald for Japan and the USA. He obtained a result contradicting the general understanding that the Japanese labour market is more flexible than that of the USA. Pay is not responsive to unemployment. My judgement on this seemingly contradictory result is as follows. Montgomery considers the relationship between unemployment and wages through regional data, including regional labour mobility, while other writers investigate flexibility based on the relationship between employment, working hours, labour supply, and wages, without referring to the movement in unemployment. Also, these writers do not pay serious attention to regional data, except for Sakurai and Tachibanaki (1992), who investigated the issue of regional mismatch in labour allocations. Three important points may be raised. First, there is little fluctuation in the published rate of unemployment; therefore, it is somewhat risky to measure the unemployment elasticity of pay on the basis of the published rate of unemployment (see my discussion of the Philips curve above). Several authors, including myself, have attempted to investigate the causes of such low fluctuation in the published rate of unemployment, and these causes are regarded as the source of labour market flexibility. Second, one of the most important aspects is that flexibility which preserves employment, and thus avoids dismissal or discharge, is evaluated highly. A higher fluctuation in working hours in response to a fluctuation in outputs has been confirmed as the most important element of labour flexibility. Third, it was concluded previously that the real-wage effects on the demand for labour in Japan were weak; this is consistent with the finding of Montgomery to a certain extent. In sum, non-Japanese economists regard a change in the rate of published unemployment as an important economic variable which can be used for measuring labour flexibility, while many Japanese economists consider that other economic variables rather than unemployment should be assessed to measure labour flexibility. Alternatively, it would be possible to obtain a consistent result if common were procedures employed to investigate labour market flexibility in Japan. In other words, not all dimensions are labour-flexible in Japan: some are flexible and others are rigid.

11.4. OTHER ASPECTS OF FLEXIBILITY RELATED TO WAGES AND LABOUR COSTS

11.4.1. Nenko Wages and Equality

Japanese wage determination is characterized by the *nenko* wage system: the wage rate is determined largely by employees' tenures and ages (see Tachibanaki, 1975; 1982; Hashimoto and Raisian, 1985). Every country has a similar system (see also Koike, 1981); the only difference is that the Japanese case is much more apparent than in other countries. Several implications of the system for the performance of the labour market are considered.

First, since the growth rate of wages by tenure and age is high, the wage level is low among younger people and high among older people. This is, incidentally, the main reason for the higher unemployment rate of older people (aged over 55), 4.3 per cent in recent years. Curiously, the rate of unemployment of younger people (aged 15–24) is not low (about 4.5 per cent). This is due largely to supply-side factors (see Tachibanaki, 1984*b*; 1984*c*).

Secondly, wage distribution among the *same* age group is quite equal because of the *nenko* system, although the wage distribution among all employees may be quite unequal because samples of both younger and older workers are included in the total number of employees; this is obvious, because the wage level of nearly all employees is proportional to their tenures and ages. It is also found that education and occupation are not major variables in differentiating the wage rate of employees (see Tachibanaki, 1975; 1982; Atoda and Tachibanaki, 1991). These features provide employees with a feeling of equal treatment by employers; this equal treatment gives incentives for corporate loyalty and hard working, especially to workers with lower educational and occupational attainment. This supports the argument of Lazear (1989). I believe that this is one of the reasons why labour productivity has been high in general.

Several questions arise concerning this interpretation. For example, how is the incentive of educated and skilled workers evaluated? The American literature emphasizes the incentive for qualified and supervisory workers, who should receive higher wages (see e.g. Calvo and Wellisz, 1979; Rosen, 1982; Brown, 1994). Incentives for qualified workers are not provided by monetary rewards, at least currently, in Japan by comparison with the USA. There is an incentive by bonus payments, as noted previously; this is still minor, and does not have a strong impact.

One important problem remains. Does productivity of workers increase in proportion to tenure at a firm? Since the *nenko* system implicitly assumes that the above is true, it is important to investigate whether it is empirically supported. Otherwise, firms may by paying higher wages than required, or workers may be receiving lower wages than their contributions. Unfortunately, no rigorous studies have investigated the relationship between wages and marginal productivity in relation to the *nenko* system; flexibility due to this system may be evaluated accurately only when the relationship is made clear empirically.

Another question may be posed: several studies (e.g. Klau and Mittelstadt, 1985) show that the average inter-industry wage differential is the highest in Japan among the OECD countries, and ascribe this to flexibility of the wage structure. This may be inconsistent with the equal wage distribution as proposed previously. Chapter 5 found that a great part of the large inter-industry wage differentials should be explained by the difference in age and sex compositions of employees in each industry, and the difference in size of firm. Thus, the highest inter-industry wage differentials in Japan ought to be discounted to a great extent. I do not deny, however, that some degree of inter-industry wage differentials due to the difference in productivities in industries contributes to the flexibility of wage payments to a very limited extent in Japan.

11.4.2. Minimum-Wage Law

Minimum-wage law specifies that the minimum wage should be determined by each prefecture. Since economic conditions differ considerably by region, such a decentralized system can be evaluated positively as flexibility. Moreover, the minimum-wage law is not obeyed strictly by employers, and penalties are almost nonexistent. In sum, it is hard to believe that the minimum-wage law has been an obstacle to hiring new employees. This is contrary to American or European experiences, in which some adverse effects are often mentioned.

11.4.3. Male–Female Wage Differentials

Several studies (e.g. Tachibanaki, 1975; Kawashima and Tachibanaki, 1986) and Chapters 3 and 9 above conclude that the most significant variable in wage differentials is sex (male–female differences). A large part of male–female wage differentials are discriminatory against women in wage payment and promotion: they do not receive the payments that correspond to their contribution to the firm. Currently, about one-third of the labour force is female. Firms benefit considerably from paying lower wages to women, since labour costs are saved. Although this is not flexibility, it is an important element which has helped Japanese firms in cost performance. Alternatively, firms could enjoy lower cost at the sacrifice of female workers.

11.4.4. Non-wage Labour Costs

It is well documented that Europe suffers a heavy burden of non-wage labour costs, in particular statutory social-security contributions to health and pension programmes. This heavy burden has meant labour-cost rigidity for firms, and is supposed to be one of the most important reasons for the high unemployment rate in Europe (see e.g. Layard et al., 1991; Layard and Nickell, 1994). This issue must be argued in relation to various aspects, such as the problem of the incidence of the employer's contribution to social-security schemes, and fixed labour costs (see e.g. Hart, 1984). Here, only a brief comment on Japan is made with respect to non-wage labour costs.

It is said that Japan and the USA are two countries among the industrialized nations where the low rate of non-wage labour costs has contributed to higher employment. I understand that the USA has a national consensus that services such as medical care and pension programmes should be arranged privately. Statutory social-security programmes organized by public authorities are not very significant. This is the main reason why the US shows a low rate of non-wage labour costs.

Japan is somewhat different. In principle, Japan wanted to adopt the welfare state system, in the European sense, about twenty years ago. The government modified the social-security system completely, by considerably raising the level of state pensions and medical benefits, and was proud of having achieved the European standard in these areas. This achievement, however, was not supported by a rigorous budgetary background. The aggregate pension and medical payment was very low because the proportion of retirees to the total population was quite low at the time. Since the growth rate of the economy was quite high, huge revenues from both general taxes and social-security contributions could be collected without necessarily assigning high rates of social-security contribution both to employers and to employees. In sum, the government wanted to introduce the notion of a welfare state only on the payment side, without a sound budgetary or actuarial calculation. This mistake was made some twenty years ago; thus, firms have not in the past been asked to contribute adequately to the social-security system. This is the main reason why the statutory employer's contribution has been lower in Japan. Although sympathy for the government is possible because of the unanticipated stagflations after the two oil crises, it was a serious mistake. It is no longer possible to enjoy such low non-wage labour costs in the future, since the share of non-wage labour costs is rising along with the ageing trend.

11.5. CONCLUDING REMARKS

This chapter has examined labour market flexibility and wage determination in Japan, with some comparisons with Europe and the USA. In particular, labour adjustments, labour demand, and labour cost were examined, with particular emphasis on the relationship with wage determinations. I find that labour market flexibility is observed in Japan for the following reasons. First, working hours, including overtime hours, are fairly flexible in response to a change in outputs. Second, wages, including bonus payments, are also flexible, although the degree of flexibility is lower than that of working hours. Third, there is a consensus among employers and employees that layoffs or discharges are an instrument of last resort for adjusting human resources. These factors have been quite effective in reducing the rate of unemployment and in minimizing change in the rate of unemployment. It should be emphasized, nevertheless, that this labour market flexibility was accompanied by some costs which may be regarded as the sacrifice. Such costs have been borne by females, part-time workers, new job-seekers ('outsiders' in the terms of Lindbeck and Snower, 1989), workers in smaller firms, and some others. Also, it is important to point out that some dimensions are not so flexible in the working of labour markets: representatively, this can be seen from a low unemployment elasticity of wages when regional data are applied. There must be some other dimensions and areas which are fairly rigid rather than flexible.

12
Conclusions

This book has investigated wage determinations and wage differentials in Japan, covering not only the period of rapid economic growth but also subsequent developments. Although the subject-matter is fairly narrow, it has important links with the working of the labour market, and these links have been investigated. Therefore, this book has examined not only the issue of wages but also the mechanism of the labour market in general. Some important aspects of this market, which can be regarded as one of the main causes of superior economic performance in terms of a lower unemployment rate, surviving well during the two oil crises, and other achievements, were addressed and discussed. Some economists attribute them to labour market flexibility; the book has examined both the benefit and the cost of this flexibility.

One important concern has been the general assumption that wage distribution or, more broadly, income distribution in Japan is fairly equal. This implies that the degree of wage differentials must be fairly small. Since this study did not set out to test this assumption by an extensive international comparative study, it is impossible to state that Japan's wage distribution is less unequal than those in other countries. Instead, recent international comparative studies (e.g. Tachibanaki and Yagi, 1995) propose that the degree of inequality in income distribution in Japan is currently comparable to those in Euro-American countries, although it is true that it was lower in the past. Therefore, it should be difficult to suppose that wage distribution today in Japan is fairly equal, by comparison with Euro-American countries.

One important point regarding wage distribution is that it is crucial to specify what samples are used to study it. More concretely, it is vital to know whether entire samples, including both older and younger people, are considered, or only a particular group, say 30-year-old male white-collar workers and university graduates. The former are likely to show an unequal wage distribution under the Japanese system of seniority and paternalism, while the latter are likely to show an equal wage distribution under the Japanese equality-oriented system. Male and female wage differentials also belong to the former category.

The book first examined a change in wage differentials for entire samples in the time-series context within Japan, studying whether or not the degree of wage differentials has changed. Particular attention was paid to the cause of such changes, if any, and at the same time to the effects responsible for such changes. Wage differentials were explained by a large number of variables, including demographic variables such as age and sex and firm-specific variables.

The variables examined here are sex, occupation, education, size of firm, job tenure (called 'experience' or 'length of service' in some places), and age. The time-series study was intended to clarify which of these variables became important and which became less important in explaining changes in wage differentials. The main statistical tool was the analysis of variance method.

Wage differentials have many dimensions: a number of variables differentiate wage figures. Some economists are interested in male/female wage differentials; others are interested in inter-industrial wage differentials. Many are interested in the impact of formal education and on-the-job training on the determination of wages and earnings. Inter-size or inter-scale wage differentials have received special attention in Japan. The book has investigated the quantitative role of each variable in the determination of wage differentials. Its most important contribution has been to derive a pure wage differential due to one such variable after controlling for an extremely large number of variables, since it is possible that a spurious wage differential due to such a variable may be observed. The pure effect of industry and that of firm size were estimated separately.

One important feature in the analysis of the pure effect of either industry or size of firm is that data used are individual observations of wages and demographic variables, rather than average wage figures per cell, which are cross-classified by various demographic variables. The latter form of data was used for the time-series change in wage differentials in Chapter 3. Data availability of individual observations enabled economists to undertake a more systematic and bias-free analysis of wage determinations and wage differentials, and at the same time to derive a pure effect of either industry or size of firm on wage differentials, using rigorous statistical methods. Chapters 7 and 8 also used individual observations of wages and other personal characteristic to investigate the issue of wage determination, although their data sources differed from those in Chapters 3, 4, and 5.

Availability of individual observations also enables economists to construct a more complicated theoretical model to account for real economic behaviour, and to carry out a more rigorous empirical study by applying skilful statistical methods. Chapters 7 and 8, it is hoped, belong to these categories, since the latter developed a theoretical wage determination which incorporates several stylized facts in Japan and the former applied a typical econometric model of discrete choice.

Several main conclusions can be drawn from the studies in this book, among many findings obtained. Since each chapter has described the causes and implications of these findings extensively, this section does not repeat them, but presents only the results which contribute to the understanding of wage determination and wage differentials in Japan in relation to the labour market mechanisms.

12.1. The male/female difference is the most significant determinant, and its main cause is discrimination against women. This result is observed when both males and females are included in the sample. In particular, it appears for raw data which have not been adjusted for any weights of demographic factors or qualifications. In other words, simple nominal wage figures, with no adjustment for other qualifications such as job tenure, education, or occupation, which pertain to both males and females, suggest that sex is the most influential among many factors in wage differentials.

This book, specifically Chapter 9, attempted to discover what happens if other qualifications are common between males and females. It is possible, for example, to insist that the average job tenure of females is shorter than males because of obvious and occasional interruptions of working activities peculiar to females. Under the seniority payment system in Japan, women would receive lower wage payments than men because of their shorter job tenures. Would they receive the same amount of wages if length of service (i.e. job tenure) were the same for men and women? Several other qualifications, education, size of firm, etc., were also investigated.

It was found that the differences in qualifications between males and females were not responsible for wider wage differentials between males and females. The most important element is the differential *treatment* of worker qualifications between males and females. Employers do not treat employees equally between males and females in the determination of their wages. Take one example, educational attainment. Wage payments are different for men and women even if their formal schooling levels are the same. In other words, the rate of return on education differs by sex. The same story holds for the other qualifications and characteristics. We call it discrimination.

Discrimination against women is rooted in contemporary Japanese industrial relations. Every country in the world has such a tendency; its degree in Japan, however, is higher than in other industrialized countries, and it has helped Japanese firms in cost performance by international standards. Some economists may say that this is one of the dimensions of labour market flexibily in view of the female role as a buffer in labour adjustments and lower wage payments; I judge that it is not flexibility. Nevertheless, it is not easy to reduce the degree of discrimination, partly because females themselves contribute marginally to it and largely because of its social, historical, and cultural roots. Japanese society has started to recognize the problem; but it will take at least a decade or two to eliminate discrimination, and this will require intensive social discussion and, of course, legal implementation.

12.2. Education, size of firm, and job tenure are the main variables which determine wage figures. Besides the difference between men and women, the following three variables turned out to be influential on the determination of wages, and thus wage differentials: education, size of firm, and job tenure. The last variable may be replaced by age; alternatively, a combination of job tenure and age can be one main determinant of wages, although the latter is less significant than the former.

These three variables are crucial for the determination of wages only when male data are examined. Male wage figures, examined carefully in Chapters 4, 7, 8, and 10, can provide discrimination-

Conclusions

free wage figures. Also, nearly all male observations are unaffected by significant interruptions of labour market activity, unlike female observations. Consequently, the examination of male wage figures can give us a reliable source from which to derive a pure quantitative effect of each variable on wage differentials.

The second conclusion merely indicates that the three variables (or four, if age is included separately) are important for the determination of wages. The economic significance and implications of each variable are described in the main text; a brief summary will be provided separately here. Finally, it is noted that Chapter 8, which constructed a theoretical model of wage determination consisting of only three variables, education, size of firm, and job tenure, was fairly successful in explaining empirical wage figures for male employees who have stayed with the same employers. This supports indirectly the hypothesis that these three variables are important in the determination of wages, at least for males who have never changed employers.

12.3. Both job tenure and age have particular implications for wage determinations. It is common to believe that the importance of job tenure arises from economic rationality, while that of age arises from a paternalism peculiar to Japan. The former includes the theory of human capital (in particular, specific human capital) and the effort–incentive theory (sometimes called 'bonding theory'). These two theories are able to show that wages grow with job tenure; unfortunately, there is no efficient and simple method by which to identify which theory is more plausible, given the empirical evidence that the growth rate of wages is an increasing function of job tenure, unless information on individual productivity in a firm is available. The author's judgment on this issue in Japan is that the effort–incentive theory is somewhat more plausible than the specific human-capital theory, in view of the following two observations. First, the slope of wage growth by job tenure is considerably steeper in Japan than in other countries where the specific human-capital argument is applied. The difference in the growth rate of wages between Japan and the rest of world can be attributed to the contribution of the effort–incentive theory. Second, the level of retirement allowances is quite high in Japan. Retirement allowances can be explained by a typical example of the bonding theory. I do not claim, however, that specific human capital has no significance in explaining the positive growth rate of wages by job tenure; *nenko joretsu* (the seniority system) could be explained by the argument of specific human capital, as described in the main text. It would be fair to conclude that both the specific human-capital model and the effort—incentive theory are appropriate, with a somewhat stronger effect of the latter than the former.

One interesting interpretation of the importance of age is the 'living-cost hypothesis', implying that employers pay higher wages to older employees because the latter have greater financial responsibilities. Age is a symbol of the degree of consumption; it is quite natural that the greater the age, the higher will be the necessity of expenditure. This hypothesis was popular among many specialists, including marxian economists, who were influenced by the Germany type of social policy. (See Ohta and Tachibanaki, 1996*b*.) From a different angle, age may be evaluated on the basis of paternalism. As was found in the main text, the influence of job tenure was somewhat stronger than that of age in wage differentials. Therefore, economic rationality (either human capital or effort–incentive) dominates paternalism, or the social-policy argument.

12.4. Size of firm has a peculiar effect as a determinant of wages, and the ability-to-pay and/or rent-sharing hypotheses are responsible for the inter-size wage differentials. The reasons for this peculiarity is as follows. First, it was believed that the effect of firm size was the most salient feature of wage differentials, and that it was unique to Japan; there have been controversies concerning the causes and implications of inter-size wage differentials. Second, the influence of firm size on wage differentials is negatively correlated with the movement of business cycles. When the economy is in a boom (or a recession), the wage differential due to size is smaller (or larger). In sum, the differentials are affected by business cycles.

Chapter 4 attempted to estimate a pure effect of firm size on wage differentials after controlling for a large number of qualification variables. It obtained the result that a substantial difference remained even after the control; and it was concluded that the ability-to-pay and/or rent-sharing hypotheses were likely to be responsible for this.

One important point regarding the size of firm is that its effect is intrinsic in the determination of wages for the following reason: when the size of firm is used as a control variable, it does substantially reduce the degree of spurious wage differentials by other variables. For example, Chapter 5 showed that inter-industry wage differentials were reduced substantially in the presence of firm size as a control variable. And Chapter 9 presented the empirical result that wage differentials between competitive industries and non-competitive (concentrated) industries are explained largely by the wage differentials by the size of firm. In other words, the former industries consist mainly of smaller firms whose wage levels are intrinsically lower, while the latter consist mainly of larger firms whose wage levels are intrinsically higher.

In sum, larger Japanese firms are able to pay considerably higher wages than smaller firms, for various reasons which were explained in detail in Chapter 4. It is supported by the ability-to-pay hypothesis; the mutual interests of employers and employees can explain its mechanism. Also, it is the rent-sharing hypothesis, which signifies a certain degree of co-operative behaviour by the two sides.

12.5. Industrial differences are relatively minor in the determination of wage differentials. Also, the compensating difference in wages is not observed. Chapters 5 and 9 presented the empirical result that wage differentials by industries were substantially reduced after controlling for a large number of quality variables. It is possible to conclude, therefore, that the effect of industrial differences on nominal wage figures, which is very large statistically, is spurious. In other words, pure industrial wage differentials are substantially smaller than spurious industrial wage differentials. Chapter 9 found that the pure inter-size differential is responsible for the spurious inter-industry difference, i.e. between competitive and concentrated sectors.

Chapter 5 found that the compensating difference in wage payments between industries which have better working conditions and those whose working conditions are worse was not observed. Employees with less favourable working conditions have to accept an additional unfavourable treatment, lower wages. This observation is similar to the case of women, who have to accept several simultaneous and unfavourable treatments in the fields of wages, employments, promotions, etc.

12.6. *Education (i.e. formal schooling) is an important determinant of wages only for a particular demographic group, notably male white-collar employees. Also, it works as a screening variable for promotion in the firms.* Education in Japan has various facets. A notorious social phenomenon is to be found in severe competition for entrance examinations at various stages of formal schooling, from college level even down to elementary school level. It is possible to assume that Japanese people desire to obtain more educational attainment, because this raises earnings capacity considerably. More education here implies two dimensions. The first dimension is to obtain a higher graduation level among various graduation levels such as high schools, junior colleges, universities, and graduate schools, and the second dimension is to enter into a more prestigious school, and in particular university.

It is true that Japanese people are anxious to satisfy the above two dimensions. It is important, however, that earning capacity is not raised by education as much as people in Japan expect: Chapter 3 showed that education was significant only for male white-collar workers in the determination of wages; Chapter 9 found that the degree of male/female wage differential would not be narrowed even if the educational level of women were raised. Chapter 10 proposed that position in wage distribution was more important than educational attainment in difference in lifetime earnings. Various empirical observations thus suggest that education is not as important for the determination of wages and earnings as people believe or expect. This does not necessarily imply, however, that education does not matter at all; it is true that the average wage is higher when the formal schooling level is higher. In this sense, education matters to a slight extent in the determination of wages.

How can we assess the role of education in Japan, where the demand for education is incredibly high, under the observed condition that formal education is not so important in raising earning capacity? One immediate answer is that Japanese people do not know the real story yet, or that they still believe the false hypothesis that education raises earnings capacity considerably.

Several more plausible and scientific answers can be suggested. First, education plays an important role when both occupation and position (hierarchy) in a firm are taken into account, as the empirical result in Chapter 7 showed. Although only two classifications in occupation in Chapter 3, blue-collar and white-collar workers, did not provide us with a clear interpretation of the role of education in the determination of earnings, a large number of different occupations considered in Chapter 7 showed a more clear-cut influence of occupation on earnings. Much more importantly, education determines the occupational class to a greater extent, if we consider a large number of different occupations.

Second, education performs a screening role in the promotion hierarchy of a firm, as we see in Chapter 7. Concretely speaking, it was found that only junior college and university graduates could start on the promotion ladder; junior and senior high-school graduates were largely excluded from that entry point. If the top executive level (i.e. board members) is examined, the university from which a candidate for an executive position graduated is significant (see e.g. Tachibanaki, 1995a). These two phenomena strongly support the hypothesis that education, both graduation level and name of university, is used as a screening or a filtering device.

Third, education is not yet an extremely important determinant of wages and earnings, contrary to common belief, despite the first and second answers above. Chapter 7 showed an enormous difference in earnings between employees who were promoted to higher positions and those who were not. This fact may be regarded as a counter-example to the third proposition, in view of the screening role of education. The last part of Chapter 7 described in some detail the argument that it was not a counter-example, so I shall not repeat the argument here. In conclusion, education is a less important determinant of wages and earnings than has popularly been believed, although it does have some effect.

Fourth, it is necessary to add the fact that education is also judged by non-pecuniary standards in Japan; it would require sociological, psychological, and even religious discussions to support this proposition. Several familiar examples are as follows. More education offers a higher chance of making a good marriage. In a family whose members have all completed college education, it may be considered shaming for a member not to possess a college degree. A similar thing may apply in a district where many inhabitants have higher educational gualifications. It is also important to note that some people desire more knowledge and academic achievement without showing any interest in earnings capacity.

Since this book belongs to the sphere of economics, we shall not develop such discussions. One important reason for the increased demand for education is to be found in such sociological and psychological factors, and in pure educational motives.

12.7. *Positions (or hierarchies) play a significant role in firms or organizations. In particular, earnings are differentiated by positions to a larger extent.* Chapter 7 presented evidence for the above. Internal competition for higher positions is very severe because the number of these positions is limited. Obviously, competition for executive positions is the most severe. One reason for such severe competition arises from the fact that the internal labour market is one of the most salient features in Japan: promotion is given mainly to those currently employed in the firm, in particular in larger firms. Severe competition among the same class of entrants to a firm persists for a long period, ten to fifteen years, and possibly longer. Careful monitoring and evaluation of employees are carried out during such a period to select productive employees who can be promoted. Since all junior-college and university graduates among white-collar workers are in line for promotion, as described previously, all these employees worked hard in expectation of future promotion. I believe that this is one of the reasons for efficient and productive management in Japanese large firms. Blue-collar employees also worked for the same reason, although their final level of promotion will be much lower. It is natural that employers should pay considerably higher wages to employees, both white-collar and blue-collar, who perform well, and who are then promoted.

The above mechanism worked fairly well during the period of strong industrialization and rapid economic growth after the Second World War, when per capita income level was lower. Less-educated employees, who had a smaller chance of promotion because of the screening role of education, also worked hard to receive the highest wages possible, in view of their lower living standard. The Japanese economy produced a high standard of living. Some employees, both educated and less-educated, white-collar and blue-collar, have started to feel dissatisfaction with severe internal competition among employees and with the hard-work ethic (see e.g. Ishikawa, 1994; Tachibanaki, 1996*b*). The main reason is that Japanese people now enjoy a high level of consumption, except for poor housing in urban areas, and so demand more free time in place of hard working. Thus, it is possible to predict that the growth rate of productivity will decline; some economists, including myself, find that signs of this were already apparent a decade ago.

12.8. Equality was regarded highly as an acceptable principle in the Japanese society. *This virtue was operative in many fields of industrial relations and management.* Equality (or fairness) has various facets. It happens that a system which is regarded as equality in one country (or society) may be judged as inequality in another country (or society). Let us take the example of the *nenko joretsu*, or seniority system. This system is judged as equality in Japan because wages grow with employees' length of service. It is fair because everybody can accumulate his or her length of service in one company, regardless of qualifications such as education and occupation and, more importantly, regardless of productivity. This system, however, may be assessed as unfair in the rest of the world because it treats productive and less productive workers equally. This may in fact be unfair; some people believe that productive workers should receive higher wages than less productive workers, even if their length of service is the same.

This equal treatment offers a higher incentive to all employees in Japan; it avoids a disincentive for employees who are treated less favourably, but it may damage the incentive for qualified and productive employees. Japanese society and firms believe that the loss due to the latter outweighs the gain due to the former; consequently, equal treatment of employees has been adopted to seek a higher gain.

We have to add several reservations. First, equality is stressed only among certain group members: males, educated, full-time workers, or workers in larger firms, or other privileged groups. Females, less-educated, part-time workers, or workers in smaller firms, or others, are treated much less favourably, as shown in various chapters of this book. In sum, only the insiders can enjoy the merit of equality. Alternatively speaking, 'equality' benefits the insiders at the expense of the outsiders.

Second, a certain portion of Japanese people have started to think that the Japanese way of equality—such as equal treatment of productive and less productive workers which derives from, for example, the seniority system—is in fact unfair, proposing that it is fair only when the able are rewarded highly and the less able not so highly. Equality may be judged differently as time goes on. This second reservation is crucial in predicting the future course of industrial relations in Japan (see e.g. Tachibanaki, 1992*b*; 1996*b*).

12.9. *Labour market flexibility, in terms of the relationship between wages and employment, is not so high as popularly believed.* It is true that labour market flexibility in Japan is high in comparison with other industrialized countries. It has helped Japan to have a much lower rate of unemployment, and to show little fluctuation in the rate of unemployment. The most important element of labour market flexibility in Japan is flexible working hours, in particular overtime hours, in response to a change in output. This is responsible for a better performance in the labour market, which is indicated by a lower rate of unemployment with little fluctuation. Several other elements of labour market flexibility, pointed out in Chapter 11, have worked quite well in the past to produce a relatively better performance in the Japanese macroeconomy.

One interesting empirical result regarding labour flexibility is that wage flexibility, which is observed statistically not only in semi-annual bonus payments but also regular monthly wages, although its degree of flexibility is smaller than that of working hours, did not contribute much to lowering the rate of unemployment. Many empirical studies (except for several studies which deal with regional data) have supported the above finding. Various reasons for this result have been presented and discussed.

12.10. *Future research*. This chapter has presented several representative conclusions derived from the analyses carried out in this book, and provided brief comments on them. Several important subjects which were not covered in this book, and future works, are described briefly.

First, it is important to accumulate studies on the determination of female wages and, more broadly, on female labour behaviour, in view of the fact that women account for about one-third of the total labour force. Second, a large number of economic variables, which affect wages, are interrelated to a certain extent; thus, it is necessary to construct a theoretical wage and labour model which takes account of such a interlinked determination. Also, it would be desirable to consider a more explicit introduction into a model of both individual employers' and employees' behaviour. Third, the effect of unions has been ignored almost entirely, except for minor treatment in Chapter 4. Although it is predicted that the influence of unions will be weak, it is necessary to take into account the role of unions and its effect on wages and other variables. Fourth, it would be interesting to combine economic analysis with sociological and psychological approaches, in particular in considering the effect of education and occupation. Fifth, the collection of new data sources, in particular information on individual productivity and performance in a firm, and panel data on individual wages and work history, is needed to enrich our understanding of wage determination and labour behaviour in Japan. Sixth, it is time to pay more attention to non-wage payments, because their share in total compensation is not negligible, and is increasing. Data of non-wage payments are much inferior to those of wages, unfortunately. Finally, a more serious international comparative study of the subjects covered in this book would enrich our understanding of the issue of wages and related subjects. See a new international study on wage differentials by Tachibanaki (1996a).

References

ABEGGLEN, JAMES G. (1958). *The Japanese Factory: Aspects of Its Social Organization*. Glencoe, Ill.: Free Press.

ABRAHAM, K. G., and HOUSEMAN, S. (1989). 'Job Security and Work Force Adjustment: How Different are US and Japanese Practices?', *Journal of Japanese and International Economics*, 3: 500–21.

ABRAHAM, K. G., and FARBER, H. S. (1987). 'Job Duration, Seniority, and Earnings', *American Economic Review*, 77 (June): 278–97.

—— and MEDOFF, J. M. (1985). 'Length of Service and Promotion in Union and Non-union Work Groups', *Industrial and Labour Relations Review*, 38(3): 408–20.

AITCHISON, J. A., and BROWN, J. A. C. (1957). *The Lognormal Distribution*. Cambridge: Cambridge University Press.

AKERLOF, G. A. (1982). 'Labor Contracts as Partial Gift Exchange', *Quarterly Journal of Economics*, 97: 543–69.

—— and YELLEN, J. L. (1986). *Efficiency Wage Models of the Labour Market*. Cambridge: Cambridge University Press.

ALTONJI, J. G., and SHAKOTKO, R. A. (1987). 'Do Wages Rise with Job Senority?', *Review of Economic Studies*, 54: 437–59.

AMEMIYA, T. (1975). 'Qualitative Response Models', *Annals of Economic and Social Measurement*, 4: 363–72.

—— (1985). *Advanced Econometrics*. Oxford: Basil Blackwell.

AOKI, M. (1988). *Information, Incentives and Bargaining in the Japanese Economy*. Cambridge: Cambridge University Press.

ARISAWA, H. (1957). 'Is It Possible to Solve the Employment Problem by Expanding the Economy?', *Sekai*, 135 (Mar.): 34–44 (in Japanese).

ARROW, K. J. (1973). 'Higher Education as a Filter', *Journal of Public Economics*, 2: 193–216.

ASANUMA, B. (1989). 'Manufacture–Supplier Relationships in Japan and the Concept of Relation-Specific Skill', *Journal of the Japanese and International Economies*, 3: 1–30.

ATODA, N., SURUGA, T., and TACHIBANAKI, T. (1988). 'Statistical Inference of Functional Forms in Income Distribution', *Economic Studies Quarterly*, 39: 14–40.

—— and TACHIBANAKI, T. (1991). 'Earnings Distribution and Inequality over Time: Education vs. Relative Position and Cohort', *International Economic Review*, 32(2): 475–89.

References

Averitt, Robert T. (1968). *The Dual Economy: The Dynamics of American Industry Structure*. New York: Horton.

Ball, R. J., and Cyr (1966). 'Short Term Employment Functions in British Manufacturing Industry', *Review of Economic Studies*, 33: 179–207.

Baran, Paul A., and Sweezy, Paul M. (1966). *Monopoly Capitalism: An Essay on the American Economic and Social Order*. New York: Monthly Review Press.

Barger, W. (1971). 'The Measurement of Labor Input: US Manufacturing Industries 1948–66', Ph.D. thesis, Harvard University.

Beck, E. M., Horan, Patrick M., and Tolbert, Charles M. (1978). 'Stratification in a Dual Economy: A Sectoral Model of Earnings Determination', *American Sociological Review*, 43 (Oct.): 704–20.

Becker, G. S. (1964). *Human Capital: A Theoretical and Empirical Analysis with Special Reference to Education*. Columbia, NY: Columbia University Press.

Bell, L. A., and Freeman, R. B. (1985). *Does a Flexible Industry Wage Structure Increase Employment? The US Experience*. NBER Working Paper No. 1604, Cambridge, Mass.: National Bureau for Ecomomic Research.

Blanchflower, D. G., and Oswald, A. J. (1994). *The Wage Curve*. Cambridge, Mass.: MIT Press.

——and Garrett, M. D. (1990). 'Insider Power in Wage Determination', *Economica*, 57: 363–70.

Blinder, Alan S. (1973). 'Wage Discrimination: Reduced Form and Structural Estimates', *Journal of Human Resources*, 8(4) (Fall): 436–55.

Bluestone, Barry, Murphy, William M., and Stevenson, Mary (1973). *Low Wages and the Working Poor*. Ann Arbor, Mich.: Institute of Labor and Industrial Relations, University of Michigan.

Blumenthal, T. (1966). 'The Effect of Socio-Economic Factors on Wage Differentials in Japanese Manufacturing Industries', *Economic Studies Quarterly*, 17: 53–67.

Bowles, S., and Gintis, H. (1976). *Schooling in Capitalist America*. New York: Basic Books.

Bowman, M. J., and Anderson C. A. (1963). 'Concerning the Role of Education in Development', in C. Geertz (ed.), *Old Societies and New States: The Quest for Modernity in Asia and Africa*. New York: Free Press.

Branson, W. H., and Rotemberg, J. J. (1980). 'International Adjustment with Wage Rigidity', *European Economic Review*, 13: 309–32.

Brechling, F. P. R. (1965). 'The Relationship between Output and Employment in British Manufacturing Industries', *Review of Economic Studies*, 32: 187–216.

BRECHLING, F. P. R., and O'BRIEN, P. (1967). 'Short-Run Employment Functions in Manufacturing Industries: An International Comparison', *Review of Economics and Statistics*, **49** (July): 277–87.

BRISCOE, G., and PEEL D. A. (1975). 'The Specification of the Short-Run Employment Function', *Bulletin of the Oxford Institute of Economics and Statistics*, **37**: 115–42.

BROWN, C. (1983). 'Are Those Paid More Really No More Productive?', Princeton Working Paper No. 169 (Princeton, NJ).

—— (1994). 'Pay and Performance', in T. Tachibanaki (ed.), *Labour Market and Economic Performance: Europe, Japan and the US* London: Macmillan.

—— and MEDOFF, J. (1989). 'The Employer Size–Wage Effect', *Journal of Political Economy*, **97**(3): 1027–59.

BROWN, H. B. (1977). *The Inequality of Pay*. Oxford: Oxford University Press.

BRUNELLO, G., and WADHWANI, S. (1989). 'The Determinants of Wage Flexibility in Japan: Some Lessons from a Comparison with the UK Micro-Data', LSE, Working Paper No. 1116, Centre for Labour Economics, London School of Economics.

CALVO, A. C., and WELLISZ, S. (1979). 'Hierarchy, Ability and Income Distribution', *Journal of Political Economy*, **87**(5) (Oct.): 991–1010.

CARMICHAEL, H. L. (1983). 'Firm-Specific Human Capital and Promotion Ladder', *Bell Journal of Economics*, **14**: 251–8.

—— (1990). 'Efficiency Wage Models of Unemployment: One View', *Economic Inquiry*, **28**(2) (Apr.): 269–95.

CARNOY, M. (1994). 'Education and Productivity', in T. Husen and T. N. Postlethwaite (eds.), *The International Encyclopedia of Education*. Oxford: Pergamon Press.

—— and RUMBERGER, RUSSEL W. (1976). *Education and Public Sector Employment*. Palo Alto, Calif.: Center for Economic Studies.

CARRUTH, A. A., and OSWALD, A. J. (1989). *Pay Determination and Industrial Prosperity*. Oxford: Oxford University Press.

CHAMPERNOWNE, D. G. (1953). 'A Model of Income Distribution', *Economic Journal*, **63**: 318–51.

CHRISTOFIDES, L. N., and OSWALD, A. J. (1992). 'Real Wage Determination and Rent-Sharing in Collective Bargaining', *Quarterly Journal of Economics*, **107**(3): 985–1002.

CORCORAN, M., and DUNCAN, G. J. (1979). 'Work History, Labour Force Attachment, and Earnings: Differences between the Races and Sexes', *Journal of Human Resources*, **14**: 3–20.

CREEDY, J. (1974). 'Income Changes over the Life Cycle', *Oxford Economic Papers*, **26**: 405–23.

—— (1977). 'The Distribution of Lifetime Earnings', *Oxford Economic Papers*, **29**: 412–29.

——and HART, P. E. (1979). 'Age and the Distribution of Earnings', *Economic Journal*, 89: 280–93.
DALLAL, G. E. (1992). 'The Computer Analysis of Factorial Experiments with Nested Factors', *American Statistician*, 46: 246–8.
DENNY, K., and MACHIN, S. (1991). 'The Role of Profitability and Industrial Wages in Firm-Level Wage Determination', *Fiscal Studies*, 12: 34–45
DEVINE, T. J., and KIEFER, N. M. (1993). 'The Empirical Status of Job Search Theory', *Labour Economics*, 1(1): 3–24.
DICKENS, W. D., and LANG, K. (1992a). *Labor Market Segmentation, Wage Dispersion and Unemployment*. NBER Working Paper No. 4073. Cambridge, Mass.: National Bureau of Economic Research.
——(1992b). *Labor Market Segmentation Theory: Reconsidering the Evidence*. NBER Working Paper No. 4087, Cambridge, Mass.: National Bureau of Economic Research.
——and KATZ, L. F. (1987). 'Inter-industry Wage Differences and Industry Characteristics', in K. Lang and J. Leonard (eds.), *Unemployment and the Structure of Labour Markets*. Oxford: Basil Blackwell.
DOERINGER, PETER B., and PIORE, MICHAEL J. (1971). *Internal Labor Markets and Manpower Analysis*. Lexington, Mass.: D. C. Heath.
DORE, R. A. (1993). 'Japanese Capitalism, Anglo-Saxon Capitalism: How Will the Darwinian Contest Turn Out?', in F. Burton and N. Campbell (eds.), *The Global Kaisha: Strategic and Organizational Issues*. London: Routledge.
DUNCAN, O. D., FEATHERMAN, A., and DUNCAN, B. (1968). *Socioeconomic Background and Occupational Achievement: Extensions of a Basic Model*. Washington, DC: US Dep. of Health, Education and Welfare.
EDEN, B., and PAKES, A. (1981). 'On Measuring the Variance–Age Profile of Lifetime Earnings', *Review of Economic Studies*, 48: 385–94.
EDIN, P. A., and ZETTERBERG, J. (1992). 'Inter-industry Wage Differentials: Evidence from Sweden and a Comparison with the United States', *American Economic Review*, 82: 1341–9.
EDWARDS, RICHARD C. (1979). *Contested Terrain: The Transformation of the Workplace in the Twentieth Century*. New York: Basic Books.
——REICH, MICHAEL, and GORDON, DAVID M. (1975). *Labor Market Segmentation*. Lexington, Mass.: D. C. Heath.
EHRENBERG, R. G. (1971). *Fringe Benefits and Overtime Behavior*. Lexington, Mass.: D. C. Heath.
FREEMAN, R. F., and WEITZMAN, M. J. (1987). 'Bonuses and Employment in Japan', *Journal of the Japanese and International Economies*, 1: 168–94.
FRIEDMAN, M., and KUZUNETS, S. (1954). *Income from Independent Professional Practice*. New York: National Bureau of Economic Research.

GAREN, J. E. (1985). 'Worker Heterogeneity, Job Screening, and Firm Size', *Journal of Political Economy*, 93: 715–39.

GIBBONS, R., and KATZ, L. (1992). 'Does Unmeasured Ability Explain Inter-industry Wage Differentials?', *Review of Economic Studies*, 59: 515–35.

GORDON, DAVID M., EDWARDS, RICHARD, and REICH, MICHAEL (1982). *Segmented Work, Divided Workers*. New York: Cambridge University Press.

GORDON, R. J. (1982). 'Why US Wage and Employment Behaviour Differs from That in Britain and Japan', *Economic Journal*, 92 (Mar.): 13–44.

GREEN, F., MACHIN, S., and MANNING, A. (1992). *The Employer Size–Wage Effect: Is Monopsony the Explanation?* Discussion Paper No. 79, Centre for Economic Performance. London.

GRILICHES, Z. (1976). 'Wages and Earnings of Very Young Men', *Journal of Political Economy*, 84(2): 569–86.

——(1977). 'Estimating the Returns to Schooling: Some Econometric Problems', *Econometrica*, 45: 1–22.

—— and MASON W. (1972). 'Education, Income and Ability', *Journal of Political Economy*, 80(2): 74–103.

GRUBB, D., JACKMAN, R., and LAYARD, R. (1983). 'Wage Rigidities and Unemployment in OECD Countries', *European Economic Review*, 21: 11–39.

GUNDERSON, M. (1989). 'Male–Female Wage Differentials and Policy Responses', *Journal of Economic Literature*, 27: 46–72.

HALL, R. (1970). *Wages, Income and Hours of Working in the US Labor Force*, MIT Working Paper No. 62, Cambridge, Mass.

——(1975). *The Rigidity of Wages and the Persistence of Unemployment*. Brookings Papers on Economic Activity 2, Washington, DC: Brookings Institution.

——(1980). *Employment Fluctuations and Wage Rigidities*. Brookings Papers on Economic Activity 3, Washington, DC: Brookings Institution.

HAMADA, K., and KUROSAKA, Y. (1984). 'The Relationship between Production and Unemployment in Japan: Okun's Law in Comparative Perspective', *European Economic Review*, 25: 71–94.

—— ——(1986). 'Trends in Unemployment, Wages and Productivity: The Case of Japan', paper presented at the Conference on the Rise in Unemployment, Brighton, Sussex.

HAMERMESH, D., and REEDS, A. (1993). *The Economics of Work and Pay*. New York: HarperCollins.

HAMERMESH, D. S. (1976). 'Econometric Studies of Labor Demand and Their Application to Policy Analysis', *Journal of Human Resources*, 2 (Summer): 310–29.

——(1980). 'Commentary', in J. J. Siegfried (ed.), *The Economics of Firm Size, Market Structure, and Social Performance*. Washington DC: Federal Trade Commission.

——(1993). *Labour Demand*. Princeton, NJ: Princeton University Press.

HART, O., and HOLMSTROM, B. (1987). 'The Theory of Contracts', in T. Bewley (ed.), *Advances in Economic Theory*. Cambridge: Cambridge University Press.

HART, P. E. (1976a), 'The Comparative Statics and Dynamics of Income Distribution', *Journal of the Royal Statistical Society*, **139**: 103–25.

——(1976b). 'The Dynamic of Earnings', *Economic Journal*, **86**: 551–65.

——and PRAIS, S. J. (1956). 'The Analysis of Business Concentration: A Statistical Approach', *Journal of the Royal Statistical Society*, **119**, ser. A: 150–81.

HART, R. A. (1984). *The Economics of Non-wage Labour Costs*. New York: George Allen & Unwin.

——and McGREGOR, P. G. (1982). *The Returns to Labour Services in West German Manufacturing Industry*. Berlin: International Institute of Management.

HASHIMOTO, K., and SURUGA, T. (1990). 'Substitution Between Capital and Labor Inputs Differentiated by Educational Attainment in Japanese Manufacturing Industries', *Journal of the Japan Statistical Society*, **20**: 227–33.

HASHIMOTO, M. (1979). 'Bonus Payments, On-the Job Training and Lifetime Employment in Japan', *Journal of Political Economy*, **87**: 1086–1104.

——and RAISIAN, J. (1985). 'Employment Tenure and Earnings Profiles in Japan and the United States', *American Economic Review*, **75**: 721–35.

————(1988). 'The Structure and Short-Run Adaptability of Labour Markets in Japan and the United States', in R. H. Hart (ed.), *Employment, Underemployment and Labour Utilization*. Boston: Unwin Hyman.

————(1992). 'Aspects of Labor Market Flexibility in Japan and the United States', in K. Koshiro (ed.), *Employment Security and Labor Market Flexibility*. Detroit: Wayne State University Press.

HAUSE, J. C. (1974). *The Covariance Structure of Earnings and the On-the-Job Training Hypothesis*. NBER Working Paper No. 25, Cambridge, Mass.: National Bureau of Economic Research.

HAYAMI, H. (1986). 'Wage Determination in Japan under Changing Conditions in the World Economy', *Monthly Journal of the Japan Institute of Labour*, **28** (June): 16–26 (in Japanese).

HECKMAN, J. (1979). 'Sample Selection Bias as a Specification Error', *Econometrica*, **47**: 153–62.

HIGUCHI, Y., SEIKE, A., and HAYAMI, H. (1986). 'Labor Market: A Change in Male–Female Labor Supply', in K. Hamada, M. Kuroda, and A. Horiuchi (eds.), *Macroeconomic Analysis in Japan*. Tokyo: University of Tokyo Press (in Japanese).

HOLMLUND, B., and ZETTERBERG, J. (1991). 'Insider Effects in Wage Determination: Evidence from Five Countries', *European Economic Review*, 35: 1009–34.

HOLMSTROM, B. (1982). 'Moral Hazard in Teams', *Bell Journal of Economics*, 13: 324–40.

—— and MILGROM, P. (1991). 'Multitask Principal-Agent Analyses: Incentive Contracts, Asset Ownership, and Job Design', *Journal of Law, Economics and Organization*, 7 (special issue): 24–52.

HÜBLER, O. (1984). 'Zur empirischen Uberpüfung Alternativer Theorien der Verteilung von Arbietseinkommen', in L. Bellman, K. Gerlack, and O. Hübler (eds.), *Lohnstruktur in der Bundesrepublik Deutschland*. Frankfurt a. M.: Campus.

IDSON, T. L., and FEASTER, D. J. (1990). 'A Selectivity Model of Employer-Size Wage Differentials', *Journal of Labor Economics*, 8: 99–122.

ISHIDA, M. (1990). *Social Sciences of Wages: Japan and the UK*. Tokyo: Chuo-keizai-sha (in Japanese).

ISHIKAWA, T. (1989). 'A Theoretical Consideration for Wage Dual Structure', in M. Tsuchiya and Y. Miwa (eds.), *Small-Size Enterprises in Japan*. Tokyo: University of Tokyo Press (in Japanese).

—— (1991). *Income and Wealth*. Tokyo: Iwanami-shoten (in Japanese).

—— (1994). 'Interindustry and Firm Size Differences in Job Satisfaction Among Japanese Workers', in T. Tachibanaki (ed.), *Labour Market and Economic Performance: Europe, Japan and the USA*. London: Macmillan.

JAMISON, D., and LAU, L. (1982). *Farmer Education and Farm Efficiency*. Baltimore: Johns Hopkins University Press.

JENCKS, C. (1972). *Inequality*. New York: Basic Books.

JOHNSON, N. L., and KOTZ, S. (1970). *Continuous Univariate Distribution* (2 vols.). New York: John Wiley.

JOVANOVIC, B. (1979). 'Job Matching and the Theory of Turnover', *Journal of Political Economy*, 87: 972–89.

—— (1984). 'Matching, Turnover and Unemployment', *Journal of Political Economy*, 92: 108–22.

KATZ, L. (1986). 'Efficiency Wage Theories: A Partial Evaluation', in S. Fischer (ed.), *NBER Macroeconomics Annual*. Cambridge, Mass.: MIT Press.

KATZ, L. E., and REVENGA, A. L. (1989). 'Change in the Structure of Wages: The United States vs. Japan', *Journal of the Japanese and International Economies*, 3: 522–33.

KATZ, L. F., and SUMMERS, L. H. (1989). *Industry Rents: Evidence and*

Implications. Brookings Papers on Economic Activity, Microeconomics, Washington, DC: Brookings Institution.

KAWASAKI, S., and McMILLAN, J. (1987). 'The Design of Contracts: Evidence from Japanese Subcontracting', *Journal of the Japanese and International Economies*, 1: 327–49.

KAWASHIMA, YOKO (1983). 'Wage Differentials Between Women and Men in Japan'. Ph.D. thesis, Stanford University.

—— and T. TACHIBANAKI (1986). 'The Effect of Discrimination and of Industry Segmentation on Japanese Wage Differentials in Relation to Education', *International Journal of Industrial Organization*, 4: 43–68.

KEMPTHORNE, O. (1951). *The Design and Analysis of Experiments*. New York: John Wiley.

KLAU, F., and MITTELSTADT, A. (1985). *Labour Market Flexibility and External Prime Shocks*. OECD Working Papers No. 24, Paris.

KOIKE, K. (1981). *Skill Formation in Japan*. Tokyo: Yuhikaku (in Japanese).

KOMIYA, R. (1989). *The Modern Chinese Economy: A Comparison with Japan*. Tokyo: University of Tokyo Press (in Japanese).

—— and K. Yasui (1984). 'Japan's Macroeconomic Performance Since the First Oil Crisis: Review and Appraisal', *Carnegie–Rochester Conference Series on Public Policy*, 20: 69–114.

KOSHIRO, K. (1992). 'Bonus Payments and Wage Flexibility in Japan', in K. Koshiro (ed.), *Employment Security and Labour Market Flexibility*. Detroit: Wayne State University Press.

KRUGER, A., and SUMMERS, L. H. (1988). 'Efficiency Wages and Inter-Industry Wage Structure', *Econometrica*, 56(2): 259–93.

KURATANI, M. (1973). A Theory of Training, Earnings, and Employment: An Application to Japan'. Ph.D. thesis, Columbia University.

LANG, K., and DICKENS, W. T. (1992). *Labour Market Segmentation, Wage Dispersion and Unemployment*. NBER Working Paper Series No. 4073, Cambridge, Mass.: National Bureau of Economic Research.

—— and KAHN, S. (1990). 'Efficiency Wage Models of Unemployment: A Second View', *Economic Inquiry*, 28(2) (Apr.): 296–306.

LAYARD, P. R. G., and NICKELL, S. J. (1985). *Unemployment, Real Wages and Aggregate Demand in Europe, Japan and the US*. Discussion Paper No. 214, Centre for Labour Economics, London School of Economics.

———— (1994). 'Unemployment in the OECD Countries', in T. Tachibanaki (ed.), *Labour Market and Economic Performance: Europe, Japan and the US* London: Macmillan.

———— and JACKMAN, R. (1991). *Unemployment*. Oxford: Oxford University Press.

LAZEAR, E. (1979). 'Why Is There Mandatory Retirement?', *Journal of Political Economy*, 84: 1261–84.

LAZEAR, E. (1981). 'Agency, Earnings Profiles, Productivity, and Hours Restrictions', *American Economic Review*, 71: 606–20.
—— (1989). 'Pay Equality and Industrial Politics', *Journal of Political Economy*, 97: 561–80.
—— and ROSEN, S. (1981). 'Rank-Order Tournaments as Optimum Labor Contracts', *Journal of Political Economy*, 89: 841–64.
LEE, L. F. (1978). 'Unionism and Wage Rates: A Simultaneous Equations Model with Qualitative and Limited Dependent Variables', *International Economic Review*, 19: 415–33.
LESTER, R. A. (1967). 'Pay Differentials by Size of Establishment', *Industrial Relations*, 7: 57–67.
LILLARD, L. A. (1977). 'Inequality: Earnings vs. Human Wealth', *American Economic Review*, 65: 42–53.
—— and WEISS, Y. (1979). 'Components of Variation in Panel Earnings Data: American Scientists 1960–70', *Econometrica*, 47: 437–54.
—— and WEISS, R. J. (1978). 'Dynamic Aspects of Earnings Mobility', *Econometrica*, 46: 985–1012.
LINDBECK, A., and SNOWER, D. J. (1989). *The Insider–Outsider Theory of Employment and Unemployment*. Cambridge, Mass.: MIT Press.
MCFADDEN, D. (1974). 'Conditional logit analysis of qualitative choice behavior', in P. Zarembka (ed.), *Frontiers in Econometrics*, New York: Academic Press.
—— (1976). 'Quantal Choice Analysis: A Survey', *Annals of Economic and Social Measurement*, 5: 363–90.
MACLEOD, W. B., and MALCOMSON, J. M. (1988). 'Reputation and Hierarchy in Dynamic Models of Employment', *Journal of Political Economy*, 96 (Aug.): 832–54.
MADDALA, G. S. (1983). *Limited-Dependent and Quantitative Variables in Econometrics*. Cambridge: Cambridge University Press.
—— and LEE L. (1976). 'Recursive Models with Qualitative Endogenous Variables', *Annals of Economic and Social Measurement*, 5: 525–45.
MAIRESSE, J. (1984). 'Comments on K. Hamada and Y. Kurosaka', *European Economic Review*, 25: 99–105.
MALCOMSON, J. M. (1984). 'Work Incentives, Hierarchy, and Internal Labor Markets', *Journal of Political Economy*, 92: 486–507.
MALINVAUD, E. (1976). *Statistical Methods of Econometrics*. Amsterdam: North-Holland.
MARSHALL, R. C., and ZARKIN, G. A. (1987). 'The Effect of Job Tenure on Wage Offers', *Journal of Labor Economics*, 5: 301–24.
MASTERS, S. H. (1969). 'An Interindustry Analysis of Wages and Plant Size', *Review of Economics and Statistics*, 51: 341–5.
MEDOFF, J. L., and ABRAHAM, K. G. (1980). 'Experience, Performance, and Earnings', *Quarterly Journal of Economics*, 96: 703–36.

MELLOW, W. (1982). 'Employer Size and Wages', *Review of Economics and Statistics*, **64**: 495–501.

MILGROM, P., and ROBERTS, J. (1992). *Economics, Organization, and Management*. New York: Prentice-Hall.

MILLER, R. A. (1984). 'Job Matching and Occupational Choice', *Journal of Political Economy*, **92**: 1086–1120.

MINAMI, R. (1972). 'Transformation of the Labor Market in Postwar Japan', *Hitotsubashi Journal of Economics*, **13**: 57–72

MINCER, J. (1962). 'On the Job Training: Costs, Return and Some Implications', *Journal of Political Economy*, **120**: 50–79.

——(1970). 'The Distribution of Labor Incomes: A Survey with Special Reference to the Human Capital Approach', *Journal of Economic Literature*, **7**: 1–26.

——(1974). *Schooling, Experience and Earnings*. New York: NBER Columbia University Press.

——(1984). *Labor Mobility, Wages and Job Training*. Washington, DC: US Dept. of Labor.

——and HIGUCHI, Y. (1988). 'Wage Structures and Labour Turnover in the United States and Japan', *Journal of the Japanese and International Economies*, **2**: 97–133.

——and JOVANOVIC, B. (1981), 'Labour Mobility and Wages', in S. Rosen (ed.), *Studies in Labor Markets*. Chicago: University of Chicago Press.

MINFORD, P. (1983). 'The Labour Market in an Open Economy', *Oxford Economic Papers*, **35** (Nov.): 531–68.

MINISTRY OF LABOUR (1986). *Annual White Paper on the Labour Market* (in Japanese). Tokyo.

MIYAZAWA, K. (1976). *Input–Output Analysis and the Structure of Income Distribution*. Berlin: Springer.

MIZUNO, A. (1973). *The Theory of Dynamics in Wage Structure*. Tokyo: Shinhyoronsha (in Japanese).

——(1985). 'Wage Flexibility and Employment Fluctuation', in R. Nakamura, S. Nishikawa, and Y. Kosai (eds.), *The Economic System in Contemporary Japan*. Tokyo: University of Tokyo Press (in Japanese).

MONTGOMERY, E. D. (1993). *Patterns in Regional Labor Market Adjustment: The United States and Japan*. NBER Working Paper No. 4414, Cambridge, Mass.: National Bureau of Economic Research.

MORISHIMA, M. (1991). 'Information Sharing and Collective Bargaining in Japan: Effects on Wage Negotiation', *Industrial and Labor Relations Review*, **44**(3): 469–85.

MURAMATSU, K. (1983). *Labour Market Analysis in Japan: The Internal Labour Market*. Tokyo: Hakuto-shobo (in Japanese).

——(1984). 'The Effect of Trade Unions on Productivity in Japanese Manufacturing Industries', in M. Aoki (ed.), *The Economic Analysis of the Japanese Firm*, Amsterdam: North-Holland.

MURAMATSU, K. (1985). 'The Impact of Wages on Employment: A Survey', *Academia*, 871 (July): 1–25 (in Japanese).

—— (1986). 'Discharge and Its Alternatives', in M. Mizuno, T. Matsugi, and Th. Dams (eds.), *Mechanization and Employment: A Comparison between Japan and West Germany*. Nagoya: Nagoya University Press (in Japanese).

MURPHY, K. M., and WELCH, F. (1992). 'The Structure of Wages', *Quarterly Journal of Economics*, 108 (Feb.): 285–326.

NADIRI, M. (1968). 'The Effects of Relative Prices and Capacity on the Demand for Labor in the US Manufacturing Sector', *Review of Economic Studies*, 35 (July): 273–88.

—— and ROSEN, S. (1974). *A Disequilibrium Model of Demand for Factors Production*. New York: National Bureau of Economic Research.

NAKAMURA, J. (1983). 'The Role of the Labour Market for Solving the Problem of Stagflation', *Economic Studies Quarterly*, 34 (Aug.): 147–55 (in Japanese).

—— (1984). 'Macroeconomic Policy and Employment-Unemployment', in K. Koike (ed.), *Contemporary Unemployment*. Tokyo: Dobunkan (in Japanese).

NAKAO, TAKEO (1980). 'Wages and Market Power in Japan', *British Journal of Industrial Relations*, 18(3): 365–8.

NAOI, M. (1977). 'Classifications of Occupations and Measurement' (in Japanese), in *SSM* (1975).

NICKELL, S. (1982). *Research into Unemployment: A Partial View of the Economic Literature*. Discussion Paper No. 131, Centre for Labour Economics, London School of Economics.

—— and ANDREWS, M. (1983). 'Unions, Real Wages and Employment in Britain, 1951–79', *Oxford Economic Papers* (Nov.): 507–30.

—— —— (1984). 'An Investigation of the Determinants of Manufacturing Employment in the United Kingdom', *Review of Economic Studies*, 51(4) (Oct.): 529–58.

—— and WADHWANI, S. (1990), 'Insider Forces and Wage Determination', *Economic Journal*, 100: 496–509.

ODAKA K. (1984). *An Analysis of the Japanese Labour Market*. Tokyo: Iwanami-shoten (in Japanese).

OHASHI, I. (1989*a*). 'On the Determinations of Bonuses and Basic Wages in Large Japanese Firms', *Journal of the Japanese and International Economies*, 39: 451–79.

—— (1989*b*). 'Bonuses as Labour Incentive', in K. Imai and R. Komiya (eds.), *Japanese Firms*. Tokyo: University of Tokyo Press (in Japanese).

OHTA, S., and TACHIBANAKI, T. (1996). 'Skill Hypothesis versus Support of Living Condition Hypothesis on Wage Determination', in I. Ohashi and T. Tachibanaki (eds.), *Employment Adjustment, Incentives and Internal Labour Market*. London: Macmillan.

OHTAKE, F. (1986). 'On Flexibility of Real Wages', report to the Ministry of Labour, Tokyo (in Japanese).

OKUN, A. M. (1981). *Prices and Quantities*. Oxford: Basil Blackwell.

OKUNO, M. (1984). 'Corporate Loyalty and Bonus Payment: An Analysis of Work Incentives in Japan', in M. Aoki (ed.), *The Economics of Japanese Firms*. Amsterdam: North-Holland.

ONO, A. (1973). *Wage Determinations in Post-war Japan*. Tokyo: Toyokeizaishimposha (in Japanese).

——(1987). 'Two Competing Hypotheses for the Nenko Wage System: Skill or Living-Cost Compensation', *Hitotsubashi Journal of Economics*, 28 (June): 1–25.

——(1989). *Employment Practice in Japan and the Labour Market*. Tokyo: Toyokeizaishimposha (in Japanese).

OSTER, G. (1979). 'A Factor Analytic Test of the Theory of the Dual Economy', *Review of Economics and Statistics*, 61 (Feb.): 33–9.

PAINE, S. H. (1971). 'Wage Differentials in the Japanese Manufacturing Sector', *Oxford Economic Papers*, 23: 212–38.

PARSONS, D. O. (1978). 'The Autocorrelation of Earnings, Human Wealth Inequality, and Income Contingent Loans', *Quarterly Journal of Economics*, 92: 551–69.

——(1986). '*Wage Determination in the Post-Schooling Period*'. Center for Human Resources, Ohio State University.

PIORE, M. J. (1975). 'Notes for a Theory of Labor Market Segmentation', in R. C. Edwards *et al.*, *Labor Market Segmentation*. Lexington, Mass.: D. C. Heath.

PSACHALOPOULOS, G. (1975). *Earnings and Education in OECD Countries*, Paris: OECD.

ROSEN, S. (1968), 'Short-Run Employment Variation on Class-1 Railroads in the US, 1947–63', *Econometrica*, 36: 511–29.

——(1977), 'Human Capital: A Survey of Empirical Research', in R. G. Ehrenberg (ed.), *Research in Labour Economics*, i. Greenwich, Conn.: Jai Press.

——(1982), 'Authority, Control, and the Distribution of Earnings', *Bell Journal of Economics and Management Science*, 13 (autumn): 311–23.

——(1986). 'The Theory of Equalizing Differences', in O. Ashenfelter and R. Layard (eds.), *Handbook of Labour Economics*, i. Amsterdam: North-Holland.

——(1987), 'Human Capital', in J. Eatwell, M. Milgate, and P. Newman (eds.), *The New Palgrave: A Dictionary of Economics*, ii. London: Macmillan.

ROY, A. D. (1951). 'Some Thoughts on the Distribution of Earnings', *Oxford Economic Papers*, 3: 135–46.

SACKS, J. (1979). Wages, Profits and Macroeconomic Adjustment: A Comparative Study. Brookings Papers on Economic Activity No. 2

Washington, DC: Brookings Institution.

——(1983). *Real Wages and Unemployment in the OECD Countries*. Brookings Papers on Economic Activity No. 1. Washington, DC: Brookings Institution.

SAKURAI, K., and TACHIBANAKI, T. (1992). 'Estimation of Mismatch and U-V Analysis in Japan', *Japan and the World Economy*, 4: 319–32.

SANO, Y. (1969). *An Econometric Analysis of Wage Determination*. Tokyo: Toyokeizaishimposha (in Japanese).

SCHEFFÉ, H. (1959). *The Analysis of Variance*. New York: John Wiley.

SCHMIDT, P., and STRAUSS, R. P. (1975). 'Estimation of Models with Jointly Dependent Qualitative Variables: A Simultaneous Logit Approach', *Econometrica*, 43(4) (July): 745–55.

——(1976). 'The Effect of Unions on Earnings and Earnings on Unions: A Mixed Logit Approach', *International Economic Review*, 17(1) (Feb.): 204–12.

SCHULTZ, T. W. (1961) 'Investment in Human Capital', *American Economic Review*, 51: 1–17.

——(1971). *Investment in Human Capital: The Role of Education and Research*. New York: Free Press.

——(1975). 'The Value of the Ability to Deal with Disequilibrium', *Journal of Economic Literature*, 13: 827–46.

SEARLE, S. R. (1971). *Linear Models*. New York: John Wiley.

——(1987). *Linear Models for Unbalanced Data*. New York: John Wiley.

——(1994). 'Analysis of Variance Computing Package Output for Unbalanced Data from Fixed-Effects Models with Nested Factors' *American Statistician*, 48(2): 148–52.

SEIKE, A. (1985) 'The Employment Adjustment in Japanese Manufacturing Industries in the 1970s', *Keio Business Review*, 22(3): 25–57.

——(1992). 'The Employment Adjustment Patterns of Japan and the United States', in K. Koshiro (ed.), *Employment Security and Labor Market Flexibility*, Detroit: Wayne State University Press.

SHAPIRO, C., and STIGLITZ, J. (1984). 'Equilibrium Unemployment as a Worker Discipline Device', *American Economic Review*, 74: 433–44.

SHEPHERD, WILLIAM G. (1970). *Market Power and Economic Welfare*. New York: Random House.

——(1979). *The Economics of Industrial Organization*. Englewood Cliffs, NJ: Prentice-Hall.

SHIMADA, H. (1981). *Earnings Structure and Human Investrment: A Comparison Between the United States and Japan*. Tokyo: Keio Economic Observatory.

SHINKAI, Y. (1982). *Anatomy of Contemporary Macroeconomic Problems*. Tokyo: Toyokeisaishimposha (in Japanese).

SHINOHARA, M. (1961). *Growth and Cycle in the Japanese Economy*. Tokyo: Sobunsha (in Japanese).

——(1970). *Structural Changes in Japan's Economic Development*. Economic Research Series No. 11, Institute of Economic Research, Hitotsubashi University, Tokyo.

SHINOZUKA, E. (1989). *Employment Adjustment in Japan*. Tokyo: Toyokeizaishimposha (in Japanese).

——and ISHIHARA, E. (1977a). 'Employment Adjustment after the Oil Crisis: A Comparison of Four Countries and Firm-Size Differentials', *Japanese Economic Studies*, 6 (Aug.) (in Japanese).

——(1977b). 'Employment Adjustment in Japanese Manufacturing Industries: 1971–83', *Japanese Economic Studies*, 15 (Mar.): 61–72 (in Japanese).

——(1980). 'Recent Employment Adjustment by Firm-Size Differentials', in R. Nakamura and S. Nishikawa (eds.), *Contemporary Labour Market Analysis*. Tokyo: Sogorodo-kenkyu-sho (in Japanese).

SIMON, H. A. (1975). 'The Compensation of Executives', *Sociometry*, 20: 32–5.

SOLIGO, R. (1966). 'The Short-Run Relationship between Employment and Output', *Economic Essays*, 6 (Spring): 161–215.

SPENCE, M. (1973). 'Job Market Signalling', *Quarterly Journal of Economics*, 87: 355–74.

SSM (1977). *Social Stratification and Mobility Report*, ed. K. Tominaga. Tokyo: University of Tokyo Press (in Japanese).

STAFFORD F. P. (1980). 'Firm Size, Workplace Public Goods, and Worker Welfare', in J. J. Siegfried (ed.), *The Economics of Firm Size, Market Structure, and Social Performance*, Washington, DC: Federal Trade Commission.

STIGLITZ, J. E. (1975). 'Incentives, Risk and Information: Notes Towards a Theory of Hierarchy', *Bell Journal of Economics and Management*, 6 (Autumn): 552–79.

STOIKOV, V. (1973). 'The Structure of Earnings in Japanese Manufacturing Industries: A Human Capital Approach', *Journal of Political Economy*, 91: 340–55.

SYMONS, J. (1985). 'Relative Prices and the Demand for Labour in British Manufacturing', *Economica*, 52: 37–50.

——and LAYARD, R. (1984). 'Neoclassical Demand for Labour Functions for Six Major Economies', *Economic Journal*, 94 (Dec.): 788–99.

TACHIBANAKI, T. (1975). 'Wage Determinations in Japanese Manufacturing Industries: Structural Change and Wage Differentials', *International Economic Review*, 16(3): 562–86.

——(1980). 'Education, Occupation and Earnings: A Recursive Approach for France', *European Economic Review*, 13: 103–22.

——(1981). 'Social Mobility: A New York', *Quality and Quantity*, 15: 317–423.

——(1982). 'Further Results on Japanese Wage Differentials: Nenko

Wages, Hierarchical Position, Bonuses and Working Hours', *International Economic Review*, 23(2) (June): 447–61.

——(1984a). 'Labor Mobility and Job Tenure', in M. Aoki (ed.), *The Economic Analysis of the Japanese Firm*. Amsterdam: North-Holland.

——(1984b). 'Measurement of Unemployment, International Comparisons and the Effect of Unemployment Compensation on the Duration of Unemployment', in K. Koike (ed.), *Contemporary Unemployment*. Tokyo: Dobunkan (in Japanese).

——(1984c). 'The Youth Unemployment Problem' *Monthly Journal of The Japan Institute of Labour*, 26 (Dec.): 12–22 (in Japanese).

——(1987a). 'Labour Market Flexibility in Japan in Comparison with Europe and the US', *European Economic Review*, 31: 647–84.

——(1987b). 'The Determination of the Promotion Process in Organizations and of Earnings Differentials', *Journal of Economic Behaviour and Organization*, 8: 603–16.

——(1988). 'Education, Occupation, Hierarchy, and Earnings', *Economics of Education Review*, 7: 221–9.

——(ed.) (1992a). *Assessment, Promotion and Wage Determination*. Tokyo: Yuhikaku (in Japanese).

——(1992b). 'Higher Land Price as a Cause of Increasing Inequality: Changes in Wealth Distribution and Socio-economic Effects', in J. O. Haley and K. Yamamura (eds.), *Land Issues in Japan: A Policy Failure*. Seattle: Society for Japanese Studies.

——(1992c). 'Why Are Wages in Finance and Insurance Industry in Japan so High?', in A. Horiuchi and N. Yoshino (eds.), *Financial Analysis for Mordern Japan*. Tokyo: University of Tokyo Press (in Japanese).

——(ed.) (1993a). *The Economics of Trade Unions*. Tokyo: Toyokeizaishimposha (in Japanese).

——(1993b). *Earning Stratification and Education*. Mimeo.

——(1993c). 'Social and Economic Background of the Lower Rate of Unionization in Japan', in Tachibanaki (1993a).

——(1994a). 'Education. Occupation and Earnings', in T. Husen and T. N. Postlethwaite (eds.), *The International Encyclopedia of Education*, Oxford: Pergamon Press.

——(1994b). 'Introduction', in Tachibanaki (ed.), *Labour Market and Economic Performance: Europe, Japan and the USA*. London: Macmillan.

——(1995a). 'A Road to Executives and their Role in Firms', in Tachibanaki (1995b).

——(ed.) (1995b). *Economics of Promotions in Japanese Firms*. Tokyo: Toyokeizaishimposha (in Japanese).

——(ed.) (1996a). *Wage Differentials: An International Comparison*.

——(1996b). *Public Policies and the Japanese Economy*. London: Macmillan.

——and NODA, T. (1994). *The Effect of Unions on Egalitarianism and Productivity in Japan*. Kyoto Institute of Economic Research, Discussion Paper No. 342.

——and OHTA, S. (1994). 'Wage Differentials by Industry and the Size of Firms, and the Labour Market in Japan', in Tachibanaki (ed.), *Labour Market and Economic Performance: Europe, Japan and the US*. London: Macmillan.

——and SAKURAI, K. (1991). 'Labour Supply and Unemployment in Japan', *European Economic Review*, 35(8): 1575–88.

——and TAKATA, S. (1994). 'Wealth Accumulation under Uncertainty in Income and Bequest Motive', Unpublished manuscript.

——and TAKI, A. (1990). 'Wage Determination in Japan: A Theoretical and Empirical Investigation', in H. Konig (ed.), *Economics of Wage Determination*. Berlin: Springer.

——and YAGI, T. (1995). 'Distribution of Economic Well-Being in Japan: Towards a More Unequal Society', in E. Palmer (ed.), *Income Distribution in the 1980s*. Cambridge: Cambridge University Press.

TAIRA, KOJI (1970), *Economic Development and the Labour Market in Japan*. New York: Columbia University Press.

TAKAHASHI, C., IOCHI, R., and EMI, K. (1959). *Dynamic Changes of Income and Its Distribution in Japan*. Tokyo: Kinokuniya.

TAKI, A., and TACHIBANAKI, T. (1994). 'An Analysis of Labour Mobility in Japan', in M. Okabe (ed.), *The Structure of the Japanese Economy*, London: Macmillan.

TAN, H. W. (1987). 'Technical Change and Its Consequences for Training and Earnings'. Unpublished manuscript.

TAUBMAN, P. (1975), *Sources of Inequality*. Amsterdam: North-Holland. The Netherlands.

THUROW, L. C. (1975), *Generating Inequality: Mechanisms of Distribution in the US Economy*, New York: Basic Books.

TIROLE, J. (1986). 'Hierarchies and Bureaucracies: On the Role of Collusion in Organization', *Journal of Law, Economics, and Organization*, 2: 181–214.

TOLBERT, CHARLES M., BECK, E. M., and HORAN, PATRICK M. (1980). 'The Structure of Economic Segmentation: A Dual Economy Approach', *American Journal of Sociology*, 85(5): 1095–1116.

TOPEL R. (1986). 'Local Labor Markets', *Journal of Political Economy*, 94: S111–43.

——(1991). 'Specific Capital, Mobility, and Wages: Wages Rise with Job Seniority', *Journal of Political Economy*, 99: 145–76.

TOPEL, R. H., and WARD, M. P. (1992). 'Job Mobility and the Careers of Young Men', *Quarterly Journal of Economics*, 107(2): 439–80.

WADHWANI, S., and WALL, M. (1991). 'A Direct Test of the Efficiency Wage Model Using UK Microdata', *Oxford Economic Papers*, 43: 529–

48.

WEISS, Y. (1972). 'The Risk Element in Occupational and Educational Choices', *Journal of Political Economy*, 80: 1203–13.

——(1986). 'The Determination of Life Cycle Earnings: A Survey', in O. Ashenfelter and R. Layard (eds.), *Handbook of Labor Economics*. Amsterdam North-Holland.

——and LILLARD, L. A. (1978). 'Experience, Vintage and Time Effects in the Growth of Earnings: American Scientists, 1960–70', *Journal of Political Economy* 86: 427–8.

WEITZMAN, M. L. (1984). *The Share Economy*. Cambridge, Mass.: Harvard University Press.

——(1986). 'Macroeconomic Implication of Profit Sharing', in S. Fischer (ed.), *NBER Macroeconomic Annual*. Cambridge Mass.: MIT Press.

WELCH, F. (1970). 'Education in Production', *Journal of Political Economy*, 78: 35–59.

WILLIAMSON, O. E. (1967). 'Hierarchical Control and Optimum Firm Size', *Journal of Political Economy*, 75(2): 123–38.

——(1975), *Markets and Hierarchies: Analysis and Antitrust Implications*. New York: Free Press.

WILLIS, R. J. (1986). 'Wage Determinations: A Survey and Reinterpretation of Human Capital Earnings Function', in O. Ashenfelter and R. Layard (eds.), *Handbook of Labor Economics*, Amsterdam: North-Holland.

WISE, A. D. (1975). 'Personal Attributes, Job Performance, and Probability of Promotion', *Econometrica*, 13(5–6) (Sept.-Nov.): 913–31.

YAMADA, M. (1934), *Analysis of Japan's Capitalism*. Tokyo: Iwanami-shoten (in Japanese).

YASUBA, Y. (1976). 'The Evolution of Dualistic Wage Structure', in H. Patrick (ed.), *Japanese Industrialization and Its Social Consequences*. Berkeley, Calif.: University of California Press.

YITZHAKI, S., and LERMAN, R. I. (1991). 'Income Stratification and Income Inequality', *Review of Income and Wealth*, ser. 37, No. 3: 313–29.

YOSHITOMI, M. (1981). *Japanese Economy*. Tokyo: Toyokeizai-shimposha (in Japanese).

INDEX

Abegglen, J. G., on age-related pay 187n.
ability, innate 15; and occupation 119
ability-to-pay hypothesis 64, 244–5; and size of firms 66–8; variables 109, 123–4, 130–1
Abraham, K. and Farber, H. S., on learning production function 153; on seniority 150
Abraham, K. and Houseman, S., on labour adjustment 221
Abraham, K. and Medoff, J. M., on experience and promotion 143
affirmative action 198–9
age, effect on wage determination 22, 28–9, 37, 41, 42, 47, 57, 207–11, 243–4; and experience 42; and industrial advantage 98; and job tenure 19–21; and lifetime earnings figures 211–17; and sex differences 187–8; and unemployment 231; and wage stratification 75; and WASD (weighted adjusted standard deviations) 96
agency theory 15, 16–17
agriculture, links of education and productivity 115
Aitchison, J. A. and Brown, J. A. C., on earnings distribution 203n.

Akerlof, G. A., on education and occupation 125
Akerlof, G. A. and Yellen, J. L., on efficiency wage theory 18, 110
Altonji, J. G. and Shakotko, R. A., on learning production function 153; on seniority 150
Amemiya, T. 133
analysis of variables (ANOVA) 24–5, 49; advantages of 24; estimation method 30–6; time-series change 43–8
Aoki, M., on job rank 127; on *keiretsu* firms 69
Arisawa, H., on dual structure 62
Arrow, K. J., on role of education 15, 120, 148
Asanuma, B., on *keiretsu* firms 69
aspiration 144, 148
Atoda, N., Suruga, T., and Tachibanaki, T., on earnings distribution 203
Atoda, N. and Tachibanaki, T., on significance of education 20; on wages and occupation 234
Averitt, R. T., on industry segmentation 170

Ball, R. J. and Cyr, on labour adjustment 221

Baran, P. A. and Sweezy, P. M., on industry segmentation 170
Barger, W., on analysis of variance 32–3
Beck, E. M., Horan, P. M., and Tolbert, C. M., on industry segmentation 171
Becker, G. S., on human-capital theory 15
Bell, L. A. and Freeman, R. B., on labour demand 231
Bernoulli differential equation 152–3
Blanchflower, D. G. and Oswald, A. J., 'International Wage Curve' 232–3
Blanchflower, D. G., Oswald, A. J., and Garrett, M. D., on ability to pay 64
Blinder, A. S., on discrimination 198; on mean-cost benefit 190
Bluestone, B., Murphy, W. M., and Stevenson, M., on industry segmentation 170
Blumenthal, T., on inter-scale differentials 39
bonding theory 16–17
bonus payments 7, 29–30, 39, 103, 146; and flexibility of wages 228–9; and human capital 103; and profit-sharing 103
Bowles, S. and Gintis, H., on socioeconomic background and earnings 116
Bowman, M. J. and Anderson, C. A., on primary education and productivity 115
Branson, W. H. and Rotemberg, J. J., on flexibility of wages 227
Brechling, F. P. R., on labour adjustment 221

Brechling, F. P. R. and O'Brien, P., on labour adjustment 221
Briscoe, G. and Peel, D. A., on labour adjustment 222
Brown, C., on monitoring of employees 70; on productivity 151–2
Brown, C. and Medoff, J. M., on education and occupation 125; on firm and establishment size 64, 83; on inter-scale wage differentials 21; on labour quality hypothesis 57, 62; on monitoring of employees 65, 74, 75; on selection bias 57
Brown, H. B., on occupation and earnings 117; on skills and wages 234
Brunello, G. and Wadhwani, S., on flexibility of wages 228

Calvo, A. C. and Wellisz, S., on education and promotion 143; on job rank 127; on skills and wages 234
capital : labour ratios 68–9
Carmichael, H. L., on efficiency wage hypothesis 110; on effort-incentive theory 17
Carnoy, M., on education, occupation, and earnings 113
Carnoy, M. and Rumberger, R. W., on industry segmentation 171; on mean-cost benefit 190
Carruth, A. A. and Oswald, A. J., on ability to pay 64
Champernowne, D. G., on comparative-advantage theory 14
change of jobs 155–6; and education 157–61; sex differences 187

Chicago School, on human-capital theory 15
Christofides, L. N. and Oswald, A. J., on ability to pay 64
comparative-advantage theory 14
compensating wage differentials 14, 81, 104, 117–18
competition theory 110
conflict avoidance 220
Corcoran, M. and Duncan, G. J., on discrimination 198
credentialism (educational signalling) 121–2
Creedy, J., on estimation of lifetime earnings 201, 202, 203, 205
Creedy, J. and Hart, P. E., on estimation of lifetime earnings 201, 211

Dallal, G. E., on analysis of variance 33
data collection 2
decentralized wage bargaining 1
Denny, K. and Machin, S., on ability to pay 64
Devine, T. J. and Kiefer, N. M., on job-matching theory 16
Dickens, W. D. and Katz, L. F., on ability to pay 64; on pure industrial advantages 97
Dickens, W. D. and Lang, K., on industry segmentation 171; on segmented labour market 63
discouraged workers 220
dismissal, and labour adjustment 223
dispersion in wages, and size of firm 70–7
Doeringer, P. B. and Piore, M. J., on industry segmentation 171; on internal labour market 170
Dore, R. A. 5

dummy variables 81–3
Duncan, O. D., Featherman, A., and Duncan, B., on education and social background 123

economic growth, cycles of 46; post-war 1; and recession 46–7; and wage differentials 22
economic rationality 29, 38, 42
Eden, B. and Pakes, A., on estimation of lifetime earnings 201
Edin, P. A. and Zetterberg, J., on efficiency wage theory 18
education, and change of jobs 157–61; choice of university 246, 247; costs of 119; effect on wage differentials 20, 22, 27–8, 41, 42, 45–6, 116–20, 218, 242–3, 246–8; equalizing effects of 197–9; as graduation level 27; and hierarchy 137, 246–7; and industrial advantage 98, 106–7; and job rank 127, 132; parents' levels of 134, 135, 136; and productivity 113–16; and promotion 137, 140–3, 144–5, 147–8; and sex differences 27–8, 34, 178–80, 185–6, 242; social considerations 123, 247–8, 251; and WASD (weighted adjusted standard deviations) 96–7
'educational credential' 147–8
'educational signalling' (screening hypothesis) 120–2
Edwards, R. C., on size of firm and profitability 172
Edwards, R. C., Reich, M., and Gordon, D. M., on industry segmentation 170

efficiency wage theory 17–18, 110, 232–3
effort-incentive theory (agency theory) 16–17, 150, 243
Ehrenberg, R. G., on labour adjustment 221
employer–employee relationship 1
employment, and efficiency wage theory 18; growth rate 219–20; maximization of 227, 237
Employment Status Survey 10, 149, 156–7
enterprise unions 3, 4
equality, Japanese attitudes to 249–50; of opportunity 6; in status 5–6
estimation procedures 154–6
experience, *see* job tenure
exploitation theory 62

female workers 4, 7; interruption of employment 154; participation in labour force 219; *see also* sex discrimination
finance and insurance industries 70, 92
flexibility of wage rates 227–31; and labour demand 219–20, 231–3, 250
foreign workers 46, 219
Freeman, R. F. and Weitzman, M. J., on bonus payments 229; on profit-sharing 69–70, 103
Friedman, M. and Kuzunets, S., on occupation and risk 118
fringe benefits 22

Galtonian regression towards the mean 202–3, 205–7, 209–11, 217
Garen, J. E., on inter-scale wage differentials 21; on monitoring of employees 74
gender, and age 187–8; analysis of worker characteristics 176–85; and change of jobs 187; and education 27–8, 34, 178–80, 185–6; effect on wage determination 26, 36, 37, 38, 44–5, 197–9, 236, 241–2; and industrial segmentation 189–91; and job tenure 180, 182, 186–7; and labour adjustment 222–3; mean-cost benefit 190–6; and size of firm 178, 188–9, 193; *see also* sex discrimination
Gibbons, R. and Katz, L., on labour quality 62
Gibrat, law of proportionate effect 202, 217
Gordon, D. M., Edwards, R., and Reich, M., on industry segmentation 170–1
Gordon, R. J., on conflict avoidance 220; on flexibility of wages 227, 228; on productivity 220
Green, F., Machin, S., and Manning, A., dynamic monopoly model 64; on size effects 60
Griliches, Z., on ability variables 131; on quantifying occupation 123–4
Griliches, Z. and Mason, W., on education, occupation and earnings 122
group coherence 5
Grubb, D., Jackman, R., and Layard, R., on flexibility of wages 227, 229
guest workers 46
Gunderson, M., on discrimination 198

Index

Hall, R., on labour deemand 231; on working hours 29

Hamada, K. and Kurosaka, Y., on flexibility of wages 229–30, 231; on productivity 220

Hamermesh, D., on capital–skill complementarity 69; on labour adjustment 222, 223, 231, 232

Hamermesh, D. and Reeds, A., labour economics 13

Hart, O. and Holmstrom, B., on job rank 127

Hart, P. E., on estimation of lifetime earnings 201, 202, 211

Hart, P. E. and Prais, S. J., on estimation of lifetime earnings 202

Hart, R. A. and McGregor, P. G., on labour adjustment 222

Hashimoto, K. and Suruga, T., on capital–skill complementarity 69

Hashimoto, M., on bonus payments 103, 229; on wage determination in Japan 19

Hashimoto, M. and Raisian, J. 19, 232; on flexibility of wages 228; on labour adjustment 221; on *nenko* wage system 234; on wages and job tenure 151

Hause, J. C., on estimation of lifetime earnings 201

Hayami, H., on trade unions 230

Heckman, J., on selection bias 52

hierarchy 9–10, 125; and earnings distribution 132–3, 146, 148, 248–9; and education 127, 132, 137, 246–7; and management order 129–30, 131–2; and occupation 141; significance in Japan 126–7; and size of firm 147, 148; supervisory role 131; and working hours 146

Holmlund, B. and Zetterberg, J., on ability to pay 64

Holmstrom, B., on effort-incentive theory 17

Holmstrom, B. and Milgrom, P., on effort-incentive theory 17; on job rank 127

Hubler, O., on education, occupation, and earnings 122

human-capital theory 14–15, 19, 150, 156, 243; and job-matching 119–20; on skills acquisition 114

Idson, T. L. and Feaster, D. J., on selection bias 52

incentive theory 15

industrial relations 48, 63; organization-oriented 5

industrial rent 91; *see also* rent-sharing

industrial segmentation, mean-cost benefit 190–6; and sex differences 189–91

industry differentials 245; pure advantages 91–3; spurious advantages 90

industry segmentation, analysis of worker characteristics 176–80; studies of 170–1

innate ability, and human capital 15

inter-scale wage differentials 21–2, 240

internal labour market 248

Ishida, M., on merit pay 75

Ishikawa, T., on human-capital theory 20; on industry

segmentation 171; on segmented labour market 63

Jamison, D. and Lau, L., on primary education and productivity 115
Jencks, C., on estimation of earnings 124
job rank, *see* hierarchy
job tenure, and age 19–21, 42; effect on wage determination 22, 28, 36–8, 47, 137–8, 146–7, 148, 165–8, 242–4, 249; and industrial advantage 98, 103, 107, 108; and promotion 143–4; and sex differences 180, 182, 186–7; and size of firms 62; *see also* seniority
job-matching theory 16
Johnson, N. L. and Kotz, S., on earnings distribution 203
Jovanovic, B., on job-matching theory 16

Katz, L., on education and occupation 125; on efficiency wage hypothesis 17, 110
Katz, L. and Revenga, A. L., on education and wage differentials 107
Katz, L. and Summers, L. H., on ability to pay 64; on industry differentials 93
Kawasaki, S. and McMillan, J., on *keiretsu* firms 69
Kawashima, Y., on size of firm and profitability 172
Kawashima, Y. and Tachibanaki, T., on *ad hoc* statistical approach 19–20; on education and wages 105; on male–female wage differentials 236; on size of firms 58

keiretsu (subcontracting) 62, 69
Kempthorne, O., on analysis of variance 32
Klau, F. and Mittelstadt, A., on flexibility of wages 229, 235
Koike, K., on age and job tenure 20; on *nenko* wage system 234
Komiya, R., on 'labour-managed firms' 69
Komiya, R. and Yasui, K., on flexibility of wages 228
Koshiro, K., on bonus payments 229; on flexibility of wages 228
Krueger, A. and Summers, L. H., on ability to pay 64; on efficiency wage theory 18; on industry differentials 92, 94
Kuratani, M., on wage determination in Japan 19

labour adjustment 220, 221–7; and dismissal 223; sex differences in 222–3; speed of 222, 223
labour demand, and wages 231–3
labour market flexibility, *see* flexibility of labour market
labour materials, key features 2–6
labour quality 62, 105–8; and size of firms 62, 66
labour quality hypothesis 57
labour separation rate 67
labour supply 61–2
labour turnover 20–1
labour-hoarding 223–4
'labour-managed firms' 69–70
Lang, K. and Kahn, S., on efficiency wage hypothesis 110
Layard, P. R. G. and Nickell, S. J., on unemployment 220, 236

Layard, P. R. G., Nickell, S. J., and Jackman, R., on unemployment 236; on unions 231; on wages and labour demand 232
layoffs 220
Lazear, E., on bonding theory 16; on seniority 150; on stratification and dispersion in wages 76–7
Lazear, E. and Rosen, S., on education and occupation 125; on effort-incentive theory 17; on job rank 127
leadership, Japanese attitudes to 5
Lee, L. F., on selection bias 52
length of service, equalizing effects of 197–8
Lester, R. A., on working conditions in larger firms 74
life-long employment 1, 4
lifetime earnings, and age 211–17; analysis of 201–7
Lillard, L. A., on estimation of lifetime earnings 201
Lillard, L. A. and Weiss, R. J., on estimation of lifetime earnings 201
Lindbeck, A. and Snower, D. J., on efficiency wage theory 18; on new job-seekers 238
'living wage' 29
living-cost hypothesis 244
long-term contractual relationships 5

McFadden, D. 133
Macleod, W. B. and Malcolmson, J. M., on effort-incentive theory 17
Maddala, G. S. 133
Maddala, G. S. and Lee, L. 133
Mairesse, J., on flexibility of wages 230
Malcolmson, J. M., on job rank 127
Malinvaud, E. 138
marginal-productivity theory 13–14
market power, and product concentration 173–6
marriage, influence on earnings distribution 137–8
Marshall, R. C. and Zarkin, G. A., on selection bias 52; on seniority 150
Masters, S. H., on working conditions in larger firms 74
Medoff, J. L. and Abraham, K. G., on experience and promotion 143
Mellow, W., on inter-scale wage differentials 21
merit pay system 48, 49, 75
Milgrom, P. and Roberts, J., on effort-incentive theory 17
Miller, R. A., on occupation-matching 120
Minami, R., on economy 46
Mincer, J., on human-capital theory 15, 149; on post-school education 38, 126, 138; on productivity 151–2
Mincer, J. and Higuchi, Y., on human-capital theory 79, 159; on wage determination in Japan 19; on wages and job tenure 151
Mincer, J. and Jovanovic, B., on human-capital theory 149
Minford, P., on unions 231
minimum-wage law 235
Ministry of International Trade and Industry, *Basic Survey on Manufacturing Industries* 78, 176
Ministry of Labour, *Employment*

Trend Survey 78; *Survey of Basic Trade Unions* 78; *Wage Structure Survey* 2, 78, 80, 157, 176, 180, 200
Miyazawa, K., on advantages of larger firms 63
Mizuno, A., on flexibility of wages 228; on inter-industry wage structure 79; on pure industrial advantages 97
mobility, social 134
mobility of income 201, 206, 213
mobility of labour 3, 4, 104, 119, 220
monitoring of employees 65–6, 70, 74
Montgomery, E. D., on wages and labour demand 233
Morishima, M., on trade unions 65, 220, 231
Muramatsu, K., on labour adjustment 221, 222; on union participation 103; on wages and labour demand 232
Murphy, K. M. and Welch, F., on competition theory 110

Nadiri, M., on labour adjustment 221
Nadiri, M. and Rosen, S., on labour adjustment 221
Nakamura, J., on labour adjustment 222
Nakao, T., on market power 173
Naoi, M., on prestige values 129
nenko (seniority) system 1, 4, 5; effect on earnings distribution 150
nenko-joretsu (job tenure) 28, 38, 39, 47–8, 49, 57, 234–5, 249
neoclassical theory of wage determination 79–80, 81
von Neumann and Morgenstern, on expected utility maximization 118
Nickell, S., on wages and labour demand 231–2
Nickell, S. and Andrews, M., on unions 231
Nickell, S. and Wadhwani, S., on ability to pay 64
non-wage labour costs 236–7, 251

occupation, and compensating wage differentials 117–18; effect on wage determination 22, 26, 38, 45, 116–20, 122–4; and hierarchy 141; licence to practise 117; monopoly in supply 117; relationship with education 120–4; and risk 118
occupation-matching theory 119–20
Odaka, K., on inter-scale wage differentials 21, 39; on labour supply 50
Ohashi, I., on bonus payments 229
Ohtake, F., on flexibility of wages 228
Okuno, M., on bonus payments 229
oligopoly 171–2
Ono, A., on *ad hoc* statistical approach 19, 20; on establishment variables 83; on inter-industry wage structure 79, 81; on 'living wage' 29
organization-oriented industrial relations 5
Oster, G., on market power 173
outside experience, and industrial advantage 107

overtime hours 226, 229

Paine, S. H., on inter-scale differentials 39
Parsons, D. O., on earnings distribution 217; on estimation of lifetime earnings 201; on productivity 151–2
part-time workers 4, 7, 198, 223
paternalism 29, 38, 42, 63, 187–8, 208, 243–4
performance, pay based on 6, 7
personal characteristics, pay based on 6
prestige values 129
product concentration, and market power 173–6
productivity 220, 235; declining 249; growth rate of 3, 7, 151–2; and trade unions 231; and wage levels 151
profit-sharing 69–70; and bonus payments 103
promotion, based on seniority 4, 5; and education 137, 140–3, 144–5, 147–8; and experience 143–4; and incentives 143–4
Psachalopoulos, G., on education 20, 126
pure industrial advantages 91–3; economic factors 97–105

regional wage differentials 83, 84
regression analysis 24–5
regulation of competition and business 104
rent-sharing hypothesis 64, 66, 68, 244–5
retirement allowances 16, 42, 243–4
risk, Japanese attitudes to 5; and occupation 118
Rosen, S., on compensating-difference theory 14, 118; on education and occupation 122, 125, 143; on job rank 127; on labour adjustment 221; on learning production function 153; on skills and wages 234; on theory of wages 13; on trainability 115
Roy, A. D., on comparative-advantage theory 14

Sacks, J., on flexibility of wages 227–8
Sakurai, K. and Tachibanaki, T., on discouraged workers 220; on wages and labour demand 233
Sano, Y., on inter-industry wage structure 79; on pure industrial advantages 97
Scheffe, H., on analysis of variance 30
Schmidt, P. and Strauss, R. P. 133
Schultz, T. W., on education and productivity 113, 114; on human-capital theory 15
screening hypothesis ('educational signalling') 120–2
Searle, S. R., on analysis of variance 30, 32, 33
segmented labour market 63
Seike, A., on labour adjustment 221
selection bias, and size of firm 52–7
self-employment 7, 220
sex discrimination 10, 22, 36, 170, 236, 241–2; future research 250–1; policy implications 197–9; in United

States 198–9; ways of combating 242; *see also* gender

Shapiro, C. and Stiglitz, J., on efficiency wage theory 18; on effort-incentive theory 17

Shephard, W. G., on market power 172

Shimada, H., on sex differences and worker characteristics 19, 182

Shinkai, Y., on flexibility of wages 228

Shinohara, M., on advantages of larger firms 63

Shinozuka, E., on labour adjustment 222

Shinozuka, E. and Ishihara, E., on labour adjustment 221, 222

Shunto (annual spring offensive) 1, 220, 230

size of firm 4, 10, 244–5; and dispersion in wages 70–7; effect on wage determination 21–2, 26–7, 39, 41, 46–7, 50–77, 242–3; financing activities 63; and gender 178, 188–9, 193; and hierarchy 147, 148; historical development of dual structure 61–4; influence on earnings distribution 137–8; and job tenure 62; and labour quality 62; and monitoring of employees 65–6; and profitability 172; pure size effect 57–61; and selection bias 52–7; and stratification in wages 70–6; and unionization 25, 65; and WASD (weighted adjusted standard deviations) 95–6; and working conditions 64–5

Smith, A., *The Wealth of Nations* 118

social security system 7, 220, 236–7; and retirement allowances 16, 42, 243–4

Social Stratification and Mobility survey 10, 127–31

socioeconomic background and earnings 116

special payments, *see* bonus system

Spence, M., on role of education 15, 120, 148

spurious industrial advantages 97

Stafford, F. P., on monitoring of employees 74; on working conditions in larger firms 74

Stiglitz, J. E., on job rank 127; on monitoring of employees 74

Stoikov, V., on inter-scale differentials 19, 39

stratification in wages 51; and size of firm 70–7

subcontracting (*keiretsu*) 69

Symons, J., on wages and labour demand 232

Tachibanaki, T. 3, 5, 6, 134; on *ad hoc* statistical approach 19–20; on analysis of variance 34; on bonus payments 146, 229; on economic growth and wages 22; on education 20, 76, 113, 122, 123, 126, 137; on establishment variables 83; on experience and earnings 137, 148; on finance and insurance industries 92; on future of industrial relations 250; on inter-industry wage structure 79, 81; on job tenure 62, 180; on labour supply 50; on labour turnover 20, 57; on male–female wage differentials 182, 236; on merit pay 48, 75; on *nenko* wage system 234; on regulation 104; on size of firms 58; on social mobility 134; on unemployment 234; on unions 25, 220; on variables in wage differentials 22, 23; on working conditions 65

Tachibanaki, T. and Noda, T., on trade unions 65, 103, 220, 231

Tachibanaki, T. and Ohta, S., on size of firms 57–8; on working conditions 65

Tachibanaki, T. and Sakurai, K., on discouraged workers 220; on unemployment 230

Tachibanaki, T. and Takata, S., on mobility of income 213

Tachibanaki, T. and Taki, A., on control variables 95; on human-capital theory 79

Tachibanaki, T. and Yagi, T. 6; on income distribution 239

Taira, Koji, on 'living wage' 29; on *nenko-joretsu* system 48, 188 n.

Takahashi, C., Iochi, R., and Emi, K., on earnings distribution 203 n.

Taki, A. and Tachibanaki, T., on self-employed workers 220

Tan, H. W., on productivity 151–2

Taubman, P., on estimation of earnings 124

temporary workers 198, 220, 223

Thurow, L. C., on trainability 15

Tirole, J., on effort-incentive theory 17

Tolbert, C. M., Beck, E. M. and Horan, P. M., on mean-cost benefit 190

Topel, R. H., on competition theory 110; on job-changing 155; on learning production function 153; on seniority 150

Topel, R. H. and Ward, M. P., on seniority 150

trade unions 3, 4, 251; employers' attitudes to 65; 'labour-managed firms' 69–70; participation rate 25–6, 103, 174–5; power of 220; and productivity 231; on wages and employment 230–1

trainability 15, 114–15

training 61; *see also* education

transportation and communication industries 92

unemployment 1, 3, 11, 47–8, 229, 236–7; and age 234; disguised 230; effect on wages 231–3; minimization of 227, 237; temporary layoffs 227

unions, *see* trade unions

United States, labour adjustment 223; ranking of industry differentials 92–3; sex discrimination in 198–9

universities 7, 246, 247

US Panel Study of Income Dynamics (PSID) 151

variance, analysis of, *see* analysis of variance

Wadhwani, S. and Wall, M., on efficiency wage theory 18

wage deferral theory 16–17
wage dispersion 51
Wage Structure Survey 25, 44, 51
wage-growth curve 16
WASD (weighted adjusted standard deviations) 94–7
Weiss and Lillard, on estimation of lifetime earnings 201
Weiss, Y., on earnings distribution 217; on occupation and risk 118; on theory of wages 13
Weitzman, M. L., on bonus payments 229; on profit-sharing 103
Welch, F., on education and productivity 114, 115
Williamson, O. E., on job rank 127; on promotion and incentives 144

Willis, R. J., on theory of wages 13
Wise, A. D., on aspiration 144; on job rank 127
working conditions, and size of firms 64–5
working hours 3; effect on wage determination 29, 40, 41, 83–4, 146; international comparisons 226–7; and wage flexibility 224, 233

Yamada, M., exploitation theory 62
Yasuba, Y., on labour supply 50
Yitzhaki, S. and Lerman, R. I., on stratification of group 71, 73
Yoshitomi, M., on flexibility of wages 228